Effigy

Issues in Crime & Justice

Series Editor
Gregg Barak, Eastern Michigan University

As we embark upon the twentieth-first century, the meanings of crime continue to evolve and our approaches to justice are in flux. The contributions to this series focus their attention on crime and justice as well as on crime control and prevention in the context of a dynamically changing legal order. Across the series, there are books that consider the full range of crime and criminality and that engage a diverse set of topics related to the formal and informal workings of the administration of criminal justice. In an age of globalization, crime and criminality are no longer confined, if they ever were, to the boundaries of single nation-states. As a consequence, while many books in the series will address crime and justice in the United States, the scope of these books will accommodate a global perspective and they will consider such eminently global issues such as slavery, terrorism, or punishment. Books in the series are written to be used as supplements in standard undergraduate and graduate courses in criminology and criminal justice and related courses in sociology. Some of the standard courses in these areas include introduction to criminal justice, introduction to law enforcement, introduction to corrections, juvenile justice, crime and delinquency, criminal law, and white collar, corporate, and organized crime.

Effigy

Images of Capital Defendents

Allison M. Cotton

LEXINGTON BOOKS

A division of
ROWMAN & LITTLEFIELD PUBLISHERS, INC.
Lanham • Boulder • New York • Toronto • Plymouth, UK

LEXINGTON BOOKS

A division of Rowman & Littlefield Publishers, Inc.
A wholly owned subsidiary of The Rowman & Littlefield Publishing Group, Inc.
4501 Forbes Boulevard, Suite 200
Lanham, MD 20706

Estover Road
Plymouth PL6 7PY
United Kingdom

British Library Cataloguing in Publication Information Available

Library of Congress Cataloging-in-Publication Data

Cotton, Allison M., 1969–
 Effigy : images of capital defendants / Allison M. Cotton.
  p. cm.
 Includes bibliographical references.
 ISBN-13: 978-0-7391-2551-9 (cloth: alk. paper)
 ISBN-10: 0-7391-2551-6 (cloth: alk. paper)
 eISBN-13: 978-0-7391-3009-4
 eISBN-10: 0-7391-3009-9
 1. Capital punishment—United States. 2. Defense (Criminal procedure)—United
States. 3. Prosecution—United States. 4. Jury—United States. I. Title.
 KF9227.C2C68 2008
 345.73'0773—dc22

                                                          2008013190

Printed in the United States of America

⊚™ The paper used in this publication meets the minimum requirements of
American National Standard for Information Sciences—Permanence of Paper
for Printed Library Materials, ANSI/NISO Z39.48-1992.

Dedication

I dedicate this, my first book, to my father, James A. Cotton, for all of his love and support, to my mother, Margaret MacNaughton, for imparting the skill to write it, and to my friends and colleagues, Hillary Potter, Stacy Mallicoat, and Julius Debro, who encouraged me during dinner one night at the Plum Tree in L.A.

Contents

	Acknowledgment	ix
	Preface	xi
Chapter 1	Introduction	1
Chapter 2	The Death Penalty in the United States and How Juries Operate	15
Chapter 3	The Importance of Defining the Defendant	39
Chapter 4	The Legal Fight	67
Chapter 5	The Guilt Phase: How the Defense/Prosecution Saw Their Mission	75
Chapter 6	The Penalty Phase: The Prosecution's/Defense's Mission	115
Chapter 7	Who Is the Defendant? The Prosecution's/Defense's Answer	133
Chapter 8	The Impact on Jurors	157
Chapter 9	Conclusion	185
	Bibliography	197
	Index	205
	About the Author	211

~

Acknowledgment

I would like to acknowledge someone in my life who has shown unwavering support to me as I completed this manuscript: Danny Wayne Bryant. You are my motivator and you have demonstrated authentic African-American manhood in many ways that mainstream society has not yet fully acknowledged. The story told within these pages, unfortunately, is not unusual, but you continue to surprise and delight me with your uncommonness. I love you. Thank you.

~

Preface

When a man goes on trial for his life, two things happen: (1) he becomes strangely irrelevant in the legal process that is designed to defend him, and (2) society acknowledges and responds seriously to his problems for the very first time. The man in this book, for example, was twenty-two years old when he committed the murder for which he stood charged. During his tumultuous lifetime, he had been diagnosed with health problems by numerous health practitioners, including doctors of psychiatry, psychology, and medicine. His behavioral problems stemmed from an abusive childhood and a damaged brain. Still, no amount of therapeutic referrals, threats, incarcerations, punishments, or traumas deterred his criminal path. In fact, his criminal behavior is what led local authorities and medical practitioners to acknowledge his terrible existence in the first place.

Murder is a peculiar event; a person dies because someone else deems him or her unfit to live. That seems to be the extent of the analysis employed by the victim's families, the media, most legal participants, and the community that it affects. However, little attention is paid to who the killer really *is* and why the murder happened. Sociologists are charged with the responsibility of identifying social forces in the environment that influence behavior. As such, a sociological analysis of this particular murder is undertaken here and includes an analysis of proximal and structural causes for the murder that took place. It is an unpopular view, to be sure, because psychological explanations for murder are preferable when an individual commits an act against another individual. Besides, it is easier to incarcerate or execute an individual for murder than to consider the social, economic, and political factors that may have contributed to the behavior.

The defendant in this case did not wake up that morning and decide to kill the woman living across the street from him. In fact, there is a sociological explanation for his behavior, that is, identifiable patterns in the factors that create the situation where murder took place. Oftentimes such reasons are overlooked, eschewed, ignored, or obfuscated because sympathy for the victim(s) overpowers any sense of responsibility to the perpetrator—no one cares why he killed her, only that the perpetrator deserves to be punished. But what if the murderer has already lived a life that is worse than the worst punishment our laws employ? What if the so-called capital punishment of the society would actually serve as a relief from circumstances that have, to that point, been unbearable? Is there any deterrent value in those punishments at all for such people? Does it make sense to blame the murderer for his actions in such a way as to reward him with a penalty that actually alleviates the pain of his existence? What does awkward living have to do with prevention? These issues are examined here.

Few people know or understand what actually happens in a courtroom when a man goes on trial for his life. It is a very sterile procedure, supposedly devoid of emotion, prejudice, or prediction. But how do human beings simply ignore those aspects of their personality when they enter a courtroom on a particular day, at a specified time, and with the only apparent reason being that they have been asked to do so? How do human beings consider the fate of a man who has killed someone without any knowledge whatsoever of the circumstances surrounding his behavior? It is as though the person's entire life started at the point in time when the murder took place and that nothing in that person's life matters previous to it. The legal process itself is designed to extract a story of events from the man accused, but the process limits the amount of background information that can be heard by the judge(s) or jury. Past criminal activity is sometimes inadmissible, for example, but so are past abuses, victimizations, health problems, mental episodes, awards, honors, and miscellaneous good works. But, if an accused person's past is inadmissible, how can one person (a judge) or several people (a jury) who have never met the defendant determine the best course of action for the accused person's future? That is not to say that, in the current case, these factors were not considered (because they were), but rather that it seemed almost to be a source of resentment for spectators, the victim's family, the media, and the community that the defense attorneys would spend a great deal of time talking about his background. Indeed, there were times when sentences that began with "When Donta was nine years. . ." or "When Donta was in the third grade. . ." were followed by sighs and whispers from the gallery of spectators and fidgeting from the jury. Why the uncomfortable response? Why is that not obviously relevant to the behavior being discussed at bar? After all, a person is dead and the person who did it might be executed. Do we really, as a society, believe that some people were born to kill?

Some people remember reading about abused children in the newspaper or seeing neglectful parents being led away in handcuffs following an episode of severe abuse. Very few people can probably remember the names of the victims of the abuse, though, or what happened to the children following the disposition of the parents' case. What happened to Susan Smith, for example, who buckled her children into their car seats before she pushed the car into a lake? What do you think the condition of her two little boys would be today if they had lived? In other words, what amount of therapy, love, or familial attention could reduce or destroy the memory of their mother strapping them into a car and then pushing it into a lake where they almost drowned? How would their sense of values, their sense of trust, or their ability to empathize with people in the future be affected? Whatever happened to Genie, a feral child whose parents (a blind, dependent mother and a psychotic father) strapped her to a potty chair in their Los Angeles home for the first eleven years of her life? Would it surprise you to learn that she reacted violently to attempts to feed, clothe, nurture, and play with her? In other words, child abuse is relevant to a discussion of adult violent behavior. Such issues will be discussed in this book, paying particular attention to the abuse that the murderer suffered during the course of his life.

On the other hand, where does responsibility for the actions of a murderer begin and the fault of society end in such an analysis? When does a murderer deserve the punishment he receives because he has acted with callous disregard for the life of another? This book will show that the responsibility of the murderer never ends because he made choices of his own volition, but also that the choices he made were the direct result of what he was raised to believe, a reflection of how he has been treated, and a manifestation of familial and societal failures that cannot and perhaps should not be ignored in a court of law. In short, it can be said that the murderer in the current study was improperly socialized and fell through the cracks of a social service and criminal justice system that should have helped him. Why isn't his mother on trial? Why hasn't his father been imprisoned? Why are his brothers still living in the household that spawned his rage when evidence has been presented that terrible and consistent abuse took place? And with whom will the cycle of violence in this family end?

Finally, how do people judge other people's actions when they do not live in their head? The overwhelming task of having to sit and listen to a set of facts as they are told by people who did not witness the event, about people whom they have never met before, and about circumstances that most people have never experienced, is given to ordinary citizens: our system of justice requires it. Without any expertise, experience, general knowledge of, or predilection towards the events or people that they are being asked to judge, jurors are charged with the responsibility of rendering a "reasonable" verdict. It is not so much the fact that this task is nearly impossible to accomplish (putting aside personal views and experiences to judge the very same in others), but rather the fact that most people put faith and confidence in this process is what offers a subject for scrutiny. People of supposed average intelligence, who are law-abiding, who are registered to vote or who have a registered driver's license are selected to decide whether a person committed a crime and, if so, what that person's intent was when he or she committed it. The facts of the case are presented by legal advocates who have been trained on how to pick a jury, how to persuade a jury, and how to present facts to a jury that lead to certain conclusions without arousing suspicion or prejudice. Such skills are repeatedly rehearsed in law school classes to be utilized on juries in criminal cases. In short, a certain level of juror ignorance is assumed. Apparently, the point is not for juries to make correct decisions as long as it appears as though a good faith attempt was made to do so.

Obviously, this researcher views the murderer as a victim as well as a criminal. But this book will also show that society should too. If there is any hope for preventing these types of murders in the future, an analysis of the circumstances that led up to and created it is necessary, even thought-provoking.

How I Met the Defendant

When a person first meets the defendant in this case he or she should be struck by his gentle demeanor. A man of his size is hard to ignore because he limps awkwardly, slouches, and never seems to care about or obtain clothing that fits. The scowl on his dark-skinned and scarred face is noticeable because it is outlined by a patchy goatee and topped off with an unkempt afro. His voice is deep, his speech clipped, and his face expressionless. He doesn't seem to have the energy to stand up straight because he is always leaning his 6- foot, 2-inch, 300-pound frame against a table, chair, or wall. But, when a person finally faces him and he decides to expend the effort to say something, it is kind, thoughtfully prepared, and purposeful. "How you doin'? My name is Donta" (with his hand extended to shake mine) is what he said to me the first time that we met.

As a tutor in the G.E.D. program at the Denver County Jail in Denver, Colorado, it was my job to greet new students at the desk when they filed into the tiny, crowded library of the jail. Sometimes I shook hands with the inmates, but most of the time I passed out pencils and asked the inmates to sit down until one of the tutors could get them started on their work for the evening. This day, I recognized Donta from the news broadcasts that I had seen months earlier about the gruesome crime that he had confessed to committing on the eve of my thirtieth birthday. I was stunned at the gentleness of his handshake and the politeness of his introduction because I was used to the obligatory grunts and stares of most inmates who entered the library where the class was held. It was nice to be greeted by one of the students in a pleasant manner.

As time passed with Donta in the class, I noticed that he took a leadership role. Without prompting, Donta tutored other students in subjects that he liked such as science and social studies, and he made suggestions for activities and books that he thought might enhance the class. He sat in the same seat for every class and the other inmates never challenged his routine. There were two other inmates that he spoke to on a regular basis; otherwise he kept to himself. One day (several months after our first meeting) as I watched him talk to an inmate at his table, I stared at him in disbelief that he would continue to talk when he knew that he was disturbing other inmates who were concentrating on their work, but instead of telling him to be quiet, I pulled him aside and asked him to be the subject of my study.

A few weeks later, I arranged a personal visit with Donta at the Denver County Jail, but the restrictions for personal visits were numerous in that I had to make an appointment, submit to a personal search, and wear specific clothing to get into the jail. I could only visit with Donta for 30 minutes at a time in the company of screaming babies, weepy wives, and watchful guards. The arrangement was not conducive to the kinds of conversations that I wanted to have with Donta so I contacted jail officials to inquire about "official visits" with him for the purpose of doing research. "Official visits" were usually granted to attorneys, social workers, and investigators but I was not a member of the defense team at that point in time so my requests (I applied two times) were denied. Official visitors were allowed to meet with inmates privately for as long as necessary in small, glass cubicles with a small table and two yellow plastic chairs. They were also allowed to bring writing materials into the jail so it was imperative for me to find a way to obtain official visitation rights in order to continue my research. Donta gave me permission to contact his attorneys, Randy Canney and Jim Castle. At first, my calls went unreturned, but with prompting from Donta, I finally received a call from Randy Canney, who invited me to his office to talk about the project. I met with him and I left him with a copy of my Human Research Committee (HRC) proposal, a curriculum vita, and a copy of an article I published after I obtained my master's degree. Mr. Canney agreed to discuss the matter with the other attorney on the case, Jim Castle.

A few weeks later, I met with "Randy" who offered me a position on the defense team as a researcher/investigator. As a member of the defense team, I was privy to all of the legal documents and I was able to visit with Donta in an "official" capacity. Following scrutiny of the confidentiality agreement by my attorney, I was granted access to Donta in an official capacity via a letter from Randy Canney to the jail personnel. I was given my first assignment right away: become an expert on the District of Columbia, that is, learn everything there is to learn about the murder rates, poverty rates, social service system, juvenile justice system, and the juvenile facilities in which Donta was housed during the early 1990s. I was also asked to include statistical data on the educational system and health-care system during the time that Donta lived there. This assignment was perfect for me because I had been trained in doing this kind of research and it was this type of research that I knew would be crucial to my understanding of Donta's environment and worldview. Later, I testified about what I found.

Subsequently, my visits with Donta were frequent. I met with him at least two times each week for at least one hour at a time (sometimes four hours) for the next ten months, not including appearances in court where I spoke with him briefly during breaks. I took copious notes about what he said and did during our meetings. My notes included everything from the way he looked to how his voice sounded, to what we talked about and how he felt. He never seemed to mind that I wrote everything down. In fact, at one point, it became a joke:

D: "Don't you want to write that down?"
A: "What?"
D: "I just coughed" (grinning)
A: "Whatever, man" (waving him off and smiling)

Towards the end of his trial, my notes during our jail visits tapered off. I began to jot down significant events instead of the smaller day-to-day details of our interactions. For example:

D looks depressed, but says he's not. No t-shirt today. Flip-flops, not sneakers. No gym, no care, needs shave. Called L.

I took copious notes throughout the trial, occasionally jotting or abbreviating my streams of thought. I recorded everything that was going on, everything Donta did or said, everything the attorneys, judges, jury, or court personnel did or said and everything that I was feeling or doing at the time. I even noted the courtroom temperature, items on tables, things I overheard other people saying, and other miscellaneous information. I never stopped writing.

In addition, I collected newspaper clippings from the actual news sources when possible and printed the articles from the Internet. I tape-recorded news stories, such as the verdict in the guilt phase and the verdict in the penalty phase, when possible. I interviewed several key defense witnesses when they came to town to testify on Donta's behalf. In fact, one of my tasks as a member of the defense team was to transport Linda Page (Donta's grandmother), Freddy Witherspoon (Donta's cousin), Erica Penny (Donta's ex-girlfriend), Dr. Dorothy Otnow-Lewis, and Dr. Johnathan Pincus to and from the airport and the courtroom. I jotted notes during those conversations. Also, I collected copies of legal exhibits, transcripts, records, and other items that were used for his defense. In the end, I managed to write over 400 pages of notes and I collected over 800 pages of documents, not including the trial transcripts.

The main title of the book, *Effigy*, speaks to the subject under study: "a crude figure of a hated person." Capital defendants, once tried and found guilty, as the defendant was in this case, certainly qualify as hated persons in society as evidenced by the order to either terminate their lives or to incarcerate them forever. Capital juries are required to reconcile, adjust, or settle their beliefs about the defendant upon which judgment is being rendered as a result of the competition between attorneys who describe and try to explain who the defendant really is. Accordingly, this book will serve to help the public reconcile their view of a defendant in light of the competition that unfolds in the courtroom during the trial that judged him.

CHAPTER ONE

~

Introduction

That innocent woman walking along the road, it's nothing to do with her what-soever. And the man who murdered her is building up and building up and building up until that day something triggers him and it's vomited over her, everything that happened to him since the moment he was born, [and] she be-comes the tragic recipient of the lot.

On February 25, 1999, at approximately 7:00 p.m., Peyton Tuthill was found murdered. According to the autopsy report,[1] she died of "multiple sharp force injuries" including perforation of the heart, lungs, aorta, and left diaphragm. She also had cuts on her throat, ribs, and hands. "Samples of combed and pulled pubic hair, fingernail scrapings, head hair, oral, anal, and vaginal swabs and smears, blood, and multiple samples of trace evidence from various parts of the body and clothing" were collected and submitted to the Denver Police Department crime laboratory. Preliminary information indicated that she had been stabbed to death and that her injuries were consistent with sexual assault.

A suspect, Donta Page, was quickly identified. He was a former resident of a drug and alcohol rehabilitation program (Stout Street) located across the street from the scene of the crime in the current case. He left Denver shortly after Tuthill's murder, and on February 27, 1999, was arrested in Maryland for robbery. The Denver police caught up with Page on March 11, 1999. When they spoke with him about the murder, Page said that he was responsible for the crime. He told a Denver detective that he was committing a burglary and the victim came home, surprising him.

The *Colorado v. Page* trial began in Denver on November 3, 2000. Henry Cooper and Phillip Brimmer served as prosecutors for the State. Their case centered on the bloody crime scene and the horror that the victim must have experienced during the attack. They forwarded a theory of the crime that portrayed the defendant as a cold-blooded killer whose only motivation for the murder was to avoid detection for a burglary. As such, they called numerous police personnel, residents of the neighborhood who knew the defendant, the victim's housemates who discovered the crime, and a coroner to testify about what they had seen and heard on the day of the crime. The prosecutors presented pictures and a video of the crime scene and played the defendant's audiotaped confession for the jury. The defense cross-examined some of the prosecution's witnesses, but reserved most of their comments for their presentation of evidence. In the end, the murder was the only event in the defendant's life that prosecutors used to "define" him, and the jury was urged to consider only the murder in their decisions about the case.

Randy Canney and Jim Castle, defense attorneys, presented a different theory of the crime. Their case focused on the defendant and his terrible history of physical, sexual, and emotional abuse that, it was argued, impaired the defendant's ability to control his emotions and act rationally, particularly when he was scared. His life was portrayed as a series of accidents (including his birth) that led him down a path of criminality replete with the commission of stupidly performed crimes, which quickly led to numerous arrests, and a chaotic, unstable daily life, that included periods of homelessness. Such instability, it was argued, stemmed not only from an abusive home life, but also from a documented lack of intelligence and bouts of overwhelming frustration that the defendant attempted to rectify with drugs and alcohol. As such, the defense called some of the defendant's family members and friends as well as several psychiatrists and neurologists to testify about his abusive childhood and its relationship to his later violence. In short, the defense did not challenge the defendant's responsibility for the crime, but rather maintained that "intent" behind the murder was absent because the defendant is not a normal adult. As such, they argued that justice demanded a conviction for second-degree murder, rather than first-degree murder.

A battle of the experts ensued with the introduction of rebuttal witness testimony. The prosecution began by calling witnesses to refute (1) whether the defendant was able to form a "culpable mental state" during the commission of the crime, (2) interpretation of the PET scan (defendant's brain image that showed damage) by the defense's witnesses, (3) the strength of the relationship between child abuse and later violence, and (4) whether the crime was committed deliberately as required by the first-degree murder statute. The defense objected to the qualification and credibility of the prosecution's rebuttal expert witnesses and was successful at establishing that one of them was not credible or qualified to testify in the capacity for which he was hired by the prosecution. The defense attorneys did not call rebuttal witnesses.

On November 17, 2000, Judge Joseph Meyer read his instructions to the jury. His instructions mainly advised jurors (1) not to consider the penalty in the case, (2) to only consider the charges of first-degree murder after deliberation, second-degree murder, aggravated robbery, first-degree burglary, second-degree sexual assault, and felony murder, (3) to consider insanity only if they find that the defendant was not capable of forming a culpable mental state, (4) to consider the credibility of witnesses, and (5) to weigh the expert testimony as they see fit. The defense wanted second-degree murder, which would remove the penalty of death from sentencing consideration.

Closing statements simply reiterated the cases presented, but each side attacked the theory of the crime that had been forwarded by the opponent. One prosecutor, for example, asked the jury: "Does being physically abused as a child make it right?" The alternate jurors were released following closing statements.

On November 21, 2000, the jury delivered a first-degree murder verdict and a guilty verdict on all of the other charges including aggravated robbery, first-degree burglary, and second-degree sexual assault. A hearing was set for the following day to schedule the penalty phase of the trial. In that proceeding, a panel of judges decided that Page deserved life imprisonment without the possibility of parole instead of the death penalty.

Goals

This book explores how various parties in a capital murder case, including prosecutors, defense attorneys, and the media, attempt to "define" or "portray" competing perspectives on the character of a capital defendant and try to persuade decision-makers (jurors, judges, and, less directly, the general public) to accept these definitions. Further, this qualitative research explores the relationship between those definitions and the verdict on sentencing (life imprisonment versus death) that decision-makers render. It seeks to understand how definitions of a murder defendant are presented in court, processed by the jury, and manifested in the trial outcome. The project employed a case study methodology and included documentary analysis, interviews, and analysis of accounts of the experiences of the defendant and his legal defense team. It raises three critical issues: (1) How do various parties attempt to answer the question, "Who is this defendant?" (2) What techniques or procedures are used to define him? and (3) How does the definition of him affect judges' and jurors' decisions about what to do with him? In short, the project examines the definitions, procedures, and consequences of decision-making in a capital trial.

Trials

Trials are dramatic performances presented to judges and juries. They involve actors, props, stages, choreography, and scripts. They occur in an historical and cultural context, and hence cannot be viewed in isolation. These performances are supposed to tell a story about an event that took place in a previous time and space and to portray an image of the defendant as, for example, evil and unsalvageable, or, alternatively, troubled and worthy of mercy. Judges and juries are asked to believe (or accept) one of the competing definitions.

But how do judges and jurors evaluate other people's actions? The overwhelming task of having to sit and listen to a set of facts as they are told by people who did not witness the event, about people whom the jurors have never met, and about circumstances that most people have never experienced, is given to ordinary citizens: our system of justice requires it. Usually when we make character evaluations (or judgments) we at least have *met* the person. Jurors do it with secondary information (and prosecutors have not even met the defendant). As such, the possibility of inaccurate character evaluations is high.

It is not so much the fact that putting aside personal views and experiences to judge the very same in others is nearly impossible to accomplish, but rather the fact that most people put faith and confidence in this process that makes this such a fascinating subject for scrutiny. People of supposed average intelligence, who are law-abiding, who are registered to vote, or who have a registered driver's license are selected to decide whether a person committed a crime and, if so, what their intent and premeditation was when they committed it. The current study will examine capital jury decision-making, highlighting, among other significant topics, the influence of lawyer performances on the outcome of the trial.

Of course, the facts of the case and attributions about the defendant are presented by legal advocates who have been trained on how to pick a jury, on how to persuade a jury, and on how to present facts to a jury that encourage jurors to accept their point of view. Such skills are rehearsed in law school classes. At a basic level, attorneys do not want "neutral" jurors; they want jurors who, from the start, are thought to be sympathetic to their point of view. In short, a certain level of juror bias is appreciated, although each side (prosecution and defense) is looking, in jury selection (voir dire) for a different sort of bias.

At trial, both sets of attorneys present an image of the defendant that is conducive to their goal: winning a conviction and maximum sentence (for the prosecution) or an acquittal and/or a minimum sentence (for the defense). The images could actually be placed on a continuum from somewhere between a subhuman, rabid animal (who is very dangerous) to a decent person who made some horrible mistakes. Of course, no one can ever determine who the defendant *really* is (or who anyone else *really* is), but the researcher can describe the way each side tried to portray him and infer from the verdict which argument the jury accepted or thought was better.

Suppose, for example, that the prosecution's definition of the defendant was dehumanizing; that is, he is not like us. He is not human. He has no feelings. He is rotten to the core—just a bad seed. He has few (if any) positive attributes, he cannot be rehabilitated, and given the chance, he would repeat the crime. He is unremorseful and dangerous. The prosecution's case would then focus on the bloody crime scene, the horror that the victim must have experienced as he or she was being killed, the defendant's criminal history, the defendant's bad attitude, and the defendant's missed or wasted opportunities to change and be rehabilitated. In short, the prosecution would use stereotypes, fear, and the victim's halo to establish guilt.

Suppose further that the defense's definition of the defendant was humanitarian; that is, he made some horrible mistakes, he has done good things in his life, he has experienced terrible abuse and torture from a very young age, he is loved by and brings joy to others, he never received emotional or professional help for his problems, any one of us could have committed the crime if we had experienced such abuse, and the murder is just one event in the life of the defendant—it should not totally define him. He is more than the worst thing he has ever done.

The defense's case would then focus on the defendant's entire life, in other words, not just the worst day of his life (the murder). They might begin with the childhood and call the family to testify about how abusive it was. The defense attorneys might introduce evidence of prior emotional problems as a result of the abuse and emphasize how damaging these experiences were to the defendant's ability to make judgments. Their experts would testify about the relationship between child abuse and later violence. In short, the defense would use sympathy, statistics, and credentials to overpower the image of the "savage beast" and replace it with an image of a "troubled youth." They might raise the issue of responsibility for the crime: Is the defendant 100 percent responsible (as a prosecutor might argue), or do others (family, teachers, those who failed to make available social services) also share at least a portion of the responsibility?

Rebuttal witnesses (for both the prosecution and the defense) would focus on contradicting what previous lay and expert witnesses had said. Both sides would find much to refute about the other side's witness testimony. Importantly, both lay and expert witnesses are crucial to the development of the stories that the attorneys relate at trial because they add specific details and comprehensive explanations that the attorneys are unable to provide in opening and closing statements. That is, the attorneys tell the story through witnesses. In fact, witness testimony constitutes the bulk of the evidence presented at trial even though it is presented to answer decidedly different questions from each side. The prosecution wants to focus on what the defendant did (behavioral) on the day of the crime; the defense wants to focus on who the defendant *is*, and shed light on how and why his criminality developed.

Finally, closing statements would be more forceful renditions of the images that had been constructed: that is, both the "savage beast" and "troubled youth" images would be summarized. The prosecution might begin with the crime and end with a list of bad things that the defendant had done in his life. The defense, on the other hand, would begin with the defendant's traumatic childhood and personal victimization and end with a plea for mercy. In sum, the prevailing definition of the defendant at trial would be the portrayal by attorneys that the jury or judge believed.

Sociological Explanations

A sociological approach that views a capital trial as an attempt to persuade jurors that one image of the defendant is more valid than another is an unpopular approach. Psychological explanations for murder are preferable when an individual commits an act against another individual; that is, people have a tendency to want to blame the individual instead of inviting more collective responsibility.[2] Besides, it is easier to incarcerate or execute an individual for murder (the "bad apple" theory) than to consider social and political factors that may have contributed to the behavior. Several theories, then, can inform an analysis of a capital trial. Most appropriate, however, seems an overall view of the analysis from the standpoint of social construction; that is, knowledge must be viewed as socially constructed through a series of social facts that fit together to explain a phenomena that can be perceived with common sense. Such social facts can be real or imagined in the mind of the perceiver and, in the current study, the social facts will be deemed real if they are viewed as real by the perceiver. Thus, "if men define situations as real, they are real in their consequences."[3]

Applied to capital juries, this approach suggests that jurors are perceivers of whatever reality the attorneys construct of the defendant and his life, particularly his motives, such that the portrayal of the "man on the street" is either a figment of the attorneys' imaginations or a truthful portrayal of that same man. For example, if attorneys portray the "man on the street" as an evil, vindictive person who views the world as a cold, heartless place where human life is valueless, the "man on the street" is more likely to be perceived by jurors as someone capable of cold-blooded murder. On the other hand, if the "man on the street" is portrayed as a man with mental and emotional problems that sometimes erupt in fits of unintentional violence, and the jurors view the "man on the street" as an ill person who needs special physical and mental help, they are more likely to judge the man as a victim of circumstance. Such perceptions lend themselves to conviction or acquittal of the defendant, respectively.

Attribution theory also deals with how the social perceiver uses information to arrive at causal explanations for events.[4] It examines what information is gathered and how it is combined to form a causal judgment. Causal judgments are based, in part, on whether the perceiver attributes behavior to internal or external loci.[5] If the behavior is attributed to an internal locus, that is, intelligence, strength, evilness, etc., the actor will be held responsible for the outcome of the behavior. But, if the behavior is partially attributed to an external locus, that is, weather, discrimination, child abuse, and so forth, the actor's behavior is less likely to be attributed solely to his or her responsibility.[6]

Erving Goffman's work on *The Presentation of Self in Everyday Life* (1959) offers an interesting way to view the participants and the proceedings of a death penalty trial. In it, Goffman uses the terms "performance" to refer to "all the activity of an individual which occurs during a period marked by his continuous presence before a particular set of observers and which has some influence on the observers" (p. 22), and "personal front" to refer to "items that we most intimately identify with the performer himself and that we naturally expect will follow the performer wherever he goes" (p. 23). Interestingly, the personal front includes race, gender, age, size, looks, posture, speech patterns, facial expressions, and bodily gestures and he divides them into categories of "appearance" and "manner" which provide clues as to how the individual will perform in a given role.

Importantly, another work by Goffman[7] forwards that when a gap exists between who a person *is* and what he or she *ought to be*, stigmatization results. The interaction between people who are stigmatized and normal people (although everyone is stigmatized at some point in time, according to Goffman) depends upon what kind of stigma it is. Applying Goffman's concept of *discreditable* stigma to the current case, then, "the dramaturgical problem of managing information so that the problem [perhaps future dangerousness] remains unknown to the audience"[8] is what the legal defense is all about. Exposing the problem so that it becomes known to the audience, on the other hand, is the task of the prosecution.

Emile Durkheim wrote about the functions of crime and punishment, too. Durkheim forwarded that crime is offensive because it offends society rather than because society decides that it is offensive. "An act is criminal when it offends strong and defined states of the conscience collective [a strongly defined moral consensus]."[9] The very fact that an act offends people is what defines it as criminal, in other words, and society protects itself by meting out punishments that assuage our emotional response to it. Further, there is no difference between the reasons why society meted out punishments in the past and why they are meted out today: vengeance is a time-honored tradition that focuses public outrage in a useful way; that is, people tend to reinforce their commonly held beliefs and values when criminals tread outside the boundaries that honest men have installed. "From all the similar impressions which are exchanged, and the anger that is expressed, there emerges a unique emotion, more or less determinate according to the circumstances, which emanates from no specific person, but from everyone. This is the public wrath."[10]

In short, murder is a peculiar event, creating many mysteries about why it happened, how to react to it, and what can be done to reduce the odds of recurrence. Little attention, however, is paid to who the killer really *is*. Perhaps, the image presented by the defense is more sociological than the prosecution's image, which may be more psychological. Sociologists are charged with the responsibility of identifying social forces in the environment that influence behavior. As such, a sociological analysis of this particular murder trial is undertaken in the current study, which includes an analysis of the competing images portrayed of him by the attorneys at trial. Such images, it is argued here, directly influenced the verdicts.

Capital Punishment in the United States Today

As of July 1, 2006, there are 3,366 persons on death row in the United States. According to the NAACP Legal Defense and Education Fund,[11] 42 percent of these inmates are black. Overall, between 1976 and the beginning of 2006, there were 1,057 executions in the United States. Of those, 20 percent were black defendants with white victims. Moreover, over 79 percent of completed capital cases—cases with a capital sentence outcome—involve white victims even though nationally less than 50 percent of murder victims in the country are white.[12]

It is unclear as to why "American society and most of its citizens continue to embrace capital punishment, which has been abandoned by every other developed nation in the West,"[13] but some literature suggests that it is, in part, due to America's willingness to support vengeance (by and for both society at large and the victim's family),[14] the unwillingness of some states to implement or enforce alternative sentences such as life imprisonment without the possibility of parole,[15] and America's general ignorance of death penalty procedures.[16] Lifton and Mitchell,[17] however, simply reduce the stubbornness to an "American habit for violence" (p. 238).

Further, although 97.5 percent of prosecutors in the United States are white (95.5 percent in Colorado), and 79 percent of death penalty defendants are minorities with white victims, requests for the death penalty by prosecutors, families of victims, and the media are not always granted by those charged with sentencing decisions. Still, the ultimate decision to seek the death penalty in a first-degree murder case resides solely within the prosecutor's discretion. "Prosecutors enjoy almost complete freedom to decline to charge, offer a plea bargain, or decline to seek a death sentence in any particular case."[18] As such, there is "overwhelming evidence that the primary source of arbitrary and discriminatory decision making in capital cases rests with the prosecutor."[19]

Public support for the death penalty is also motivated by political considerations[20] because "few politicians are willing to ignore the preferences of most of their constituents."[21] In fact, "political orientation has remained a stable predictor of death penalty attitudes, comparable in magnitude to sex."[22]

Finally, decisions about how to handle minority defendants are sometimes based on racial stereotypes,[23] which, in turn, can affect attributions about future dangerousness.[24] Attributions of future dangerousness have been shown to be important factors in the decision of whether to execute or incarcerate a capital defendant.

Existing Empirical Scholarship

Before 1987, no researchers paid systematic attention to decision-making by capital juries. Then, Geimer and Amsterdam published their pioneering work, which involved interviews with 54 jurors in ten capital cases in Florida.[25] The researchers found "an inherent tension between the discretion accorded capital-sentencing juries and the guidance for use of that discretion that is constitutionally required" (p. 2). Stimulated by the originality and importance of this work, in 1990 Northeastern University Criminologist William J. Bowers began a comprehensive, nationwide study of how capital juries make life and death decisions.[26] In it, his team of university-based researchers undertook to examine the extent to which jurors exercise of capital sentencing discretion is still infected with, or now cured of, the arbitrariness which the U.S. Supreme Court condemned in *Furman v. Georgia*, and the extent to which the principal kinds of post–*Furman* guided discretion statutes are curbing arbitrary decision-making—as the court said they would in *Gregg v. Georgia* and its companion cases. (p. 1043)

"*Furman v. Georgia* held that juries were imposing the death penalty in an arbitrary and capricious manner in violation of the Eighth Amendment's prohibition against 'cruel and unusual' punishment." Following the *Furman* decision, the death penalty was temporarily suspended and 629 death sentences were commuted to life sentences. In 1976, *Gregg v. Georgia* put the Supreme Court's stamp of approval on new death penalty statutes that included (1) "guided discretion" sentencing guidelines for juries, (2) bifurcated trials (splitting them into separate guilt and penalty phases), (3) automatic appellate review of convictions and sentences, and (4) some sort of proportionality review (ensuring that only the worst crimes and criminals receive the harshest sentences). In January 1977, Gary Gilmore became the first death row inmate to be executed in the United States following the *Furman*-imposed moratorium.[27]

The ongoing Capital Jury Project primarily relies on personal interviews with capital jurors as the main source of data. The capital jurors in the project are guaranteed confidentiality and are paid $20 as an incentive to participate. There are three stages to the sampling plan: selective sampling of states with guided discretion capital-sentencing statutes followed by selective sampling of bifurcated capital trials, and random selection of at least four capital jurors for interviews. Thus far, the project has yielded 30 empirical studies and six dissertations about capital jury decision-making since its inauguration in 1990.[28]

This project expands the Capital Jury Project design by using interview data from a 2000 Colorado death penalty case. The researcher has focused her attention on various attempts by attorneys to portray or define the defendant, and how those efforts were evaluated or interpreted by jurors.

The Case of Donta Page

Case study methodology was used to analyze the capital trial of the defendant, Donta Page. The research expands our knowledge of how the sentencing authorities (judge and jury) make life and death decisions by identifying images of the defendant that are presented to the judges and jurors who make guilt and sentencing decisions. These images are important to an understanding of how decisions are made about people, especially when they face criminal charges in a court of law. The images themselves are constructed by attorneys whose sole purpose in the trial is to portray the defendant in a light most favorable to their position. That is, once sentencing authorities are asked to decide whether the defendant at bar should be sentenced to death, the defendant's guilt or innocence of the capital crime is not at issue. Instead, who the defendant *is*, rather than what crime he has committed, is the focus of debate.

It is important to determine how various parties "define" the defendant because the consequences of these definitions are permanent. For example, prosecutors seeking a death sentence may attempt to portray the defendant as a "savage beast" and this definition may compete against an image of a "troubled youth" that the defense will develop. This research uses a case study, coupled with extensive participant observation, to examine how competing definitions are used. The necessity of dehumanization for death penalty sentencing has been noted by Robert Johnson.[29] He writes:

> Indeed, the point of the modern bureaucratic execution procedure is to suppress any real-life human reactions on the part of the prisoners or their executioners. Human reactions—displays of character or faith—would interfere with the efficient administration of the death penalty and indeed draw unwanted attention to the violence of the proceedings. The impersonality of the modern death penalty makes it distinctively brutal.

Theoretically, verdicts and sentencing decisions are supposed to be the result of rationale and logic, and bounded by clear statutory guidelines. Specifically, jurors are asked to make causal inferences about the defendant's violence, and what to do with him. This project offers a contrasting view, one that attempts to show that defense attorneys believe that the closer a jury or panel of judges "feels" to a defendant, the less likely they are to support his execution. That is, jurors (and judges) are less likely to sentence defendants to death when the "social distance" between them is perceived as relatively small. In fact, Howard S. Becker, in 1963, wrote that "the degree to which other people will respond to a given act as deviant varies greatly" (p. 12), particularly across time and relational variables such as "who commits the act and who feels he has been harmed by it."[30]

Prosecutors, on the other hand, "play a central, if little understood, role in the death penalty process. Their significance can hardly be overstated, for the machinery cannot grind forward at all without the original decision by a district attorney to seek a death sentence."[31] Following that decision, however, the prosecutor's focus shifts to zealously building a case against the capital defendant that contradicts the theory of the defense and widens the social distance between the defendant and the jury. Widening the social distance between the jury and the defendant increases the likelihood of conviction.

Jury verdicts and sentencing decisions, therefore, not only follow statutory guidelines, but can also be subjective. Hence, verdicts and sentencing decisions in America hinge upon interpretation of the situation and the interpretation depends upon the skills of the participating attorneys in utilizing or debunking stereotypes about the defendant to persuade a jury or panel of judges to incarcerate or execute. In the current case, the skills of the attorneys were comparable, which enhanced the competition of the images presented.

Applications

Even though interest in criminality, particularly murder, is not new, there has been little attention paid by researchers to the definitions that are applied to murder defendants that shape our understanding of who the defendant *is*. Much of the research with regard to murder defendants focuses on their victims and community responses to the stigma of murder[32] or a defendant's rights and motivations.[33] This project is unique in that it involves participant observation of a murder trial from beginning to end in a state where the decision of whether to sentence someone to death was, at the time, made by a panel of three judges. The larger issue, however, is on how attorneys construct an image of a defendant in order to win the case and that the image that prevails also wins. Further, if the image that prevails is one that also dehumanizes the defendant, he is more likely to be sentenced to death (Johnson 1998).

This research adds significantly to our knowledge about how images of a defendant influence the trial verdict, and what methods attorneys use to construct such images. The larger intellectual dimension of the current study addresses the question of who the defendant was on the day of the crime, the prosecution's approach (which lent itself to a retributive response), versus who he has been for most of his life, the defense's approach (which lent itself to a humanitarian response).

We now turn our attention to reviewing the theoretical and empirical research that informs this case study analysis.

Notes

1. The autopsy report by Dr. Thomas Henry, Denver County Coroner, was entered as an exhibit in the guilt phase of the trial.

2. William Ryan, *Blaming the Victim* (New York: Pantheon Books, 1971).

3. William I. Thomas and Dorothy S. Thomas, *The Child in America: Behavior Problems and Programs* (New York: Knopf, 1928), 52.

4. Susan T. Fiske and Shelley E. Taylor, *Social Cognition* (New York: McGraw-Hill, 1991).

5. Roger Brown, *Social Psychology*, 2nd ed. (New York: The Free Press, 1986); Susan T. Fiske and Shelley E. Taylor, *Social Cognition* (New York: McGraw-Hill, 1991).

6. F. M. Lewis and L.H. Daltroy, "How Causal Explanations Influence Health Behavior: Attribution Theory" in *Health Education and Health Behavior: Theory, Research and Practice*, ed. K. Glanz, F. M. Lewis, and B. K. Rimer (San Francisco: Jossey-Bass Publishers, 1990).

7. Erving Goffman, *Stigma: Notes on the Management of Spoiled Identity* (Englewood Cliffs, NJ: Prentice Hall, 1963).

8. George Ritzer, *Modern Sociological Theory* 4th ed. (New York: McGraw-Hill, 1996), 220.

9. Anthony Giddens, *Emile Durkheim: Selected Writings* (New York: Cambridge University Press, 1972), 123.

10. Giddens, *Emile Durkheim*, 123.

11. Information available on the Death Penalty Information Center Website www.deathpenaltyinfo.org.

12. Information available on the Death Penalty Information Center Website www.deathpenaltyinfo.org.

13. Robert Jay Lifton and Greg Mitchell, *Who Owns Death? Capital Punishment, The American Conscience, and the End of Executions* (New York: Harper Collins, 2002), xvi.

14. James R. Acker, Robert M. Bohm, and Charles S. Lanier, *America's Experiment with Capital Punishment: Reflections on the Past, Present, and Future of the Ultimate Penal Sanction* (Durham, NC: Carolina Academic Press, 1998); Samuel R. Gross, "Update: American Public Opinion on the Death Penalty—It's Getting Personal," *Cornell Law Review* 83(1998):1448–1475.

15. Gross, "Update," 1448–1475.

16. Michael Mello, *Against the Death Penalty: The Relentless Dissents of Justices Brennan and Marshall* (Boston, MA: Northeastern University Press, 1996); Robert Johnson, *Death Work: A Study of the Modern Execution Process* (Belmont, CA: Wadsworth Publishing, 1998).

17. Robert Jay Lifton and Greg Mitchell, *Who Owns Death? Capital Punishment, the American Conscience, and the End of Executions* (New York: Harper Collins, 2002).

18. Jeffrey J. Pokorak, "Probing the Capital Prosecutor's Perspective: Race of the Discretionary Actors," *Cornell Law Review* 83(1998): 1811–1820.

19. Pokorak, *Probing*, 1819.

20. David Pritchard, "Homicide and Bargained Justice: The Agenda Setting Effect of Crime News on Prosecutors," *Public Opinion Quarterly* 50(1986): 143–159.

21. James R. Acker, Robert M. Bohm, and Charles S. Lanier, *America's Experiment with Capital Punishment: Reflections on the Past, Present, and Future of the Ultimate Penal Sanction* (Durham, North Carolina: Carolina Academic Press, 1998), 26.

22. Samuel R. Gross, "Update: American Public Opinion on the Death Penalty – It's Getting Personal," *Cornell Law Review* 83:1448–1475.

23. George S. Bridges and Sara Steen, "Racial Disparities in Official Assessments of Juvenile Offenders: Attributional Stereotypes as Mediating Mechanisms,"*American Sociological Review* 63(1998): 554–570; Farrell, Ronald Farrell and Malcolm D. Holmes, "The Social and Cognitive Structure of Legal Decision-Making," *The Sociological Quarterly* 32(1991): 529–542; Victoria Lynn Swigert and Ronald A. Farrell, "Normal Homicides and the Law," *American Sociological Review* 42(1977): 16–32.

24. John H. Blume, Stephen Garvey, and Sheri Johnson, "Future Dangerousness in Capital Cases: Always at Issue," *Cornell Law Review* 86(2001): 404–410; Mark Mandell, "Overcoming Juror Bias: Is There an Answer?" *Trial* 36(2000): 28.

25. William S. Geimer and Jonathan Amsterdam, "Why Jurors Vote Life or Death: Operative Factors in Ten Florida Death Penalty Cases," *American Journal of Criminal Law* 15(1988):1–54.

26. William J. Bowers, "The Capital Jury Project: Rationale, Design, and Preview of Early Findings," *Indiana Law Journal* 70(1995): 1043–1102.

27. Samuel R. Gross and Robert Mauro, *Death and Discrimination: Racial Disparities in Capital Sentencing* (Boston, MA: Northeastern University Press, 1984); Robert Jay Lifton and Greg Mitchell, *Who Owns Death? Capital Punishment, the American Conscience, and the End of Executions* (New York: Harper Collins, 2002).

28. Stated in a telephone conversation between the researcher and William J. Bowers on December 10, 2001.

29. Robert Johnson, *Death Work: A Study of the Modern Execution Process* (Belmont, CA: Wadsworth, 1998), 50.

30. Howard S. Becker, *Outsiders: Studies in the Sociology of Deviance* (New York: Free Press, 1963), 12.

31. Robert Jay Lifton and Greg Mitchell, *Who Owns Death? Capital Punishment, the American Conscience, and the End of Executions* (New York: Harper Collins, 2002), 107.

32. Hugo Adam Bedau, *The Death Penalty in America: Current Controversies* (New York: Oxford University Press, 1997); Darnell Hunt, "Reaffirming Race: Reality, Negotiation, and the Trial of the Century," *The Sociological Quarterly* 38(1997): 399–422; Hazel May, "Who Killed Whom: Victimization and Culpability in the Social Construction of Murder," *British Journal of Sociology* 50(1999): 489–506; Hazel May, "Murderers' Relatives: Managing Stigma, Negotiating Identity," *Journal of Contemporary Ethnography* 29(2000):198–221.

33. John E. Conklin, *New Perspectives in Criminology* (Boston, MA: Allyn and Bacon, 1996); Paul Cromwell, *In Their Own Words: Criminals on Crime*, 2nd ed. (Los Angeles: Roxbury Publishers, 1996).

CHAPTER TWO

~

The Death Penalty in the United States and How Juries Operate

The Constitution, as interpreted by the courts, does not require that the accused, even in a capital case, be represented by able and effective counsel.

In the beginning, public executions served as a method of social control that was not only condoned by clergy and government officials but that were "well attended and enjoyed by the crowds."[1] In fact, "execution day served as both a warning and a celebration. . . . Civil and clerical figures offered proof that society worked properly and that God saved souls."[2] But, since public executions of the late 1800s, there has been a drastic change in the methods of execution, that is, from torturous death mechanisms like the wheel, drawing and quartering, drowning, burning at the stake (for members of the lower classes), and hanging (for members of the upper classes) during the Middle Ages[3] to lethal injection, which, though sometimes botched, does not usually result in bloody mutilations as previously observed. By the time that public hangings began to decline in the late 1800s, the preceding two centuries had already seen a turn away from more painful and prolonged types of executions. Some say that such changes indicate a general trend towards abolition of the death penalty.[4]

The gas chamber, for example, which was offered as a more humane method of execution beginning in 1921, has drawn criticism from proponents of the Eighth Amendment on the grounds that it (and the electric chair) epitomizes cruel and unusual punishment. So today no states mandate lethal gas as a form of execution. Also, the drastic reduction in the number of crimes punishable by death (from 223 crimes in England in 1800 [a.k.a. the bloody code], down to primarily one crime today—murder) indicates a general trend toward abolition of the death penalty.

Such advancements can be traced back to the Quaker establishment of prisons as alternatives to the death penalty in the eighteenth century, along with Cesare Beccaria's reform movement in 1793 that forwarded the concept of "rehabilitation" for prisoners.[5] These physical changes brought about conceptual changes in the law including degrees of murder in Pennsylvania in 1794 and the establishment of the first death penalty abolition group in 1845. By the middle of the nineteenth century, legislative bills were constantly being brought before Congress that urged abolition of the death penalty in the United States. Michigan was the first state in the Union to abolish the death penalty in 1847, followed by Wisconsin in 1857, and Iowa, Maine, and Colorado in 1897.[6]

In short, the historical view of capital punishment conjures visions of public mutilations and torture where justice was rendered swiftly and sometimes arbitrarily. But the American conscience has moved away from lynch-mob justice to a more humane treatment of prisoners that allows them to be executed with so-called dignity and with rights to appeal that ensure due process. Still, mistakes have been made and over 210 people have been released from death row in recent years,[7] in part, due to biological advances that have allowed scientific testing,[8] specifically DNA testing, to eliminate people as participants to various crimes.[9] Such DNA evidence, along with appellate review and academic research, has uncovered systemic fallibility that has freed numerous people who were condemned by and in a court of law; that is, "based on the continuing record of discovery of erroneous convictions, we fully expect future inquiry will show one or more of the 2000 persons now under death sentence to be innocent."[10]

In 1972, the U.S. Supreme Court held that juries were imposing the death penalty in an arbitrary and capricious manner in violation of the Eighth Amendment's prohibition against "cruel and unusual" punishment.[11] As a result, the death sentences of 629 prisoners in the United States were reduced to life imprisonment. Legislators soon passed revised death penalty statutes, however, most of which "guided discretion" by splitting the trial process into separate guilt and penalty phases, and included procedural guidelines for jurors that attempted to eliminate arbitrary and capricious death sentences (*Gregg v. Georgia* 1976; *Proffit v. Florida* 1976; and *Jurek v. Texas* 1976). Such guidelines as the "threshold" statute (where at least one aggravator must exist), the "balancing" statute (where jurors are required to weigh aggravators against mitigators to decide penalty), and the "directed" statute (where the death penalty can only be imposed upon capital felons under aggravating circumstances) were approved in *Gregg v. Georgia, Proffit v. Florida*, and *Jurek v. Texas*, respectively.[12]

Debate over whether the guided discretion statutes remedied the problems of arbitrariness and capriciousness that they were designed to remedy continues to this day. Indeed, major questions have been raised in a wealth of literature about the objectivity and rationality of contemporary death sentencing practices.[13]

One study, conducted by Craig Haney even asserts that "many of the procedures that govern jury decision-making are designed to sow the seeds of chaos and confusion, and ensure that juror decision-making is based on partial truths rather than on more complete knowledge and understanding of the issues."[14] In short, the literature suggests that arbitrariness and capriciousness in capital jury decision-making may still exist. In 1977, executing resumed when Gary Gilmore stopped his appeals and submitted to a firing squad in Utah.[15]

Denver and the State of Colorado

Denver, Colorado's first legal hanging took place in 1859.[16] John Stoefel, who admitted to "shooting his brother-in-law for a small bag of gold," was tried and hanged within 48 hours of committing the crime. He was characterized as a "hungarian and a heathen" and his execution was reportedly attended by 1,000 persons. In the nineteenth century, high attendance at public executions was common. In fact, punishment for capital crimes was (1) swift, usually resulting in hanging within eight to ten months of sentencing by a jury, and (2) public, "sometimes with a carnival-like atmosphere."[17] The carnival-like atmosphere surrounding public executions remained until the last legal public execution in Colorado, that of Andrew Green in 1886 for the murder of a streetcar conductor, which brought an estimated crowd of 20,000 people to the hanging in Denver.[18] Following Green's death, support for *public* executions dropped and they were moved behind the closed doors of the state penitentiary at Cañon City (toward the end of the nineteenth century) where, today, news coverage is minimal and the death penalty procedure is mysterious.[19]

Subsequently, Colorado abolished the death penalty in 1897, but that abolition only lasted for three years because in 1901 "for a conviction of first degree murder, the jury was given a choice between imposing a sentence of death or life imprisonment with hard labor."[20] Later, executions were performed with lethal gas. In fact, the first person to be executed by lethal gas in Colorado was William Kelley on June 22, 1934, but in 1988 Colorado legislators voted to change the method of execution to lethal injection.

By March of 2002, there were six people on Colorado's death row, four of whom were sentenced to death by a panel of three judges. The panel of judges was established on June 5, 1995, to rectify the reluctance of Colorado juries in sentencing capital defendants to death. "The statute moved sentencing in death penalty cases to a panel of three judges and eliminated the jury's role in the sentencing phase."[21] Colorado Senate Bill 54 revised Section 16-11-103 of the Colorado Revised Statutes, which became effective on July 1, 1995.[22] The revision survived constitutional scrutiny (that argues that a violation of the Sixth Amendment right to a jury trial occurs in the absence of sentencing by a jury) until June 24, 2002, when the U.S. Supreme Court decided in *Ring v. Arizona* (2002) that "the Sixth Amendment would be senselessly diminished if it encompassed the factfinding necessary to increase a defendant's sentence by two years, but not the factfinding necessary to put him to death. We hold that the Sixth Amendment applies to both."[23] As such, persons who have been sentenced to death by judges must now have their cases reviewed.

The Death Penalty Today

According to the NAACP's "Death Row USA" (2007), as of January 1, 2007, 3,350 persons await execution in the United States. Forty-two percent of those on death row are black, 45 percent are white, and 11 percent are Hispanic. Over 98 percent of all persons currently on death row are males. All of the inmates on death row have been convicted of murder.

Between 1976 and January 1, 2007, Texas, Virginia, and Oklahoma have led the nation in the number of executions with 379, 98, and 83 executions respectively. Thirty-four percent of those executed during that time period were black, 57 percent were white, and 7 percent were Hispanic. And, while 39 states use the death penalty as a form of punishment in the United States, 36 of those 39 use lethal injection or offer lethal injection as an option. Alabama and Nebraska are the only two states not to offer the option of lethal injection; in both, the death penalty is carried out by electrocution.[24]

The cost of the death penalty varies from state to state. In Florida, for example, $57 million was spent on death penalty cases between 1973 and 1988 to achieve 18 executions. As such, an average of $3.2 million was spent on each completed execution. Texas averages $2.3 million per death penalty case, too, which is three times the cost of incarceration for 40 years at the highest security level in that state. Colorado taxpayers have spent more than

$2.5 million on five death penalty cases, one of which ended in a death sentence.[25]

The Bureau of Justice Statistics publishes an annual report on America's death rows, the latest of which is entitled *Capital Punishment 2000*. This publication reports that 51.7 percent of U.S. prisoners under sentence of death on December 31, 2000, had less than a high school diploma or GED level of education (p. 8). Sixty-eight percent of prisoners under sentence of death were between the ages of 25 and 44 with the youngest offender being 18 and the oldest being 85 (p. 9). Also, "among prisoners executed from 1977 to 2000, the average time spent between the imposition of the most recent sentence received and execution was more than 10 years" (p. 12). Florida (375), North Carolina (238), and Georgia (135) had the highest numbers of overturned death sentences between 1973 and 2000, while Texas (45) and Florida (18) had the two highest rates of death sentence commutations (p. 15).

Legal Representation and the Role of Attorneys

To shed light on the importance of attorneys' abilities to persuade juries to adopt particular images of a defendant, we must understand the importance of quality of representation. Legal representation of indigent death penalty defendants has become an increasingly disturbing topic of debate, even though the concern is not over whether the death defendants *are* represented, but rather as to how *well* they are represented.[26] Certainly, capital sentences that are imposed when lawyers sleep during the trial, when lawyers are paid less than what they could earn by pumping gas for a living, or when lawyers lack the resources and skills to properly defend clients who are charged with capital offenses, are suspect.[27] Unfortunately, though, the representation issue boils down to funding; for example, "most fundamental is the wholly inadequate funding for the defense of indigents. As a result, there is simply no functioning adversary system in many states."[28] This state of affairs is tolerated essentially because the U.S. Supreme Court does not require anything more; that is, as long as the assigned counsel is not deemed "ineffective," the constitutional requirement has been met. "The Constitution, as interpreted by the courts, does not require that the accused, even in a capital case, be represented by able and effective counsel."[29] The case of *Strickland v. Washington* (1984), for example, only mandated that counsel be provided to defendants facing a capital crime. The competence of that counsel was not discussed.

Importantly, the outcome of a capital trial depends at least in part on the skills and resources of the attorneys involved in presenting their cases to the judge and jury who will decide whether a capital defendant lives or dies. As such, it is important to consider the limits placed on lawyers in presenting their cases, particularly the constitutional limits. Prior to *Lockett v. Ohio* (1977), for example, the sentencing judge was "not permitted to consider the defendant's character, prior record, age, lack of specific intent to cause death, and her relatively minor part in the crime"[30] before sentencing the petitioner (who was convicted of aiding and abetting a robbery which caused the death of a person) to death. In that opinion, the court held that "the limited range of mitigating circumstances [history, character, and condition of the defendant] which may be considered by the sentencer under the Ohio statute is incompatible with the Eighth and Fourteenth Amendments" because the constitution requires that "a death penalty statute must not preclude consideration of relevant mitigating factors."[31]

Concurring in the majority opinion of the Court which vacated Sandra Lockett's death sentence, Justice Byron White wrote that

> The Ohio statute, with its blunderbuss, virtually mandatory approach to imposition of the death penalty for certain crimes, wholly fails to recognize the unique individuality of every criminal defendant who comes before its courts.[32]

But, in dissenting from that portion of the opinion, Justice Rehnquist wrote:

> I think it clear from this context that the term "mitigating circumstances" was *not* so broad as to encompass any evidence which the defense attorney saw fit to present to a judge or jury. . . . By encouraging defendants in capital cases, and presumably sentencing judges and juries, to take into consideration anything under the sun as a "mitigating circumstance," it will not guide sentencing discretion but will totally unleash it.[33]

From this opinion, then, it is clear that lawyers do not have unfettered access to the jury's hearts and minds, but rather are encouraged to limit the kinds of issues they raise in a court of law even when the defendant's life is at stake. In short, evidence presented at trial must only relate to the nature of the crime or the character of the offender.

Finally, with regard to adversarial balance, early findings of the Capital Jury Project report that "jurors' responses present a picture of stark pro-prosecution one-sided-ness."[34] In fact, jurors believed that the prosecution held advantages in the areas of preparation, communication with the jury, commitment to winning the case, and fighting hard during the guilt phase of the trial. And the advantages were measured to be "great" rather than "moderate" or "slight." This disparity of counsel may be due, in part, to jurors predisposition to death as required by the "death qualified" jury, according to Bowers, as well as to the perceived "ineffectiveness of defense counsel and the proneness to favor the prosecution."[35] To that end, Bowers concludes:

> Whatever its causes, however, the implication of this perceived adversarial imbalance is that advocacy on behalf of a punishment less than death is in the hands of someone most jurors have come to regard as inferior or second rate, at least by these indicators of performance and motivation.[36]

The Problem of Racial Bias and Discrimination

Race has been one of the major predictors of who is sentenced to death in America. Although only 50 percent of homicide victims are white (NAACP Legal Defense Fund, "Death Row USA" 2002), some 80 percent of those executed in the United States since 1977 were put to death for killing white victims (NAACP Legal Defense Fund, "Death Row USA" 2002). Numerous studies have documented a disproportionate number of people sentenced to death for killing whites[37] even though the race of the defendant was found to be less significant than the race of the victim. This is one reason why Justices Thurgood Marshall and William Brennan dissented on all death penalty decisions in the United States, including those that were denied certiorari, during their tenures on the Supreme Court (1967–1991 for Marshall; 1956–1990 for Brennan) for the reason of race discrimination, among other Eighth and Fourteenth amendment issues. Still, "the most striking racial pattern in the use of the death penalty in America has been the disproportionate execution of blacks."[38]

Pre-*Furman* studies such as those conducted by Harold Garfinkel[39] and Thorsten Sellin[40] document patterns of racial discrimination where defendants who killed whites were more likely to receive the sentence of death than defendants who killed blacks. The same pattern was found in post-*Furman* studies conducted by Bowers and Pierce,[41] Marc Reidel,[42] and Hans Ziesel.[43] It should be noted that the data from these studies came from some of the states where the death penalty is most often used—Florida, Georgia, and Texas—and from states where the largest numbers of death row inmates are black (Florida and Texas).[44] In short, "the best evidence available provides strong support for the argument that, to this day, race influences the decision of who will die in Florida's [and any other state's] electric chair."[45]

The most famous race-based decision about the possibility of discriminatory death sentencing was *McCleskey v. Kemp* in 1987 where the petitioner raised 18 claims alleging that the death penalty is imposed in a racially discriminatory manner in violation of the Eighth and Fourteenth amendments to the Constitution. In that case, raw data from "the Baldus study," conducted by Professor David Baldus, a law professor at the University of Iowa, indicated that "defendants charged with killing white persons receive the death penalty in 11 percent of the cases, but defendants charged with killing blacks received the death penalty in only 1 percent of the cases."[46] In that case, the Supreme Court found methodological problems that rendered the study flawed and denied the petitioner's claim on that basis. Thus, "to prevail under the Equal Protection Clause, McCleskey must prove that the decision makers in *his* case acted with discriminatory purpose."[47]

In the small percentage of cases where whites have been executed for killing blacks in the United States, that is, "less than two-tenths of 1 percent of known executions" or 30 cases,[48] the victim held a higher social status than the defendant (when the operational definition of status included a measure of race, class, occupation, economic value, marginality, prior criminality, and community integration).[49] That is, "crimes where the victim's status ranks above the offender's status—are treated as more serious than downward crimes, and punishment is more likely to have a downward than an upward direction."[50] This pattern raises the issue of whether death penalty defendants are truly the worst miscreants in our society or simply the least socially desirable. Certainly, "a large part of the death row population is made up of people who are distinguished by neither their records nor the circumstances of their crime, but by their abject poverty, debilitating mental impairments, minimal intelligence, and the poor legal representation they received."[51]

Public Opinion

In recent years, public support for the death penalty dropped. While 80 percent of the American public voiced support in 1994, only 66 percent voiced support in February 2000.[52] The decrease in support can be attributed to decreasing belief in the deterrent value of the death penalty,[53] and perceived openness to alternative sentencing.[54]

Some data on decreasing support for the death penalty also supports the *Marshall Hypothesis*, forwarded by Justice Thurgood Marshall in his written response to the *Furman* decision in 1972,[55] which suggests that if the American public knew the truth about the death penalty, they would not support it.[56] Importantly, evidence for the validity of the Marshall Hypothesis is inconclusive, but Fox and colleagues argue that only a modification is warranted. To that end, they re-hypothesize that "if Americans were better informed about the operation of the criminal justice system, they would not be so vehement in their support of the death penalty."[57]

Further, with regard to decreasing support for the death penalty, police, including corrections officials, have denied the effectiveness of the death penalty as a law enforcement tool.[58] That is, "a clear majority of the police chiefs in the Hart Poll say that capital punishment is not an effective law enforcement tool, even though they support it philosophically."[59]

Death sentences imposed by jurors have steadily declined in recent years, too. In general and in theory, then, the public still supports the death penalty as long as they don't have to impose it, watch it, or administer the lethal mechanism.[60] Certainly, "a key to capital punishment . . . is that no one feels responsible for the killing."[61] Still, some literature suggests that data from the General Social Survey and Gallup polls, two of the premiere mechanisms for gathering information about views on the death penalty from American citizens, has, over time, changed such that the questions in most recent polls are vastly different from those in earlier polls which simply asked broad-based questions, such as "Do you believe in the death penalty for murder?"[62] Today, such questions are much more specific, for example, "Are you in favor of the death penalty for a person convicted of murder?"[63] There is some doubt as to whether the wording of the questions has anything to do with the results of such polls, but in the current case such word usage is pertinent to understanding how and why people perceive information that is read, told, or showed to them. Afterall, the current study suggests that jurors are influenced by lawyer performances and if the lawyers refer to the defendant in court as a "cold-blooded killer," for example, the image of the defendant is affected. Words are powerful communication devices, in other words, and literature on the death penalty and jury decision-making supports this assertion.

Demographic variables, specifically race and gender, have been, and continue to be, useful predictors of death penalty attitudes. Historically, blacks have supported the death penalty less than whites, and women less than men.[64] Political affiliations have also been strong indicators. For example, "on the 1996 General Social Survey, 61 percent of Democrats, 70 percent of Independents, and 85 percent of Republicans were in favor of the death penalty" (Gross 1998:1451). Westerners are more favorable towards the death penalty than easterners and midwesterners. "Strong support also appears . . . among those of high social classes with more education and higher income."[65]

However, "when Americans are asked about the death penalty in the context of particular facts, support drops. It drops sharply in the face of each of several mitigating factors that are so prevalent that at least one is probably present in almost every death penalty case."[66] In other words, it is difficult to obtain a *true* measure of general public opinion on the death penalty in the absence of a particular case even though support for the death penalty decreases, generally, when alternatives to the death penalty, such as life imprisonment without the possibility of parole, are available.[67] The decrease can be attributed to the fact that "when we learn almost anything about the killer, even irrelevant details that are perfectly consistent with homicidal mania—that he has a family, pets, hobbies—the stereotypical image is diluted and the focus shifts to the individual."[68] With this historical and cultural context, we now turn our attention to reviewing what social scientists have discovered about how jurors think.

How Juries Operate

Juries are not a random sample of the population. In fact, in some states, only registered voters are used. In Colorado, the process is similar: Once a year, all people with driver's licenses, state identification cards, and registered voters are put into a pool of names. A computer system, maintained by the State Court Administration Office, eliminates duplicate names and each potential juror is issued a number. Numbers are entered into a database in a computer and when a court calls the State Court Administration Office and requests a specific number of jurors, the computer selects that number of people randomly by number and sends out notices to appear. This system is applied to all juries that are convened in the state of Colorado, including those that are convened for the purpose of deciding capital cases. Capital juries, in other words, are no more or less qualified to hear cases involving life or death than they are to hear cases involving medical malpractice, insurance fraud, or personal injury claims, for example.

But capital jury decision-making has become increasingly complex[69] Not only are today's capital jurors expected to weigh both mitigating and aggravating factors to make their life-or-death decisions,[70] but they are also expected to ignore whatever biases with which they may enter the courtroom.[71] They are especially required to avoid any racial bias, which has sometimes been found to influence prosecutorial and jury decisions in capital cases.[72] In fact, a study conducted in 1990 by James Alan Fox and others concluded that "many of our findings and comments have implications for selecting capital juries. Certain respondent characteristics—such as race, age, and sex—are unequivocally associated with death penalty opinion."[73]

Interestingly, one study asserts that expecting jurors to ignore racial bias may be counterproductive to the goal of rendering justice because if jurors do not acknowledge the existence of the bias, its influence will continue to be overlooked. In that essay, Jody Armour asserts that "it is difficult to change an attitude that is unacknowledged" and argues that "even low-prejudiced subjects who have well-internalized non-prejudiced beliefs about blacks have cognitive structures (that is, stereotypes) that automatically produce stereotype-congruent evaluations of ambiguous behaviors when subjects cannot monitor stereotype activation consciously."[74]

The literature also suggests that it is not unusual for jurors to infect the task of making decisions about capital defendants by relying on non-legal factors that are not supposed to be part of their deliberations, such as future dangerousness,[75] pretrial publicity in the mass media,[76] and xenophobia.[77] Some studies have even found that jurors have disregarded judges' instructions in making decisions when the instructions were unclear or confusing.[78]

Other studies have found that some jurors have ignored witness testimony, particularly expert witness testimony,[79] even though it was pertinent to the establishment of guilt or innocence, mitigation and aggravation, motivation and cause. The effect, according to Myers and coauthors is that courtrooms are having to be turned into classrooms during trial even though "juries are not competent to resolve scientific evidence issues."[80] In fact, the authors suggest that "matters of complex scientific evidence should be removed from them" because the "trial process itself may be as much an impediment to jury comprehension and understanding as the complexity of the legal concepts and evidence, or the competencies of jurors." Consequently, jurors have relied upon their own understanding of human behavior to determine a defendant's guilt and/or sentence,[81] or on how the evidence is presented to them,[82] particularly their feelings about the performances of the lawyers who are participating in the case.[83]

For example, Ahlen's research on the impact of opening statements on jury comprehension suggests that the trial outcome is determined by the relative performance of attorneys at trial, particularly in their opening and closing statements. "Most litigators would agree that an effective opening statement can be a great advantage in ultimately persuading the jury. Some go as far as to say that trials are won or lost in openings."[84] He goes on to say that the pressure to deliver an "emotion-packed" opening is great because such emotion is conducive to making jurors feel responsible for the verdicts they render. "A nationally prominent civil counsel suggests that attorneys use emotion-packed language and emphasize to jurors in opening that they can control the destiny of more than just the plaintiff, but also that of the defendant." Finally, he asserts that "an effective opening statement is an essential aid to the jury's understanding of the evidence which will follow."[85]

Also, Burns argues that lawyers influence the outcome of trials by "appeal[ing] to the emotions and prejudices of jurors and with effect . . . [and] jurors are prey to this sort of manipulation and are incapable of understanding, let alone following, the instructions."[86] He goes on to suggest that trials are competitive performances that are designed to elicit compelling stories and that verdicts are the result of the performances that present an acceptable theory—juries simply decide which theory to believe. The dust cover of his book states that this is as much a result of "which lawyer can best connect with the hearts and minds of the jurors as by what the evidence might suggest." More specifically, Burns observes:

> That is one reason why trial lawyers say that the trial is a battle for the imagination of the jury. To anticipate somewhat, it is also why it is so important that the jury want to accept one account rather than another. It is one of the reasons why social scientists say that the acceptance of one theory rather than another "causes" the verdict. Trial "facts" are heavily theory-laden.[87]

On the other hand, a study conducted by Diamond and colleagues (1996) where "jurors in a simulated videotaped case involving civil or criminal law issues were studied to test juror reaction to lawyers" concluded that "a jury's choice of verdict and their reaction to attorneys and witnesses do not appear to be connected."[88] Both Diamond and colleagues (1996) and Burns (1999) express the need for further research on the relationship between lawyer performances and jury verdicts.

Besides, some literature suggests that both jury decision-making and larger public opinion on the death penalty have become politicized—divided along party lines and infected by pretrial publicity,[89] while other studies conclude that jurors who make life and death decisions sometimes make those decisions prematurely (Bowers et al. 1998; Haney 1995; and Sandys 1995), that is, "before the sentencing stage of the trial, before hearing the evidence or arguments concerning the appropriate punishment, and before the judge's instructions for making the sentencing decision."[90] Jurors are even able to thwart feeling responsible for those decisions by placing the onus on either the defendant, or the judge who oversees the trial and has the ability to override many of their decisions.[91] "Passing the buck" in such a fashion may lead to immoral and unjustifiable jury decisions.[92]

In short, the literature suggests that there is a need for research surrounding the relationship between lawyer performances and jury decisions. In fact, almost all of the literature on jury decision-making suggests that further investigation into this relationship is warranted not only because "juror motivation is under-investigated and under-reported,"[93] but also because "there is no way to guide the discretion of juries."[94] Hopefully, though, a comprehensive review of the trial process with regard to trial performances and jury decisions will uncover issues that can further be analyzed with a goal of increasing the probability of accurate results.

The Capital Jury Project

As stated in chapter 1, numerous studies have documented the influence of personal characteristics on jury decisions. Most famous, however, are the emerging results of the Capital Jury Project (CJP), which, among other significant findings, concludes that juries still use the death penalty in an arbitrary, capricious, and discriminatory manner. Early findings from the Capital Jury Project, for example, suggest that the sentencing guidelines in *Gregg*, *Proffit*, and *Jurek*, which supposedly rid the process of these maladies, instead "provide 'legal cover' to many who have already made up their minds, and 'legal leverage' for persuading the undecided."[95] The guidelines also seem to "lessen the sense of responsibility for imposing an awful punishment."[96]

Most recently, a study conducted by Bowers and colleagues, for the Capital Jury Project, asserts that "the CJP data from capital jurors themselves unmistakably demonstrate the influence of race in capital sentencing"[97] and that the "make-up of the jury, we now see, is integral to this racial influence." This, they suggest, is due to the fact that black and white jurors view the same circumstances and the same people in very different ways such that blacks move away from wanting to impose the death penalty as the trial goes on while whites tend to move towards imposing it because "white jurors often appear unable or unwilling to consider the defendant's background and upbringing in context."[98]

Further, "these data paint a picture at odds with the notion of a "deliberative jury." Instead, the authors conclude that black jurors feel that white jurors are in a hurry to reach a verdict when they get back to the jury room. "In their narrative accounts, black jurors report that their white fellow jurors came to the trial with their minds made up about punishment and that they treated evidence of mitigation as trivial or ignored it."[99] Gross and Mauro also report:

> Evidence of racial discrimination in the administration of justice . . . [and] experimental studies of jury decision making have demonstrated that individuals are more lenient toward defendants of the same race, and that the race of the

victim can affect the perceived culpability of the defendant and the recommended sentence in non-capital rape cases.[100]

Recently, the racial composition of capital juries has garnered the attention of the U.S. Supreme Court. On February 13, 2002, Sara Rimer at the
New York Times reported that the case of Thomas Miller-El, who was scheduled to be executed by the State of Texas on February 21 for shooting two
white hotel clerks during a 1985 robbery, has been granted *certiorari* by the
Court. The clemency petition alleges that "the jury the prosecutors accepted
was composed of nine whites, one Filipino, one Hispanic and one black man
who told prosecutors that he thought that execution was too easy, and that
the appropriate punishment for murderers was to 'pour some honey on them
and stake them out over an ant bed.'" At issue is whether Miller-El received
a fair trial as required by the landmark ruling in *Batson v. Kentucky* (1986).
"*Batson* held that if the defense was able to show that it appeared the prosecution was using its strikes to exclude minorities, the trial judge would require the prosecutor to explain the peremptory strikes." Miller-El's attorneys
claim that the *Batson* ruling was not applied by the appeals courts in his case.

Further, the petition alleged that a 1963 internal memo from the Dallas
district attorney's office advised prosecutors who pick juries not to take "Jews,
Negroes, Dagos, Mexicans, or a member of any minority race on a jury, no
matter how rich or how well educated." As a result, 90 percent of qualified
black jurors were excluded from juries in Dallas County from 1980–1986, according to the article. "What's at stake in this case is the fundamental right
of citizens of all races to participate in the justice system," according to
Miller-El's attorney, Jim Marcus.

Combined with previous studies from the CJP (and other sources) that
have found juries to be hasty in their decision-making,[101] wanton in their disregard for the rules,[102] and derelict in the decisions they have made based on
factors that are not supposed to be considered,[103] further research is needed
to determine how standardless the death decision-making process is and how
widespread the standardlessness is, according to Bowers.[104] The *Page* case examines the standards based on lawyer performances.

Best Arguments for Life

Controversy over capital punishment has a long-standing tradition in law and
politics, but while debate around the topic continues, the number of death
row inmates in the United States has decreased to 3,300 persons, down from
an all-time high of over 3,700 persons at the end of 2001. Proponents of life

imprisonment without the possibility of parole (LWOP), instead of the death penalty, for capital crimes insist that capital punishment is bad policy because it is inefficient, time-consuming, and ineffective. Both pre- and post-*Furman* scholarship has uncovered interesting relationships between demographic variables like race and death sentencing, which shifts the focus of some of the debates from issues of cost and deterrence to that of fairness and discrimination. As such, the best arguments for LWOP provide a cost-effective, moral, and ideological basis for eliminating the death penalty in the United States.

"Every cost study undertaken has found that it is far more expensive, because of added legal safeguards, to carry out a death sentence than it is to jail a killer for life."[105] The cost-*in*effectiveness has the additional problem of creating backlog in America's courts due to automatic appeals, the results of which (low use) do not justify the extra time and expense required to sentence a capital defendant to death. According to David Von Drehle, "America has executed approximately one in every 20 inmates sentenced to die under modern death penalty laws."[106] In short, the uncertainty of execution exacerbates the pure inefficiency of the system to which capital defendants are subject, and without certainty of punishment, any deterrent value of the punishment is ultimately diminished.

Of course, people who support LWOP argue that the death penalty fails to deter people from committing capital crimes anyway. In fact,

> Murder is not a rational act done by rational people who carefully think through the consequences of their actions. Those who murder are usually either consumed by hate or anger or are in a warped emotional state. They are demented, pathological people who, at the time they kill, do so with utter disregard for human life. Many are either high on drugs or in desperate need for more drugs. Killers are by and large anti-social people who do not respond to such behavioral disincentives not to kill as the death penalty. Acceptance of normal societal values is alien to their individual natures. In my view, for us to think that we can influence or deter them from killing through capital punishment is in and of itself irrational thought and behavior.[107]

In short, "there is no evidence that capital punishment is more effective as a deterrent to murder than incarceration"[108] and while incarceration has the benefit of reversibility, the death penalty does not. For that reason, some say, that the death penalty should be abolished in favor of LWOP: that is, it is better to err on the side of revocability than to administer a punishment in an imperfect system that, later, cannot be reversed.

Further, the discriminatory application of the death penalty should not be ignored, according to those who support LWOP. "The implication of the way in which the death penalty has been administered in this nation is the not so subliminal message that a black person's life has less value attached to it than does the life of a white person."[109] In other words, the arbitrary and capricious manner in which the death penalty has been administered in capital cases renders it unjust as exemplified in the *Furman* decision that temporarily suspended the death penalty in the United States in 1972. Thus, "it should be clear that a society that adopts the death penalty when it is likely to be applied in this way chooses to bring about injustice."[110]

Finally, revenge or "just desserts" that make Americans "feel good" as a reason to continue executing people convicted of capital crimes when it is arbitrarily, capriciously, discriminatorily, and expensively applied fails to uphold the ideals of justice that are guaranteed by the constitution of the United States. Even though the concept of "just deserts" can intellectually be justified by its emphasis on (1) retribution, which pays back an offender who has caused harm to others, (2) fairness, that attempts to maintain "a fair distribution of civic burdens" amongst its citizens, and (3) deterrence, that provides a "disincentive to commit offenses," this is only one formulation or interpretation of *lex talionis* or the eye-for-an-eye philosophy; it is not the only way to punish crime.[111] To that end, proponents of LWOP, in agreement with Justice Harry Blackmun writing in dissent of a 1994 death penalty case, "feel morally and intellectually obligated to concede that the death penalty experiment has failed."[112]

Best Arguments for Death

While proponents of LWOP argue that the death penalty is inefficient, unfair, and immoral, proponents of the death penalty ("death"), argue that the mistakes and problems that the death penalty (as currently administered) has are outweighed by the utility of ridding society of some of its worst miscreants and, perhaps, preventing more murders. That is, even if it is arbitrarily or discriminatorily applied, it should not be abolished; that is, "a just law is still just even if it is not applied consistently."[113]

Theories of punishment, according to the "death" perspective, support the death penalty as a means to upholding laws that citizens implicitly agree to abide by else they forfeit the rights that are guaranteed by those very same laws. But CJP data reports that capital jurors locate the onus for death sentencing more upon the defendant than with the law or themselves as decision-makers; that is, "more jurors believe that the greatest responsibility lies with the defendant than with the law."[114] Such theories emphasize the importance of "just deserts" over social utility as the reason for the infliction of death; that is, "justice requires the annulment of the unfair advantage."[115] Utilitarian and rehabilitative theories also suggest that the death penalty is warranted in certain circumstances and that the decision to execute appeals to higher authorities than emotion (justice, freedom, and democracy) such as the feelings of the victim's family or public conscience. In fact, "we may all deeply regret having to carry out the punishment," but that does not mean that it should not be done.[116]

Also, supporters of "death" argue that deterrence cannot be measured in any meaningful way because we cannot show that it has saved lives. As such, the death penalty should not be conceptualized as a tool of deterrence, but rather as a tool of *lex talionis*, upon which our system of justice stands. Not only does this increase the utility of capital punishment (improve our odds of maintaining a safe and free society), but it also emphasizes the value that Americans place on human life. Importantly, supporters of "death" also suggest that "our moral obligation is to risk the possible ineffectiveness of executions."[117]

Finally, future dangerousness of the defendant is a major consideration for those who support "death" in that jury decisions about the death penalty often focus upon views about the future dangerousness of the defendant. In fact, CJP data by William J. Bowers reports that

> When the questioning turned to the jury's deliberations at the guilt phase of the trial, we asked jurors about a number of specific topics they might have discussed, including some that are legally irrelevant or impermissible in determining guilt, such as the defendant's likely future dangerousness . . . considerations explicitly reserved for the later punishment phase of the trial. . . . Jurors were evidently concerned with the defendant's future dangerousness and the punishment to be imposed during their deliberation on the defendant's guilt.[118]

Future dangerousness also raises the issue of truth in sentencing, that is, whether a "life" sentence really means until the end of the person's life or a determinate amount of years in prison with the possibility of parole. Some states in the United States do not offer the alternative of LWOP for capital crimes that is, Texas, Wyoming, New Jersey, New Mexico, Kansas (Death Penalty Information website, see www.deathpenaltyinfo.org). In those states, for "death" proponents, the death penalty seems the only appropriate way to prevent the offender from ever offending in public again.

Notes

1. Robert Jay Lifton and Greg Mitchell, *Who Owns Death? Capital Punishment, the American Conscience, and the End of Executions* (New York: Harper Collins, 2002), 22.

2. Louis P. Masur, *Rites of Execution: Capital Punishment and the Transformation of American Culture 1776–1865*, (New York: Oxford University Press, 1989); See also Lifton and Mitchell, *Who Owns Death?*, 25.

3. Robert Jay Lifton and Greg Mitchell, *Who Owns Death? Capital Punishment, the American Conscience, and the End of Executions* (New York: Harper Collins, 2002), 22.

4. Hugo Adam Bedau, *The Death Penalty in America: Current Controversies* (New York: Oxford University Press, 1997); See also Lifton and Mitchell, *Who Owns Death?*, xvii.

5. Cesare Beccaria, *On Crimes and Punishments* (Indianapolis: Bobbs-Merrill, 1963).

6. Bedau, *The Death Penalty*, 1997.

7. Barry Scheck, Peter Neufeld, and Jim Dwyer, *Actual Innocence: Five Days to Execution, and Other Dispatches from the Wrongly Convicted* (New York: Doubleday, 2000); Hugo Adam Bedau and Michael L. Radelet, "The Myth of Infallibility: A Reply to Markman and Cassell," *Stanford Law Review* 41(1988): 161–170; See also the Death Penalty Information website www.deathpenaltyinfo.org.

8. Stephen B. Bright, "Counsel for the Poor: The Death Sentence Not for the Worst Crime but for the Worst Lawyer," in *The Death Penalty in America: Current Controversies*, ed. Hugo Adam Bedau (New York: Oxford University Press, 1997a), 791.

9. Robert Jay Lifton and Greg Mitchell, *Who Owns Death? Capital Punishment, the American Conscience, and the End of Executions* (New York: Harper Collins, 2002), xvii; and Frank Schmalleger, *Trial of the Century: People of the State of California v. Orenthal James Simpson* (Upper Saddle River, NJ: Prentice Hall, 1996).

10. Hugo Adam Bedau and Michael L. Radelet, "The Myth of Infallibility: A Reply to Markman and Cassell," *Stanford Law Review* 41(1988): 167.

11. *Furman v. Georgia* 408 U.S. 238 (1972), 240.

12. James R. Acker, Robert M. Bohm, and Charles S. Lanier, *America's Experiment with Capital Punishment: Reflections on the Past, Present, and Future of the Ultimate Penal Sanction* (Durham, NC: Carolina Academic Press, 1998), 7; Samuel R. Gross and Robert Mauro, *Death and Discrimination: Racial Disparities in Capital Sentencing* (Boston, MA: Northeastern University Press, 1989), 6; Carol S. Steiker and Jordan M. Steiker,. "Judicial Developments in Capital Puhishment Law," in *America's Experiment with Capital Punishment*, ed. James Acker, Robert Bohm, and Charles Lanier (Durham, NC: Carolina Academic Press, 1998), 47–76.

13. William J. Bowers and Glenn L. Pierce, "Arbitrariness and Discrimination under Post-Furman Capital Statutes," *Crime and Delinquency* 26 (1980): 626–629; Daniel Givelber, "The New Law of Murder," *Indiana Law Journal* 69(1994): 375–391; Samuel R. Gross and Robert Mauro, *Death and Discrimination: Racial Disparities in Capital Sentencing* (Boston, MA: Northeastern University Press, 1989); James Luginbuhl and Julie Howe, "Discretion in Capital Sentencing Instructions: Guided or Misguided?" *Indiana Law Journal* 70(1995): 1161–1181; Roxane J. Perusso, "And Then There Were Three: Colorado's New Death Penalty Sentencing Statute," *University of Colorado Law Review* 68(1997): 189–227; Marla Sandys "Cross Overs— Capital Jurors Who Change Their Minds about Punishment: A Litmus Test for Sentencing Guidelines," *Indiana Law Journal* 70(1995): 1183–1221.

14. Craig Haney, "Taking Capital Jurors Seriously," *Indiana Law Journal* 70(1995): 1225.

15. Samuel R. Gross and Robert Mauro, *Death and Discrimination: Racial Disparities in Capital Sentencing* (Boston, MA: Northeastern University Press, 1989), 199.

16. Olga Curtis, "Denver's First Murderer," *Empire Magazine* 5(1978):33.

17. Lifton and Mitchell, *Who Owns Death?*, 22; Perruso, "And Then There Were None," 195.

18. William M. King, *Going to Meet A Man: Denver's Last Legal Public Execution, 27 July 1886* (Niwot, CO: University of Colorado Press, 1990).

19. Roxane J. Perusso, "And Then There Were Three: Colorado's New Death Penalty Sentencing Statute," *University of Colorado Law Review* 68(1997): 189–227; Austin Sarat, "Vio-

lence, Representation, and Responsibility in Capital Trials: The View from the Jury," *Indiana Law Journal* 70(1995): 1103–1135.

20. Perusso, "And Then There Were None," 197.

21. Perusso, "And Then There Were None," 227.

22. Perusso, "And Then There Were None," 201.

23. *Ring v. Arizona*, 536 U.S. 584 (2002), 23.

24. www.deathpenaltyinfo.org.

25. www.deathpenaltyinfo.org.

26. Stephen B. Bright, "Counsel for the Poor: The Death Sentence Not for the Worst Crime but for the Worst Lawyer," in *The Death Penalty in America: Current Controversies*, ed. Hugo Adam Bedau (New York: Oxford University Press, 1997), 791.

27. Michael Mello and Paul J. Perkins, "Closing the Circle: The Illusion of Lawyers for People Litigating for Their Lives at the *Fin de Siecle*," in *America's Experiment with Capital Punishment*, ed. James Acker, Robert Bohm, and Charles Lanier (Durham, NC: Carolina Academic Press, 1998), 245–284.

28. Hugo Adam Bedau, *The Death Penalty in America: Current Controversies* (New York: Oxford University Press, 1997), 279.

29. Bedau, *The Death Penalty*, 288.

30. *Lockett v. Ohio*, 434 U.S. 889 (1977), 597.

31. *Lockett v. Ohio*, 434 U.S. 889 (1977), 608.

32. *Lockett v. Ohio*, 434 U.S. 889 (1977), 621.

33. *Lockett v. Ohio*, 434 U.S. 889 (1977), 630.

34. William J. Bowers, "The Capital Jury Project: Rationale, Design, and Preview of Early Findings," *Indiana Law Journal* 70(1995): 1098.

35. Bowers, "The Capital Jury Project," 1100.

36. Bowers, "The Capital Jury Project," 1101.

37. William J. Bowers and Glenn L. Pierce, "Arbitrariness and Discrimination Under Post-Furman Capital Statutes." *Crime and Delinquency* 26(1980): 626–629; Samuel R. Gross and Robert Mauro, "Patterns of Death: An Analysis of Racial Disparities in Capital Sentencing and Homicide Victimization," *Stanford Law Review* 37(1984): 895–911; Michael L. Radelet and Glenn L. Pierce, "Choosing Those Who Will Die: Race and the Death Penalty in Florida." *Florida Law Review* 43(1991): 1–34; Hans Zeisel, "Race Bias in the Administration of the Death Penalty: The Florida Experience," *Harvard Law Review* 95(1981): 459–460.

38. Samuel R. Gross and Robert Mauro, *Death and Discrimination: Racial Disparities in Capital Sentencing* (Boston, MA: Northeastern University Press, 1989), 17.

39. Harold Garfinkel, "Research Note on Inter and Intra-Racial Homicides," *Social Forces* 27(1949): 120–123.

40. Thorsten Sellin, *The Penalty of Death* (Beverly Hills, CA: Sage Publications, 1980).

41. William J. Bowers and Glenn L. Pierce, "Arbitrariness and Discrimination Under Post-Furman Capital Statutes." *Crime and Delinquency* 26(1980): 626–629.

42. Marc Riedel, "Discrimination in the Imposition of the Death Penalty: A Comparison of the Characteristics of Offenders Sentenced Pre-Furman and Post-Furman," *Temporal Law Quarterly* 49(1976): 230–258.

43. Hans Zeisel, "Race Bias in the Administration of the Death Penalty: The Florida Experience," *Harvard Law Review* 95(1981): 459–460.

44. NAACP Legal Defense Fund, "Death Row USA" 2002.

45. Michael L. Radelet and Glenn L. Pierce, "Choosing Those Who Will Die: Race and the Death Penalty in Florida." *Florida Law Review* 43(1991): 33.

46. Hugo Adam Bedau, *The Death Penalty in America: Current Controversies*. (New York: Oxford University Press, 1997), 254.

47. *McCleskey v. Kemp* 106 S.Ct. 3331 (1986); Bedau, *The Death Penalty in America*, 256; Gross and Mauro, *Death and Discrimination*, 162.

48. Michael L. Radelet, "Executions of Whites for Crimes against Blacks: Exceptions to the Rule?" *The Sociological Quarterly* 30(1989):535.

49. Radelet, "Executions," 531.

50. Radelet, "Executions," 531.

51. Bedau, *The Death Penalty in America*, 278.

52. George Gallup, Jr., *Gallup Poll 2000*. Wilmington, DE: SR Books, June 28, 2001; see also Robert Jay Lifton and Greg Mitchell, *Who Owns Death? Capital Punishment, the American Conscience, and the End of Executions* (New York: Harper Collins, 2002), 213.

53. Ruth D. Peterson and William C. Bailey, "Is Capital Punishment an Effective Deterrent for Murder? An Examination of Social Science Research," in *America's Experiment with Capital Punishment*, ed. James Acker, Robert Bohm, and Charles Lanier (Durham, NC: Carolina Academic Press, 1998), 157–182; Phoebe C. Ellsworth and Samuel R. Gross, "Hardening of the Attitudes: Americans' Views on the Death Penalty," in *The Death Penalty in America: Current Controversies*, ed. Hugo Adam Bedau (New York: Oxford University Press, 1997), 90–115; Michael L. Radelet and Ronald L. Akers, "Deterrence and the Death Penalty: The Views of the Experts," *The Journal of Criminal Law and Criminology* 87(1996):1–16.

54. Robert M. Bohm, "American Death Penalty Opinion: Past, Present, and Future," in *America's Experiment with Capital Punishment*, ed. James Acker, Robert Bohm, and Charles Lanier (Durham, NC: Carolina Academic Press, 1998), 25–46; James Alan Fox, Michael Radelet, and Julie L. Bonsteel "The Death Penalty Opinion in the Post-Furman Years," *New York University Review of Law and Social Change* 18 (1990):514.

55. *Furman v. Georgia* 408 U.S. 238 (1972),361.

56. James Alan Fox, Michael Radelet, and Julie L. Bonsteel "The Death Penalty Opinion in the Post-Furman Years," *New York University Review of Law and Social Change* XVIII (1990–91):511.

57. Fox et al., "The Death Penalty Opinion," 515.

58. Richard C. Dieter, "Sentencing for Life: Americans Embrace Alternatives to the Death Penalty," in *The Death Penalty in America: Current Controversies*, ed. Hugo Adam Bedau (New York: Oxford University Press, 1997), 116–134; Michael L. Radelet and Ronald L. Akers, "Deterrence and the Death Penalty: The Views of the Experts," *The Journal of Criminal Law and Criminology* 87(1996):8.

59. Richard C. Dieter, "On the Front Line: Law Enforcement Views on the Death Penalty" (A report of the Death Penalty Information Center, Washington, D.C., 1995), 14.

60. Robert Jay Lifton and Greg Mitchell, *Who Owns Death? Capital Punishment, the American Conscience, and the End of Executions* (New York: Harper Collins, 2002), xvii.

61. Lifton and Mitchell, *Who Owns Death?*, 235.

62. Robert M. Bohm, "American Death Penalty Opinion: Past, Present, and Future," in *America's Experiment with Capital Punishment*, ed. James Acker, Robert Bohm, and Charles Lanier (Durham, North Carolina: Carolina Academic Press, 1998), 27; See also Fox et al., "The Death Penalty Opinion," 514.

63. Bohm, "American Death Penalty Opinion", 27.

64. See Samuel R. Gross "Update: American Public Opinion on the Death Penalty—It's Getting Personal," *Cornell Law Review* 83(1998): 1448–1475.

65. James Alan Fox, Michael Radelet, and Julie L. Bonsteel "The Death Penalty Opinion in the Post-Furman Years," *New York University Review of Law and Social Change* XVIII (1990):503.

66. Samuel R. Gross "Update: American Public Opinion on the Death Penalty—It's Getting Personal," *Cornell Law Review* 83(1998): 1473.

67. Michael L. Radelet and Glenn L. Pierce, "Choosing Those Who Will Die: Race and the Death Penalty in Florida," *Florida Law Review* 43(1991): 1–34.

68. Gross, "Update," 1474.

69. Craig Haney, "Taking Capital Jurors Seriously," *Indiana Law Journal* 70(1995):1223–1232; James Luginbuhl and Julie Howe, "Discretion in Capital Sentencing Instructions: Guided or Misguided?" *Indiana Law Journal* 70(1995): 1161–1181; Austin Sarat, "Violence, Representation, and Responsibility in Capital Trials: The View from the Jury," *Indiana Law Journal* 70(1995): 1103–1135.

70. William S. Geimer and Jonathan Amsterdam, "Why Jurors Vote Life or Death: Operative Factors in Ten Florida Death Penalty Cases," *American Journal of Criminal Law* 15(1988):1–54. Craig Haney, "Taking Capital Jurors Seriously," *Indiana Law Journal* 70(1995):1223–1232; James Luginbuhl and Julie Howe, "Discretion in Capital Sentencing Instructions: Guided or Misguided?" *Indiana Law Journal* 70(1995): 1161–1181.

71. Jody Armour, "Stereotypes and Prejudice: Helping Legal Decision-Makers Break the Prejudice Habit" *California Law Review* 83(1995): 733–772; Gary D. Hill, Anthony R. Harris, and JoAnn Miller, "The Etiology of Bias: Social Heuristics and Rational Decision Making in Deviance Processing," *Journal of Research in Crime and Delinquency* 22(1985): 135–162; Jennifer L. Reichert, "Lawyers Face the Hurdle of Overcoming Juror Biases, Survey Shows," *Trial* 35(1999): 96–101.

72. Jody Armour, "Stereotypes and Prejudice: Helping Legal Decision-makers Break the Prejudice Habit" *California Law Review* 83(1995): 733–772; William J. Bowers, Benjamin D. Steiner, and Marla Sandys, "Death Sentencing in Black and White: An Empirical Analysis of the Role of Jurors' Race and Jury Racial Composition," *University of Pennsylvania Journal of Constitutional Law* 3(2001): 171–274; Bryan Morgan, "The Jury's View," *University of Colorado Law Review* 67(1996): 983–988; Michael L. Radelet and Glenn L. Pierce, "Choosing Those Who Will Die: Race and the Death Penalty in Florida," *Florida Law Review* 43(1991): 1–34.

73. James Alan Fox, Michael Radelet, and Julie L. Bonsteel "The Death Penalty Opinion in the Post-Furman Years," *New York University Review of Law and Social Change* XVIII (1990–91): 516.

74. Armour, "Stereotypes and Prejudice," 750–772.

75. William J. Bowers, Benjamin D. Steiner and Marla Sandys, "Death Sentencing in Black and White: An Empirical Analysis of the Role of Jurors' Race and Jury Racial Composition,"*University of Pennsylvania Journal of Constitutional Law* 3(2001): 171–274; John H. Blume, Stephen Garvey, and Sheri Johnson, "Future Dangerousness in Capital Cases: Always at Issue," *Cornell Law Review* 86(2001): 404–410; Marla Sandys, "Cross Overs—Capital Jurors Who Change their Minds About Punishment: A Litmus Test for Sentencing Guidelines," *Indiana Law Journal* 70(1995): 1183–1221.

76. Nancy M. Steblay, Jasmina Besirevic, and Solomon Fulero, "The Effects of Pretrial Publicity on Juror Verdicts: A Meta-analytic Review," *Law and Human Behavior* 23(1999): 219–235.

77. Mark Mandell, "Overcoming Juror Bias: Is There an Answer?" *Trial* 36(2000): 28.

78. Bethany K. Dumas, "Jury Trials: Lay Jurors, Pattern Jury Instructions, and Comprehension Issues," *Tennessee Law Review* 67(2000): 701–742; Valerie P. Hans, "How Juries Decide

Death," *Indiana Law Journal* 70(1995): 1233–1240; Neil A. Rector, Michael Bagby, and R. Nicholson, "The Effect of Prejudice and Judicial Ambiguity on Defendant Guilt Ratings," *The Journal of Social Psychology* 133(1993): 651.

79. Shari Seidman Diamond, Jonathan D. Casper, Cami L. Heiert, and Anna-Maria Marshall, "Juror Reactions to Attorneys at Trial," *Journal of Criminal Law and Criminology* 87(1996): 17–47; Bethany K. Dumas, "Jury Trials: Lay Jurors, Pattern Jury Instructions, and Comprehension Issues," *Tennessee Law Review* 67(2000): 701–742; Vicki L. Fishfader, Gary N. Howells, Roger C. Katz, and Pamela S. Teresi, "Evidential and Extralegal Factors in Juror Decisions: Presentation, Mode, Retention, and Level of Emotionality," *Law and Human Behavior* 20(1996): 565–572; Jeremy Rose, "How Jurors See Expert Witnesses," *Trial Lawyer* 22(1999): 420–426.

80. Robert D. Myers, Ronald S. Reinstein, and Gordon M. Griller, "Complex Scientific Evidence and the Jury," *Judicature* 83(1999): 150–157.

81. Scott Bell, "Hearts and Minds: For Success at Trial, Appeal to a Jury's Rationality as well as its Sympathy," *Los Angeles Daily Journal* 110:1(S); Joseph M. Fast, and Ray Doyle "A View from the Jury Box," *For the Defense* 37(1995): 20–21; Robyn Packard, "Judging Jurors." *Canadian Lawyer* 20(1996): 12–15.

82. Neil J. Vidmar and Regina A. Schuller, "Juries And Expert Evidence: Social Framework Testimony," *Law and Contemporary Problems* 52(1989): 133–176.

83. Michael J. Ahlen, "Opening Statements in Jury Trials: What Are the Legal Limits?" *North Dakota Law Review* 71(1995): 701–720; James W. McElhaney, "Finding the Right Script: Trial Lawyers Must Fit Their Cases to the Belief Patterns of Juries," *American Bar Association Journal* 81(1995): 90–92; Bryan Morgan, "The Jury's View," *University of Colorado Law Review* 67(1996): 983–988; Brian Reeves, "Jurors Judge Lawyers," *Kentucky Bench and Bar* 61(1997): 24–25.

84. Ahlen, "Opening Statements," 701.

85. Ahlen, "Opening Statements," 719.

86. Robert P. Burns, *A Theory of the Trial* (New Jersey: Princeton University Press, 1999), 32.

87. Burns, *A Theory*, 192.

88. Shari Seidman Diamond, Jonathan D. Casper, Cami L. Heiert, and Anna-Maria Marshall, "Juror Reactions to Attorneys at Trial," *Journal of Criminal Law and Criminology* 87(1996): 17.

89. Samuel R. Gross "Update: American Public Opinion on the Death Penalty – It's Getting Personal," *Cornell Law Review* 83(1998): 1448–1475; Nancy M. Steblay, Jasmina Besirevic, and Solomon Fulero, "The Effects of Pretrial Publicity on Juror Verdicts: A Meta-Analytic Review," *Law and Human Behavior* 23(1999): 219–235.

90. William J. Bowers, Marla Sandys, and Benjamin D. Steiner, "Foreclosed Impartiality in Capital Sentencing: Jurors' Predispositions, Guilt-Trial Experience, and Premature Decision-Making," *Cornell Law Review* 83(1998): 1477.

91. Valerie P. Hans, "How Juries Decide Death," *Indiana Law Journal* 70(1995): 1233–1240; Craig Haney, "Taking Capital Jurors Seriously." *Indiana Law Journal* 70(1995): 1223–1232; Joseph L. Hoffman, "Where's the Buck? Juror Misperception of Sentencing Responsibility in Death Penalty Cases," *Indiana Law Journal* 70(1995): 1137–1160; Austin Sarat, "Violence, Representation, and Responsibility in Capital Trials: The View from the Jury," *Indiana Law Journal* 70(1995): 1103–1135.

92. Joseph L. Hoffman, "Where's the Buck? Juror Misperception of Sentencing Responsibility in Death Penalty Cases," *Indiana Law Journal* 70(1995): 1137–1160.

93. William S. Geimer and Jonathan Amsterdam, "Why Jurors Vote Life or Death: Operative Factors in Ten Florida Death Penalty Cases." *American Journal of Criminal Law* 15(1988): 5.

94. Geimer and Amsterdam, "Why Jurors Vote," 7.

95. William J. Bowers, "The Capital Jury Project: Rationale, Design, and Preview of Early Findings," *Indiana Law Journal* 70(1995): 1102.

96. Bowers, "The Capital Jury Project," 1102.

97. William J. Bowers, Benjamin D. Steiner and Marla Sandys, "Death Sentencing in Black and White: An Empirical Analysis of the Role of Jurors' Race and Jury Racial Composition,"*University of Pennsylvania Journal of Constitutional Law* 3(2001): 259.

98. Bowers, "Death Sentencing," 260.

99. Bowers, "Death Sentencing," 260.

100. Samuel R. Gross and Robert Mauro, *Death and Discrimination: Racial Disparities in Capital Sentencing* (Boston, MA: Northeastern University Press, 1989), 111.

101. William J. Bowers, Marla Sandys, and Benjamin D. Steiner, "Foreclosed Impartiality in Capital Sentencing: Jurors' Predispositions, Guilt-Trial Experience, and Premature Decision-Making," *Cornell Law Review* 83(1998): 1476–1556; Craig Haney, "Taking Capital Jurors Seriously." *Indiana Law Journal* 70(1995): 1223–1232; Marla Sandys "Cross Overs – Capital Jurors Who Change their Minds About Punishment: A Litmus Test for Sentencing Guidelines" *Indiana Law Journal* 70(1995): 1183–1221.

102. Scott Bell, "Hearts and Minds: For Success at Trial, Appeal to a Jury's Rationality as well as its Sympathy," *Los Angeles Daily Journal* 110:1(S); Joseph M. Fast, and Ray Doyle "A View from the Jury Box," *For the Defense* 37(1995): 20–21; Robyn Packard, "Judging Jurors." *Canadian Lawyer* 20(1996): 12–15; Randall T. Salekin, James R.P. Ogloff, Cathy McFarland, and Richard Rogers, "Influencing Jurors' Perceptions of Guilt: Expression of Emotionality During Testimony," *Behavioral Sciences and the Law* 13 (1995): 293–305; Neil J. Vidmar and Regina A. Schuller, "Juries And Expert Evidence: Social Framework Testimony," *Law and Contemporary Problems* 52(1989): 133–176.

103. William J. Bowers, Benjamin D. Steiner and Marla Sandys, "Death Sentencing in Black and White: An Empirical Analysis of the Role of Jurors' Race and Jury Racial Composition," *University of Pennsylvania Journal of Constitutional Law* 3(2001): 171–274; John H. Blume, Stephen Garvey, and Sheri Johnson, "Future Dangerousness in Capital Cases: Always At Issue." *Cornell Law Review* 86(2001): 404–410; Mark Mandell, "Overcoming Juror Bias: Is There an Answer?" *Trial* 36(2000), 28; Marla Sandys "Cross Overs—Capital Jurors Who Change their Minds About Punishment: A Litmus Test for Sentencing Guidelines" *Indiana Law Journal* 70(1995): 1183–1221; Nancy M. Steblay, Jasmina Besirevic, and Solomon Fulero, "The Effects of Pretrial Publicity on Juror Verdicts: A Meta-Analytic Review," *Law and Human Behavior* 23(1999): 219–235.

104. Bowers, "Death Sentencing," 171–274.

105. David Von Drehle, "Miscarriage of Justice: Why the Death Penalty Doesn't Work," *The Washington Post Magazine* 33(1995): 33–36.

106. David Von Drehle, "Miscarriage of Justice: Why the Death Penalty Doesn't Work," *The Washington Post Magazine* 33(1995): 33–36.

107. James McCloskey, "The Death Penalty: A Personal View," *Criminal Justice Ethics* 15(1996):70–75.

108. Victor Kappeler, Merle Blumberg, and Gary Potter, *The Mythology of Crime and Criminal Justice*, 2nd ed. (Prospect Heights, IL: Waveland, 1996), 325; see also Ruth D. Peterson and Willam C. Bailey, "Is Capital Punishment an Effective Deterrent for Murder? An Examination

of Social Science Research," in *America's Experiment with Capital Punishment*, ed. James Acker, Robert Bohm, and Charles Lanier (Durham, North Carolina: Carolina Academic Press, 1998), 157–182.

109. James McCloskey, "The Death Penalty: A Personal View," *Criminal Justice Ethics* 15(1996): 53.

110. Louis P. Pojman and Jeffrey Reiman, *The Death Penalty: For and Against* (Lanham, MD: Rowman and Littlefield Publishers, 1998), 123.

111. Pojman and Reiman, *The Death Penalty*, 69.

112. Acker, James R., Robert M. Bohm, and Charles S. Lanier. *America's Experiment with Capital Punishment: Reflections on the Past, Present, and Future of the Ultimate Penal Sanction.* Durham, NC: Carolina Academic Press, 1998, p. 8.

113. Pojman and Reiman, *The Death Penalty*, 56.

114. William J. Bowers, "The Capital Jury Project: Rationale, Design, and Preview of Early Findings." *Indiana Law Journal* 70(1995): 1094.

115. Louis P. Pojman and Jeffrey Reiman, *The Death Penalty: For and Against* (Lanham, MD: Rowman and Littlefield Publishers, 1998), 11.

116. Pojman and Reiman, *The Death Penalty*, 7–26.

117. Pojman and Reiman, *The Death Penalty*, 41.

118. William J. Bowers, "The Capital Jury Project: Rationale, Design, and Preview of Early Findings," *Indiana Law Journal* 70(1995): 1087.

CHAPTER THREE

~

The Importance of Defining the Defendant

A researcher wanders through the landscape and enters into conversations with the people encountered . . . explores the many domains of the country . . . roaming freely around the territory . . . [and] asks questions that lead the subjects to tell their own stories of their lived world.

The Importance of "Defining" the Defendant

The problem with the Capital Jury Project research is that it does not sufficiently address the role of stereotypes in defining the defendant. It also ignores attributions of personality and disposition that contribute to discussions about future dangerousness that are not suppose to be part of the jury's deliberations. As such, capital defendants who fit certain stereotypes are more likely to be found guilty and more likely to be sentenced to death during a capital trial, not necessarily because of the crime they allegedly committed, but rather because of the kind of person the jury deems them to be.

The Role of Stereotypes

Stereotypical images of defendants are not new. Many researchers have found stereotypes to play a large role in the decisions made by people, particularly in hypothetical situations versus real ones.[1] J. Frank Yates, for example, studied how people often make decisions about other people based on "likelihood judgments" and Nancy Cantor and Walter Mischel concluded that categorizing other people simplifies the world for humans.[2] Further, Jody Armour attacks the "unconscious racism" model that prevents attorneys from bringing the issue of prejudice into the open at trial by suggesting that "colorblind formalism is counterproductive in reducing discrimination."[3]

Instead, Armour suggests that attorneys be allowed to state that their clients represent stereotyped groups and to urge jurors to suppress ingrained stereotypes because "references in court that challenge jurors to reexamine and resist their automatic discriminatory tendencies may actually enhance, rather than impede, the rationality and fairness of legal proceedings."[4] Unfortunately, the influence of stereotypes of black defendants on legal decision-making, including sentencing decisions is well documented.[5]

Theoretical Implications

Social Constructionism

Several theories can inform an analysis of a capital trial. Most appropriate, however, seems an overall view of the analysis from the standpoint of social construction: that is, knowledge must be viewed as socially constructed through a series of social facts that fit together to explain phenomena that can be perceived with common sense. Such social facts can be real or imagined in the mind of the perceiver and, in the case under study here, the social facts will be deemed real if they are viewed as real by the perceiver. Thus, "if men define situations as real, they are real in their consequences."[6]

In their seminal book, *The Social Construction of Reality: A Treatise in the Sociology of Knowledge*, Berger and Luchman assert that "everyday life presents itself as a reality interpreted by men and subjectively meaningful to them as a coherent world." If we define "reality" as "phenomena that we recognize as having a being independent of our own volition," and "knowledge" as "the certainty that phenomena are real and that they possess specific characteristics," an analysis of a death penalty trial must take whatever is said and done in the trial as a source of knowledge and attempt to extract meaning from those events.[7] Whatever is said, for example, can be used as a source of information. Whatever is done, then, must also be taken as a source of information. These sources of information must be taken together and reported as "what happened" in the trial as fact, not opinion. In fact, Berger and Luchman contend that

> The "sociology of knowledge" must concern itself with whatever passes for "knowledge" in a society, regardless of the ultimate validity or invalidity (by whatever criteria) of such "knowledge." And insofar as all human "knowledge" is developed, transmitted and maintained in social situations, the sociology of

knowledge must seek to understand the processes by which this is done in such a way that a taken-for-granted "reality" congeals for the man in the street.[8]

Applied to capital juries, this approach suggests that jurors are perceivers of whatever reality the attorneys construct of the defendant and his life, particularly his motives, such that the portrayal of the "man on the street" is either a figment of the attorneys' imagination or a truthful portrayal of that same man. For example, if attorneys portray the "man on the street" as an evil, vindictive person who views the world as a cold, heartless place where human life is valueless, the "man on the street" is more likely to be perceived by jurors as someone capable of cold-blooded murder. On the other hand, if the "man on the street" is portrayed as a man with mental and emotional problems that sometimes erupt in fits of unintentional violence, and the jurors' view the "man on the street" as an ill person who needs special physical and mental help, they are more likely to judge the man as a victim of circumstance. Such perceptions lend themselves to conviction or acquittal of the defendant, respectively.

If images of a capital defendant are constructed by attorneys whose performances pit one view of the man against the other in a battle to define him, for example, it would not contradict the precepts of the social construction of reality perspective because "knowledge must always be knowledge from a certain position."[9] That is to say that "social groups vary greatly in their capacity thus to transcend their own narrow position."[10] As such, the battle to define the defendant (and to win that battle) is difficult and may require attorneys to overcome inherent biases that the jury may hold. Berger and Luchmann explain thusly:

> The reality of everyday life is organized around the "here" of my body and the "now" of my present. This "here and now" is the focus of my attention to the reality of everyday life. What is "here and now" presented to me in everyday life is the *realissiumum* of my consciousness. I experience everyday life in terms of differing degrees of closeness and remoteness, both spatially and temporally. Closest to me is the zone of everyday life that is directly accessible to my bodily manipulation. This zone contains the world within my reach, the world in which I act so as to modify its reality, or the world in which I work . . . [and] my attention to this world is mainly determined by what I am doing, have done or plan to do in it.[11]

Further, Berger and Luchmann assert that reality consists of signals presented in language which is "capable of 'making present' a variety of objects that are spatially, temporally and socially absent from the 'here and now.'"[12] In other words, it is perfectly reasonable to portray an image of a defendant and the events that brought him to trial using language.

Interestingly, this view of reality also suggests that "any action that is repeated frequently becomes cast into a pattern, which can then be reproduced with an economy of effort and which, ipso facto, is apprehended by its performer as that pattern."[13] In fact, "habitualization carries with it the important psychological gain that choices are narrowed . . . [and] this frees the individual from the burden of 'all those decisions,' providing a psychological relief that has its basis in man's undirected instinctual structure."[14] In short, decision-making by human beings is inherently wrought with bias, like stereotypes, that make it easier for us to live our lives. In other words, if murders in our society are usually performed by people who are characterized as unscrupulous, evil beasts who pose a threat to society at large, why expend the energy to view a capital defendant differently?

For example, much of the literature on prior-record evidence suggests that jurors (and mock jurors) "informed of the defendant's prior conviction were more likely than jurors who had no information about prior record to convict the defendant on subsequent charges."[15] That is to say, when jurors believe or even know for a fact that a defendant has been involved in previous crimes, rather than look at the evidence presented at trial in the case they are empanelled to hear, they may "need less evidence to be convinced of the defendant's guilt beyond a reasonable doubt."[16] Several studies attest to the fact that juries and mock juries show the same propensity towards making assumptions about defendants at trial, based in part or entirely upon prior-record evidence.[17] In the current study, the defense attorneys, therefore, had the additional task of overcoming juror biases that perhaps place capital defendants in a category of the unsalvageable and irrelevant, qualified for incarceration or execution. "Institutionalization occurs whenever there is a reciprocal typification of habitualized actions by types of actors."[18]

In short, the more that a capital defendant can be portrayed as "typical" as compared to other defendants similarly situated, the more likely he is to be found guilty and incarcerated or executed. Similarly, the more "atypical" a defendant can be portrayed, the less likely guilt and incarceration or execution will be assessed.[19] Attribution theory also suggests that decisions about people are made utilizing an assessment of the typicality of their actions, but it forwards that a more complex cognitive process is involved.

Attribution Theory
Attribution theory deals with how the social perceiver uses information to arrive at causal explanations for events.[20] It examines what information is

gathered and how it is combined to form a causal judgment. Causal judgments are based, in part, on whether the perceiver attributes behavior to internal or external loci.[21] If the behavior is attributed to an internal locus, that is, intelligence, strength, evilness, and so forth, the actor will be held responsible for the outcome of the behavior. But, if the behavior is partially attributed to an external locus, that is, weather, discrimination, child abuse, and so forth, the actor's behavior is less likely to be attributed solely to his or her responsibility.[22]

Sentencing decisions, for example, particularly death penalty decisions made by juries and, in the current case, by a panel of judges, are based on whether the defendant is judged by them to be internally or externally influenced, according to Fritz Heider's original formulation of the theory.[23] Jones and Davis expanded the original formulation of the theory to include dispositions and intentions (personality traits, attitudes, and so forth) to make causal inferences.[24] And Harold Kelley extended the attribution process to include both multiple and single events.[25] Both the guilty verdict and the decision to incarcerate, not execute, the defendant in the current case can be viewed as resulting from causal inferences made by the jury and judges about the internal and external loci of the defendant: the defendant's disposition and intent, and the validity of the judgments as portrayed by the attorneys at trial.

The prosecuting attorneys and the defense attorneys both attempted to prove or disprove that the aforementioned criteria were met or not met, respectively. A decision to execute, it is argued, would require that the judges attribute an internal loci, an evil or mean disposition, and attributional validity—a low or high degree of consensus, a low or high degree of distinctiveness, and a low or high degree of consistency between the actions of the defendant and the actions of other actors similarly situated. For example, if "high consensus" means that most people engage in the behavior under discussion, for example eating, drinking, laughing, and "high distinctiveness" means that the situation is unique, for example at a funeral, at a ball game, at a party, and "high consistency" means that the behavior and the situation frequently occur together, for example, laughing at a ball game, eating at a party, the actor's behavior will be judged to be due to the situation, not the actor.

There are several combinations that fit the "causal calculus" outlined above. Each combination leads the perceiver to different conclusions and, consequently, different attributions of responsibility. Internal attributions suggest that the actor is highly responsible for the behavior under discussion. External attributions suggest that the situation was unique and that the actor is less responsible for the behavior because of the unique circumstances in which he found himself. The combination that attributes the most responsibility for behavior to the actor or, in the current case, the defendant, is high consensus, where most people like the defendant are capable of murder; low distinctiveness, where the defendant has been in violent or criminal situations before; and high consistency, where the defendant has been involved in violent and criminal behavior frequently in the past. This combination (HLH) suggests that the defendant/actor is highly responsible for the murder because the locus of control is internally attributed.

On the other hand, if jurors decide that there is low consensus (people like the defendant are not capable of murder), high distinctiveness (violence and criminality are unusual for people like the defendant), and low consistency (people like the defendant do not usually act violently in surprising situations), an LHL pattern, the defendant would be held less responsible for his actions and perhaps acquitted of the charge of first-degree murder because the locus of control would be attributed externally (perhaps to something that the victim did to cause her own death). In short, internal and external attributions depend entirely upon how the jury views the defendant and how the jury views the situation the defendant was in. The task for the prosecutors in the current case was to define the defendant so as to internally attribute the crime, whereas the task of the defense attorneys was to define the situation so as to externally attribute the crime. As such, the battle to define the defendant (and the crime) by the attorneys resulted in competing definitions of who the defendant *is*, not what the defendant did.

The current study argues that the effort to attribute internal locus—an evil disposition—partially failed, but that instead of a failure of those who made the decisions, it is a failure of the attribution process: the process does not account for bias at its various levels. One such bias, called the "fundamental attribution error," refers to the tendency to "underestimate the impact of situational factors and to overestimate the importance of internal dispositional factors."[26] People are inherently biased in their decision-making about people, in other words, oftentimes assuming that conditions or circumstances are under the control of individuals more often than they really are. To characterize the process as purely rational and lacking prejudice, then, is unwarranted. Even more unwarranted is the implicit notion that people do not judge other people on the basis of stereotypes alone.

Who Is He? The Work of Goffman

Erving Goffman's work *The Presentation of Self in Everyday Life* (1959) offers an interesting way to view the participants and the proceedings of a death penalty trial, too. In it, Goffman uses the terms "performance" to refer to "all the activity of an individual which occurs during a period marked by his continuous presence before a particular set of observers and which has some influence on the observers," and "personal front" to refer to "items that we most intimately identify with the performer himself and that we naturally expect will follow the performer wherever he goes."[27] Interestingly, the personal front includes race, gender, age, size, looks, posture, speech patterns, facial expressions, and bodily gestures and he divides them into categories of "appearance" and "manner" which provide clues as to how the individual will perform in a given role.

Such roles are already established and "whether his acquisition of the role was primarily motivated by a desire to perform the given task or by a desire to maintain the corresponding front, the actor will find that he must do both."[28] In other words, lawyers are performing a role in court and they are using the appropriate front to carry it off. Likewise, the defendant is performing a role and using a front as the trial progresses and the same goes for the jury and judges. Participants in a trial, therefore, are witnessing *dramaturgy* at all times and they are judging the performances of others just as they would a play that is being performed for them at a theater. As such, "interaction," according to Goffman, "is seen as very fragile, maintained by social performances. Poor performances or disruptions are seen as great threats to social interaction just as they are to theatrical performances."[29] Thus, attorneys are under great pressure to perform well during their presentation of the case lest they be judged poorly by the jury, which will cause them to lose the trial.

The defendant was not allowed to actively "perform" during the trial except that his attendance was required. His behavior was rehearsed: he was told to look and dress a certain way so as to enhance his performance in the courtroom absent any speech or meaningful communication such as testimony, which he did not give. In short, the defense attorneys in the current case were performing *for* the defendant or on his behalf. His own performance was scrutinized by the jury, but it could be called a "staged performance" since he was not allowed to speak or move except in limited ways that were designed to create a certain image of him. This may be called the "idealized performance," according to Goffman, because the defendant was told to look remorseful and humble to the jury by keeping his eyes lowered, by not talking to anyone, and by not writing or reading during the trial proceedings. Idealized performances tend to "play up ideal values which accord to the performer a lower position than he covertly accepts for himself."[30]

Importantly, another work by Goffman forwards that when a gap exists between who a person *is* and what he or she *ought to be*, stigmatization results.[31] The interaction between people who are stigmatized and normal people (although everyone is stigmatized at some point in time, according to Goffman) depends upon what kind of stigma it is. Applying Goffman's concept of *discreditable* stigma to the current case, then, "the dramaturgical problem of managing information so that the problem [perhaps future dangerousness] remains unknown to the audience,"[32] is what the legal defense is all about. Exposing the problem so that it becomes known to the audience, on the other hand, is the task of the prosecution.

In *Presentation*, Goffman goes on to suggest that people oftentimes find themselves on "performance teams" where "individuals cooperate in staging a single routine."[33] The defense and the prosecution both represent examples of performance teams in the current case: that is, each side collaborated on and even rehearsed their parts in "fostering a given definition of the situation."[34] In so doing, they entrusted each other with various tasks that needed to be accomplished during the trial—for example, each attorney was responsible for presenting evidence, giving arguments, questioning witnesses, and so forth—that would portray an image of the defendant and a theory of the crime that was appropriate to winning the trial. If, for example, one of the attorneys for the prosecution had stood at the podium and delivered a closing argument that suggested to the jury that the defendant should be set free, a disruption in the performance would have taken place and a mistrial could have been obtained.

Importantly, each team also assumes the role of an audience during the others' performance. For example, when the defense is delivering an argument to the judge and jury, the prosecution is expected to remain silent until they finish, except for when they decide to raise an objection to what is being said or done. At that point, they become the center of attention until the judge, who manages the entire social interaction, rules on the objection. As such, Goffman asserts that dramaturgy is multifaceted with team members playing different roles, with different fronts, at various times throughout the proceeding.

During the trial, it can be said that both sets of attorneys fought for control over the social setting, too. When one side had the jury's attention, they performed, and when the other side took the floor, they tried to outperform the other. Goffman explains that "control of the setting may give the controlling team a sense of security."[35]

Additional Thoughts on Crime and Punishment

Michel Foucault argues that the trial process more than simply evaluates crimes but also (functionally) evaluates criminals:

> It is no longer simply: 'What law punishes this offence?' but: 'What would be the most appropriate measures to take? How do we see the future development

of the offender? What would be the best way of rehabilitating him?' A whole set of assessing, diagnostic, prognostic, normative judgements concerning the criminal have become lodged in the framework of penal judgment.[36]

Reflecting upon the purpose of tortuous executions in the 1700s, that is, to procure confessions, Foucault goes on to suggest that the trial plays a role in reaffirming the sovereignty of people in power. Criminals were viewed as threats to the state's eminent rule. Thus, public executions served a "juridico-political function."[37] In the modern day, aspects of Foucault's thought can be found in the circus-like atmosphere surrounding the execution of Timothy McVeigh, who was convicted and sentenced to death for the bombing of the Alfred P. Murrah federal building in Oklahoma City in 1995. Thousands of people attended the McVeigh execution by way of live television broadcasts, while hundreds of victims' families, when denied the right to watch on closed-circuit television, waited patiently outside the walls of the prison where the execution took place to hear word that the lethal injection had been administered. Americans patriotically commented about the McVeigh execution following word-for-word and minute-by-minute accounts of the incident, including his last words and the gestures he used to say good-bye, as if American society had suddenly been made safe following McVeigh's dispatch from it. Foucault suggests that the satisfaction with which society views such spectacles are less the result of planned justice and more the result of citizens' conceding power to the machinery of politics over which they have no control.

> Its aim is not so much to re-establish a balance as to bring into play, as its extreme point, the dissymetry between the subject who has dared to violate the law and the all-powerful sovereign who displays his strength . . . there must be an emphatic affirmation of power and of its intrinsic superiority . . . by breaking the law, the offender has touched the very person of the prince [the state] . . . the ceremony of punishment, then, is an exercise of 'terror' . . . if severe penalties are required, it is because their example must be deeply inscribed in the hearts of men.[38]

In the current case, the capture, judgment, and subsequent incarceration of the defendant, Donta Page, provided localized evidence that the juridico-political machinery is functioning properly. To be sure, the sight of his shackles and police escorts, televised comments of attorneys throughout the process, and quoted statements made by jurors in news articles at the conclusion of the trial proved to the public that he was being prosecuted to the fullest extent of the law. As such, coverage of the actual words being spoken in the courtroom and the actual decisions that were being made by jurors and judges took a backseat to the media propaganda that assured Denver residents that the judicial process was being implemented. Besides, "this enables us to understand some of the characteristics of the liturgy of torture and execution—above all, the importance of a ritual that was to deploy its pomp in public. Nothing was to be hidden of this triumph of the law."[39]

Emile Durkheim wrote about the functions of crime and punishment. Durkheim forwarded that crime is offensive because it offends society rather than because society decides that it is offensive. "An act is criminal when it offends strong and defined states of the conscience collective [a strongly defined moral consensus]."[40] The very fact that an act offends people is what defines it as criminal, in other words, and society protects itself by meting out punishments that assuage our emotional response to it. Further, there is no difference between the reasons why society meted out punishments in the past and why they are meted out today. Vengeance is a time-honored tradition that focuses public outrage in a useful way: that is, people tend to reinforce their commonly held beliefs and values when criminals tread outside the boundaries that honest men have installed. "From all the similar impressions which are exchanged, and the anger that is expressed, there emerges a unique emotion, more or less determinate according to the circumstances, which emanates from no specific person, but from everyone. This is the public wrath."[41]

Obviously, Durkheim assumes that people care about their community. They want to protect it. They want it to succeed. They want to be a part of it and to contribute to its sustenance. As such, "tradition, and religious beliefs, serve as brakes upon even the strongest of governments."[42] Crime and punishment can be viewed as two such traditions that fortify norms. The absence of norms (anomie) and procedures for maintaining those norms (sanctions) is unacceptable. Government is charged with the responsibility of establishing itself as a method of social control because "a transgression is correspondingly more shocking if the offended being is superior in nature and dignity to the transgressor. The more something is held in respect, the more abhorrent is a lack of respect."[43] Further, social solidarity requires citizens to sell out to the ideals of the group, which necessitates the virtual denial of individual rights. When someone violates the group's norms in favor of his or her own, society is threatened and it is, therefore, the job of government to step in and protect the conscience collective.

In the current case, the defendant, Donta Page, violated the rights of one of society's citizens by imposing his individual will upon the actions of another. Society, according to Durkheim, has no choice but to impose itself (represented by government) between him and society as a "conciliator of private interests,"[44] not as a third party, but rather as a body of laws that attach Page and the victim to the conscience collective. Page must be dealt-with, in other words, because "if we have a strong inclination to think and act for ourselves, we cannot be as strongly inclined to think and act as others do"[45] and society will become unstable. Instability is the worst possible state of affairs for a society, according to Durkheim.

Conclusions and Hypotheses

Overall, the current study focuses on what goes on in the courtroom during a death penalty trial. Specifically, the conclusions drawn here provide answers to the following questions: (1) How do attorneys attempt to portray an image of the defendant? and (2) How is that image related to the guilt decision? In answering these questions, I examine the historical and cultural context of jury decision-making as well as the theoretical and empirical context of how people make decisions.

Based on a sociological framework that embraces reality as knowable and understandable from social facts that can be presented and perceived as stimuli for further action (a.k.a. the social construction of reality), the answers formulated here suggest that images of a defendant, whether real or imagined, can be created from the performances of lawyers, and that the decisions made about the defendant based on those images created are socially relevant not only because the defendant's life is affected by them, but also because society accepts and validates the image with incarceration or execution. It is, therefore, hypothesized that the ultimate incarceration of the defendant, Donta Page, signifies an unwillingness to terminate a life that, at some point had, or in some way still has, value.

The theoretical literature offered here also lends itself to an analysis of a capital trial where the performances of attorneys pit one view of the defendant against the other in a battle to define him. Therefore, the author hypothesizes that the performance and lawyers that the jury accepts and believes, respectively, will be the performance and lawyers on the winning side of the verdict. Similarly, the portrayal of the defendant that the judges accept will be the portrayal of the defendant that is manifested in the sentence.

With regard to the jury's task of attributing responsibility for crime and rendering a verdict based on that attribution of guilt, the author discusses the influence of stereotypes on jury decisions based on automatic responses to certain characteristics (such as gender, race, and prior-record evidence) that have historically criminalized and, hence, incarcerated poor black men. That is to say, stereotypes play an important role in the current study because poor black men are oftentimes viewed as violent criminals because of the type of *people* they are perceived to be, rather than because of the kinds of situations in which they find themselves (as a result of poverty and discrimination, for example).

And while people in our society criminalize black men by frequently internally attributing their behavior, society does the opposite to whites, particularly those who are affluent. That is to say that rich white people who murder are rarely viewed as having engaged in that behavior because they are innately evil, but rather because they found themselves in a situation, for example, the wrong crowd, temporary insanity, under the influence of drugs and alcohol. As such, rich white people are held less responsible for their behavior because of the situation they were in, rather than because of the kind of people they are. Hence, incarceration and/or execution are not viewed as necessary punishments for rich whites and those punishments are less frequently conferred upon them.

Finally, Goffman's view of control and its accompanying security in social settings by actors in a performance may manifest itself in the jury verdict too, because it is hypothesized here that the team of attorneys who possessed the most control over the social setting (the courtroom) is also the team who won the case.

Methodology

Case Study
Case studies in social science research are useful. In fact, "the study of the single case or an array of several cases remains indispensable to the progress of the social sciences,"[46] particularly where qualitative data is being used. Advantages of case study research include the ability to (1) collect fundamental insight into everyday phenomena, (2) provide richness and depth to the description of social life, (3) study people in their natural settings, and (4) do detailed analysis of the people and settings to which the case study methodology is applied.

> In the social science literature, most case studies feature: descriptions that are complex, holistic and involving a myriad of not highly isolated variables; data that are likely to be gathered at least partly by personalistic observation; and a writing style that is informal, perhaps narrative, possibly with verbatim quotation, illustration and even allusion and metaphor.[47]

Certainly, the use of case study methodology is appropriate means by which to examine the intricacies of a courtroom procedure, one in which the death penalty, a wholly complex issue in itself, could result. In this way, case study methodology not only allowed the researcher to describe the events of the process, but also to experience them firsthand so that the narrative, including verbatim quotation from the trial transcript, could evolve into a vivid portrayal of the complex procedure. In fact, many sociological case studies have added to our understanding of the human condition: *Tally's Corner*,[48] *Street Corner Society*,[49] *Asylums*,[50] and *Tearoom Trade*[51] serve as outstanding examples of some of the most memorable and respected products of qualitative methodology in general and case study methodology in particular.

Participant Observation

One technique useful in case studies is participant observation. According to Lofland and Lofland, participant observation is warranted when the research examines a many-sided and relatively long-term relationship with a human association in its natural setting. Certainly, "your overall goal is to collect the richest possible data. Rich data mean, ideally, a wide and diverse range of information collected over a relatively prolonged period of time."[52] In addition, participant observation can be used to gain intimate familiarity with a setting and allows the researcher to engage in face-to-face interaction with the settings participants. Lofland and Lofland also assert that participant observation, combined with interviewing, allows researchers to directly apprehend social events in their natural setting.[53] Being embedded with those who are being studied allows the researcher to learn intensive information about the participants. In sum, "field research is a matter of going where the action is and simply watching and listening. You can learn a lot merely by paying attention to what's going on."[54]

Interviews

Qualitative interviewing is a much less structured form of interview because the questions are not prepared in advance:

> A qualitative interview is an interaction between an interviewer and a respondent in which the interviewer has a general plan of inquiry but not a specific set of questions that must be asked in particular words and in a particular order. A qualitative interview is essentially a conversation in which the interviewer establishes a general direction for the conversation and pursues specific topics raised by the respondent. Ideally the respondent does most of the talking.[55]

With the Defendant

I first met the defendant six months after his arrest in the Denver County Jail. At the time, I was teaching a G.E.D. class at the jail as a volunteer and Donta was one of approximately ten students to enroll in the class that month. The first time that I met with the defendant in the current case, for example, I had no idea what I wanted to ask him or what he was going to say. I simply went to visit him one day in the spring of 1999 and chatted informally with him for a while about the food, the temperature in the jail and outside, and the noise at the Denver County Jail, where he was being held. That initial conversation led to numerous others as we soon developed a rapport that, later, led to my education of him including but not limited to his views on life and death, sex, women, fatherhood, family, violence, drugs, homosexuality, perversion, rape, child abuse, molestation, and guns.

In the beginning, Donta found it difficult to talk in a relaxed dialogue. Over several months, however, we both felt more comfortable with each other, talking about our lives, about the case, or about our interactions with the defense team. These initial interactions were informal conversations, not directed interviews. We taught each other about our lives. We shared a common age, race, and American ethnicity, but not much else. Bridging the "social distance" took time. I am female; he is male. I was brought up by loving parents; he was violently abused. I was raised by two parents, he by one. I had a college degree; he had a G.E.D. My family was solidly middle class, his impoverished. And, when we met, he knew that even in the best-case scenario, he would live the rest of his life in prison.

Eventually we started each interview with funny stories about our friends/cellmate or family. We often laughed about things that happened in the jail on a daily basis such as the deputy sheriffs and their occasionally bizarre treatment of the inmates. Jail is not usually a place where you would expect to hear much laughter, but after speaking with the defendant over a period of months before his trial began, I learned to find humor in even the most depressing situations.

One way to gain rapport with the defendant was through the use of humor. To be sure, the humor served several functions simultaneously, such as providing a nice break from the intensity of conversation or as a defense mechanism about our depressing surroundings (a jail) and mission (facing a death penalty trial). One time when I was interviewing the defendant privately in a small glass-encased room with plastic chairs and a heavy metal door that clanged shut, for example, the power in the jail suddenly shut off. For about 45 seconds, I was alone, in the dark, with a killer. Neither of us moved in the darkness until the automatic generator powered up and the fluorescent lights flickered on. When I looked at the defendant, supposedly having stifled my fear, he was laughing hysterically at how scared he thought I looked. When the color supposedly returned to my face (and as a black woman, it is hard to imagine a pale face) the defendant did an imitation of the shower scene in the movie *Psycho*, and instead of being afraid, I laughed until my stomach hurt. The interview ended shortly thereafter because I suddenly had to use the ladies' room.

Through these unstructured conversations and "qualitative interviewing," I gained a sense of how the defendant viewed his own life and circumstance independent of what the world thought of it and him. I say this because even when I went to the jail with an idea of what I wanted to talk about, sometimes it was not discussed because the defendant was not in the mood or perhaps in a better mood than what the subject of discussion would have allowed. At such times, I was able to switch gears and learn about him in the way that he was willing to teach me without feeling guilty about not sticking to an interview schedule. In this way, I served what Steinar Kvale calls the role of an "interview traveler," where a researcher "wanders through the landscape and enters into conversations with the people encountered . . . explores the many domains of the country . . . roaming freely around the territory . . . asks questions that lead the subjects to tell their own stories of their lived world."[56]

That is not to say that my interviews with the defendant were always unfocused. There were many times when I was forced to ask pointed and difficult questions (either for the attorneys or for myself). At these times, I tried to use a relaxed method of approaching the topic. "Hey D, you never told me what your mom said about your grades when you got suspended," "Greta [investigator] told me that you told her that someone else was in the house with you. Is that the person who raped the girl?" or "Do you ever wonder what your life would have been like if you had never gotten involved with drugs?" Such questions seemed to steer the conversation in a general direction, but oftentimes ended up in a place that I had not anticipated. For example, we would end up talking about cheerleaders or go-go clubs or movies he had seen instead of the topic I wanted to discuss—his mother's attitude, his previous criminality, or his lack of vision for his future. At times, I had to refocus the conversation "because field research interviewing is so much like normal conversation, you must keep reminding yourself that you are *not* having a normal conversation."[57]

Often, I forced myself to act ignorant of certain things that I was more or less knowledgeable of in order to urge the defendant to explain it to me in his own way. "What's a dime bag?" "What's the difference between a sawed-off shotgun and an automatic?" or "What's a hollow-point bullet?" Lofland and Lofland call this role the "socially acceptable incompetent"[58] and suggest that it can be advantageous for researchers to act as though they do not understand situations and need the help of someone they are studying to "grasp the most basic and obvious aspects of that situation."[59] In other words, the researcher plays the "quintessential student role."[60]

Of course, there were disadvantages to playing this role, particularly with a streetwise person such as the defendant, Donta Page. First, because I had so much to learn about his lifestyle and history, the defendant chose not to trust me with some of the secrets he may have revealed about himself to a person from his neighborhood. In this way, I believe the defendant left out certain details about his life and offered, instead, a more socially acceptable explanation, or even an "I don't know." Second, at times, the defendant was unusually condescending to me when explaining certain matters of his life, challenging my intelligence, and causing me to react defensively. Sometimes this caused a rift in our relationship and I found myself staying away from him for a period of time to repair my ego.

Third, I gained a reputation with the other inmates in the jail as a "cream puff" (a name he often called me in front of other inmates), insinuating that I knew nothing about the "real" world, which probably decreased the amount of respect that I received from them, although I never felt disrespected by the inmates or him. My naivete and the consequent diminished respect was not obvious in the jail because it is a very controlled setting, but I believe on the street it would have served as a liability. Finally, there were times when I *forgot* to act ignorant and perhaps surprised the defendant with information or comprehension that he thought I lacked. This served to hinder my ability to extract information from him for periods of time because, where he's from, if a person "surprises" you with his behavior, you don't know that person, and he or she is not to be trusted. Needless to say, I had to "start over" with Mr. Page several times.

With Other Members of the Defense Team

The interviews I conducted with members of the defense team, for example, investigators, paralegals, attorneys, and witnesses, were much more instrumental because of the time constraints placed on my interactions with them. For example, my interactions with the attorneys were limited to hearings, meetings, and conferences with the defendant where a specific agenda (created without my input) had already been set. At such times, I would always take notes about what was being said or done, I would do the work that I was asked to do, but occasionally, I would be able to ask a question such as "Why are we doing that?" "What does that mean?" or "How does that help us?" with regard to legal strategy and terminology or "What should I be looking for?" "How should I approach it?" or "What purpose will this serve?" with regard to my own assignments. Such questions allowed me to fill in the big picture of what my role would be in the trial and to learn more about how the attorneys would be presenting the case. Obviously, as a newcomer to the criminal court system, I was their student.

The attorneys were always very open and honest with me. They would take the time to explain the legal strategy, their expectations, odds, probabilities, counterstrategies, hopes, dreams, and worst-case scenarios. For example, one time I was summoned to one of the attorneys' offices to view a video of one of the maximum-security prison facilities in Colorado where the defendant could have been placed. As we viewed the video, which showed a clean workshop, nutritious cafeteria food, clean housing facilities, and a large, well-equipped recreation area, I asked the attorneys why we were watching the video. They sadly explained that the prosecution planned to enter the video as evidence that prison is a nice place to live and that the defendant did not deserve to be placed in such a facility; he should be executed instead. Following the video, the defense team discussed ideas about how to counter the argument by the prosecution that the defendant deserved execution with a plea for mercy and presentation of evidence that the defendant was, in fact, a good candidate for incarceration because he had done well in prison before.

Therefore, I was treated like a full-fledged member of the team and at no time did I feel as though anything was "none of my business." In fact, I believe that the attorneys were amateur social science researchers themselves and actually understood the process of experiential learning that I was going through. One time, an attorney had to actually force me to take a copy of a large exhibit that I did not think was useful to my endeavor, but later became extremely important: the brief about proportionality evidence in Colorado that was submitted to the court to prove that prosecutors seek the death penalty more often on black defendants with white victims than on other types of defendants.

They constantly shoved copies of exhibits, transcripts, social welfare data on the defendant, interview reports, videotapes, pictures, and contact information at me that they thought would be useful. "Allison needs a copy of this," and "Allison, do you want this?" were oftentimes stated during breaks in the trial or meetings. Sometimes the paralegals and investigators would sit next to me during trial proceedings and ask me if I understood what was going on. Most of the time, I did, but if I did not, they were readily available to answer my questions. And at all times, they seemed grateful for my presence in court, for my work on the case, and for the comfort that I seemed to provide to the defendant by visiting him at the jail. In short, I believe that in a very short period of time, I became an *active* member of the defense team, according to Patricia and Peter Adler:

> With active membership, the researcher moves clearly away from the marginally involved role of the traditional participant observer and assumes a more central position in the setting. Researchers who adopt active membership roles do more than participate in the social activities of group members; they take part in the core activities of the group (to the extent that these core activities can be defined and agreed upon by group members). In so doing, they generally assume functional, not solely research or social, roles in their settings. Active-member-researchers (AMRs), therefore, relate to members of the setting in a qualitatively different way than do researchers in peripheral membership roles. Instead of merely sharing the status of insiders, they interact as colleagues: co-participants in a joint endeavor.[61]

With Jurors

One part of human inquiry that is especially intriguing to some social scientists is the realm of knowledge called experiential reality.[62] That is, people tend to believe what they hear and see and they tend not to believe what they do not hear and see. In order for a social scientist to convey an experience to an audience that was absent from the topic of discussion (the trial), then she or he must convey it in such a way as to not contradict common sense. For that reason, an interview methodology for the jurors in the *Page* case was chosen to add richness and depth to the case study. Each juror who agreed to be interviewed was offered $30 for their honest response to questions about jury selection, their deliberations, the attorneys, the judge, the defendant, the crime, and some general crime-related questions. Their experiences were tape-recorded and transcribed and the results of those interviews are included in later chapters of the book.

Interestingly, juror interviews have recently become a very important part of research on the death penalty process, particularly because of the Capital Jury Project (CJP) and its effort to examine guided discretion statutes, among other legal issues surrounding such cases.[63] Much of the research prior to the CJP focused on jury simulation instead of actual juror experiences[64] and although the simulations allow researchers to control research settings and manipulate variables, new research has steered away from the artificiality of the simulations to the riveting, real-life accounts of actual jurors and the decisions they have had to make about life and death. Craig Haney reports that the articles "make for spellbinding reading as one follows the jurors through the process that leads them first to grapple with the awesome responsibility they have been given, and then to choose with other jury members life or death for a fellow citizen."[65]

The interviews I conducted with the jurors in the *Page* case were loosely structured. In fact, I used selected questions from the CJP questionnaire that I thought captured the data that I was interested in examining. Initially, the jurors were contacted through the mail via a letter from the author asking each juror to contact me for an interview about the *Page* jury experience. Each juror that contacted me was then scheduled for an interview at his or her convenience and each was paid $30 after signing the confidentiality agreement. Two (out of the 12) jurors from the *Page* case agreed to be interviewed. Both of the interviews were tape-recorded and transcribed for analysis. The 22-item instrument was administered by me in an informal setting with each juror and the interviews lasted for an average of 35 minutes. Five additional interviews were procured from investigators' notes on the case when jurors were interviewed following the verdict in the case.

Data Collection

During the interviews with the defendant and the defense team, and during the trial, I took copious notes. I began the research with an "open" role in mind; that is, I had no intention of hiding or even downplaying the fact that I was participating in the trial as a researcher. In the beginning, I asked the participants in the study if they minded my note taking, but eventually, I stopped asking for permission because my role expanded into that of a recorder and corresponding secretary.

At first, when I interviewed the defendant at the jail, I would try to write down everything that he said and did, from the way that he looked to how his voice sounded, to what we talked about and how he (and I) felt on any given day. He never seemed to mind that I wrote everything down.

Towards the end of the trial, the volume of my notes during our jail visits tapered off because my interests became more focused. I only took notes on big events or circumstances that struck me as different from the ordinary.

I took copious notes throughout the trial, too, occasionally jotting or abbreviating my streams of thought. I recorded everything that was going on, everything the defendant did or said, everything the attorneys, judges, jury, or court personnel did or said, and everything that I was feeling or doing at the time. I even noted the courtroom temperature, items on tables, things I overheard other people saying, and other miscellaneous information. I never stopped writing.

I interviewed several key defense witnesses when they came to Denver to testify on the defendant's behalf. In fact, one of my tasks as a member of the defense team was to transport Linda Page (defendant's grandmother), Freddy Witherspoon (defendant's cousin), Erica Penny (defendant's ex-girlfriend), and Dr. Dorothy Otnow-Lewis and Dr. Johnathan Pincus (defense experts) to and from the airport and the courtroom. I made notes of those conversations when time allowed.

Importantly, the defense attorneys made sure that the family of the defendant and the expert witnesses knew that I was a researcher and that I was participating in the case in that capacity as well as an investigator. I was often introduced to such people as a "Ph.D. student" or a "doctoral student" who was helping with the case, and I believe that paved the way towards making the people feel comfortable with me and with my constant note taking.

I collected documents that might be used in the trial, including medical records, school records, criminal justice reports, and social welfare reports relating to the defendant. I took notes during the trial proceedings, such as jury selection and preliminary hearings, and I obtained a copy of the trial transcript from the guilt phase of the trial.

Data Analysis

Extensive notes were taken and they (along with the trial transcripts) were analyzed with an open coding system; that is, the notes and transcript were read line by line as a data set looking for patterns and categories that helped to make sense of what was going on in the setting. This process was difficult and tedious in that each line-by-line reading of the notes generated different sets of categories and codes for the same set of circumstances. The observations were collapsed into categories and patterns of sociological significance that were conducive to interpretation.

For example, when the prosecutors made statements directing the jury's attention to what happened on the day of the crime and *only* on the day of the crime, the code "DAY" was used to refer to how the prosecution's case centered around one day in the life of the defendant. Similarly, when the defense attorneys made statements about the defendant's background or lifestyle, the code "LIFE" was used to refer to how the defense broadened the scope of the jury's purview (coded "VIEW") to include circumstances in the defendant's life that may have contributed to his criminality. Additional codes like "INTERNAL" and "EXTERNAL" were used to depict statements that directly related to internal or external attributions of responsibility for the crime, both of which made up the categorical code of "DEF" or "defendant" and were analyzed together as part of the theoretical analysis. In other words, two lists were made of the defendant: one that listed the internal attributions portrayed at trial and another that listed the external attributions. Two lists were made for the "VIEW" from the jury that was being talked about; one was of the day of the crime, and the other was of the entire life of the defendant.

Such codes helped to answer the two main questions I sought to understand in the current study, that is, (1) How do attorneys attempt to portray an image of the defendant? and (2) How is that image related to the guilt decision? Again, it is hypothesized in the current study that the lawyers who presented the most convincing evidence of internal or external attribution of the defendant and the most convincing view of what happened to cause the crime (whether on that day or throughout the defendant's life) represented the side of the argument that won the case. Perhaps it was the side of the argument that jurors did not have to reach as far to believe, too.

As a data set, generalized questions were posed by the researcher upon review of the notes. Questions, such as those proposed by Robert M. Emerson, Rachel I. Fretz, and Linda L. Shaw, proved useful:

> What are people doing? What are they trying to accomplish? How do members talk about, characterize, and understand what is going on? What assumptions are they making? What do I see going on here? What did I learn from these notes? Why did I include them?[66]

Such questions helped to streamline the difficult task of creating a meaningful scene from the observation that could be interpreted in a sociological way by emphasizing process rather than cause, by focusing on the mundane issues in the setting, and by clarifying the meaning or significance of what was recorded by the researcher and why, that is, "Why did I include them?"

Theoretical memos about the various codes and the patterns and categories that arose from the coding were written (only those that gave rise to a larger analytic issue), which then helped to create themes for the final product, for example:

SOCIAL DISTANCE —the jury did not have far to go to believe that the defendant was an evil monster. It wasn't a stretch. The stereotypes surrounding large, poor black men with a prior record all but characterized him that way before the trial began. Of course he did it! That's how black men act. The "normal primitive" stereotype is alive and well. The jury could be lazy and arrive at that conclusion without any guilt on their part. A stretch for them would have been to believe that society and all of its malfunctioning systems created the monster they saw. Blaming society is not an acceptable or reasonable conclusion to draw, but it is the conclusion the defense attorneys attempted to draw.

Several themes were selected for inclusion in the current study, but many were set aside for separate consideration. Focused coding with the actual physical grouping of themes and codes helped to organize the pieces of this work. Integrative memos were written to elaborate on the new codes and themes that arose from the focused coding and links between themes appeared that ultimately framed the analysis. For example,

XENOPHOBIA is common

↓

Much SOCIAL DISTANCE between juror and criminal feels safe

↓

PSYCHOLOGICAL explanations are easier than SOCIOLOGICAL ones

↓

INTERNAL attributes are easier, safer, and more common than EXTERNAL attributes

↓

GUILT has been rationalized and the story makes sense

The trial transcript offered a more concrete data source to use to understand how attribution theory works, though. Patterns of internal and external attributions of responsibility to the defendant became increasingly clear as the transcript was cross-referenced with the notes that had been previously coded. In other words, each section of the transcript was marked that offered an analysis of either internal attributions or external attributions not only in the words that were spoken by the attorneys, but also in the motions and gestures that were used, the exhibits that were shown, and/or the evidence that was offered. Each set of attorneys was clearly trying to establish internal or external attribution to the defendant at all times during the trial.

Author/Defendant Relationship

I met Donta in the fall of 1999, six months after the crimes occurred, when he joined a G.E.D. class at the Denver County Jail where I was a tutor. Having seen the crime reported on television in February (including photographs of him when he was arrested), when we met, I was initially surprised by his gentle demeanor and his sense of humor. I soon came to realize that he was more intelligent than his test scores in my class revealed. At that point, I became interested in Mr. Page's progress toward the diploma, particularly his aptitude for science and geography. Seven months after our initial meeting, I asked him if I could follow his case on a more systematic level for the purpose of conducting this study. He enthusiastically agreed to introduce the question to his attorneys.

Donta Page was twenty-two years old when, in February 1999, he raped and killed a twenty-four-year-old white woman in Denver, Colorado. Donta Page is black. He was an ex-convict, on parole, from a ten-year sentence in Baltimore, Maryland, for armed robbery. Donta told a judge that he wanted to "change his life" in a letter written from his jail cell in Maryland, according to a newspaper article written by Lynn Bartels of the *Rocky Mountain News* (March 21, 1999):

> I've hit the bottom and there is no where to go but up from here. . . . I really want to be a productive member of society and make up for the pain I've caused. . . . I was living the life or so I thought, but the life I was living was a fool's life. . . . I sit and think what type of role model I am to them [his two younger brothers]. I know now what I have to do. I have to be there for my brothers. Your honor, I'm 22 years old and I have a long life ahead of me and don't want to spend it going in and out of institutions, like most of the men in here.

According to the same article, "he told the judge in his August 1998 letter that a reason he wanted to attend Denver's Stout Street Foundation rehab program was that there was a long waiting list to get into the prison's drug programs. Page said he had planned to go to college but then started committing crimes, including dealing drugs." Donta Page was released from prison in Maryland on October 12 and arrived at the Stout Street Center in Denver, Colorado, on October 15, 1998. Page had never been to Colorado and did not know anyone in the state when he arrived. After being expelled from the program (four months later) for bad behavior, he raped and killed twenty-four-year-old Peyton Tuthill, a white woman, during a burglary of her house when she came home and surprised him during the crime. Ms. Tuthill was an employee of the Cherry Creek Mortgage Company.

Following my conversation with Donta about studying his case, I attempted to gain approval from the Human Research Committee (HRC) for the case study project. Approval was denied, however, because prisoners are a protected class of citizens. Their interests have to be represented by a community spokesperson at the HRC meeting and even then, they are entitled to extra protection for things they may say or do as a part of the research that may make them vulnerable to additional or related prosecution (that is, I would need to have an attorney present at all of my interactions with the defendant in order to protect his rights). These regulations are not only understandable, but of immense use in protecting prisoners from abuse. Nonetheless, they would render my work (as a pure scholar) all but impossible. By combining the scholar role with that of a legal assistant, however, not only would the proper concerns of the HRC be met (supervision by an attorney), but I would also have the permission of the attorney and client to talk unobserved.

In August 2000, defense attorneys Randy Canney and Jim Castle agreed to allow me to assist them as an investigator and researcher for the defense following much persuasion by me and the defendant and scrutiny of my academic background. This solved my problem with HRC approval because the role that I would play as an investigator was voluntary and could be subsumed under the category of "my life." Just as any human being is free to study her or his own children in the role of "mother" without HRC approval, I was, then, free to study the defendant in the role of "investigator" on his defense team and I took full advantage of the opportunity by signing a confidentiality agreement with the attorneys and the defendant which held me legally responsible until the end of the trial for maintaining strict confidence with the information I received. Furthermore, my work was closely supervised by the "research subject's" lawyers. In short, unlike 98 percent of qualitative studies, I was not free to divulge any of the circumstances of the case or any confidential information until after the defendant had been acquitted or convicted and sentenced.

A Note on Researcher Objectivity and Neutrality

Obviously, the role I played as a defense investigator was not a neutral one because not only did I work for the defense in the current case, but I also continue to work towards the abolition of the death penalty in the United States in my own life. As such, the current project utilizes notes and observations taken from the perspective of an individual who wholeheartedly defended a murderer, not because of the person I believed him to be, but rather as an endeavor to investigate my personal belief in the wrongfulness of execution and in the arbitrary, capricious, and discriminatory manner in which I believe murderers are judged and sentenced, particularly those whose lives have already executed their human spirit and will to live.

I make no pretense of neutrality in the fight over the death penalty. In fact, neutrality is not at all required by social scientists.[67] Certainly, "there is no position from which sociological research can be done that is not biased in one or another way."[68] Instead, the goal of research should be to avoid sentimentality, to "use our techniques impartially enough that a belief to which we are especially sympathetic could be proved untrue,"[69] and to state clearly the limits of the research to prevent them from being used inappropriately. Certainly, "the fact that a scientist has reasons for his choice of problems other than a thirst for knowledge or a love of truth scarcely implies that his inquiry will be biased."[70] We now turn our attention to the major discoveries of this research project.

Notes

1. Jody Armour, "Stereotypes and Prejudice: Helping Legal Decision-Makers Break the Prejudice Habit," *California Law Review* 83(1995): 733–772; Richard E. Nisbett, "The Dilution Effect: Nondiagnostic Information Weakens the Implications of Dignostic Information," *Cognitive Psychology* 13(1981): 248–272.

2. J. Frank Yates, *Judgment and Decision Making* (Englewood Cliffs, NJ: Prentice Hall, 1990); Nancy Cantor and Walter Mischel, "Prototypes in Person Perception," *Advances in Experimental Social Psychology* 12(1979): 3–4.

3. Jody Armour, "Stereotypes and Prejudice: Helping Legal Decision-makers Break the Prejudice Habit" *California Law Review* 83(1995): 733.

4. Armour, "Stereotypes and Prejudice," 733.

5. Jody Armour, "Stereotypes and Prejudice: Helping Legal Decision-makers Break the Prejudice Habit" *California Law Review* 83(1995): 733–772; George S. Bridges and Sara Steen, "Racial Disparities in Official Assessments of Juvenile Offenders: Attributional Stereotypes as Mediating Mechanisms,"*American Sociological Review* 63(1998): 554–570; Ronald Farrell and Malcolm D. Holmes, "The Social and Cognitive Structure of Legal Decision-Making," *The Sociological Quarterly* 32(1991): 529–542; Gary D. Hill, Anthony R. Harris, and JoAnn Miller, "The Etiology of Bias: Social Heuristics and Rational Decision Making in Deviance Processing," *Journal of Research in Crime and Delinquency* 22(1985): 135–162; Victoria Lynn Swigert and Ronald A. Farrell, "Normal Homicides and the Law," *American Sociological Review* 42(1977): 16–32.

6. William I. Thomas and Dorothy S. Thomas, *The Child in America: Behavior Problems and Programs* (New York: Knopf, 1928), 572.

7. Peter L. Berger and Thomas Luchmann, *The Social Construction of Reality: A Treatise in the Sociology of Knowledge* (New York: Doubleday, 1966), 1–19.

8. Berger and Luchmann, *The Social Construction*, 3.

9. Berger and Luchmann, *The Social Construction*, 10.

10. Berger and Luchmann, *The Social Construction*, 10.

11. Berger and Luchmann, *The Social Construction*, 22.

12. Berger and Luchmann, *The Social Construction*, 22.

13. Berger and Luchmann, *The Social Construction*, 53.

14. Berger and Luchmann, *The Social Construction*, 53.

15. Edith Green and Mary Dodge, "The Influence of Prior Record Evidence on Juror Decision-Making," *Law and Human Behavior* 19(1995): 68.

16. Green and Dodge, "The Influence," 68.

17. E. Borgida and R. Park, "The Entrapment Defense: Juror Comprehension and Decision-making," *Law and Human Behavior* 12(1988): 19–40; A. Doob and H. Kirshenbaum, "Some Empirical Evidence on the Effect of Section 12 of the Canada Evidence Act Upon the Accused," *Criminal Law Quarterly* 15(1972): 88–96; R.L. Wissler and M.J. Saks, "On the Inefficacy of Limiting Instructions: When Jurors Use Prior Conviction Evidence to Decide on Guilt," *Law and Human Behavior* 9(1985): 37–48.

18. Berger and Luchmann, *The Social Construction*, 54 .

19. Victoria Lynn Swigert and Ronald A. Farrell"Normal Homicides and the Law." *American Sociological Review* 42(1977): 16–32.

20. Susan T. Fiske and Shelley E. Taylor, *Social Cognition* (New York: McGraw-Hill, 1991).

21. Roger Brown, *Social Psychology*, 2nd ed. (New York: The Free Press, 1986); Susan T. Fiske and Shelley E. Taylor, *Social Cognition* (New York: McGraw-Hill, 1991).

22. F. M. Lewis and L. H. Daltroy, "How Causal Explanations Influence Health Behavior: Attribution Theory," in *Health Education and Health Behavior: Theory, Research and Practice*, ed. K. Glanz, F. M. Lewis, and B. K. Rimer, (San Francisco, CA: Jossey-Bass Publishers, 1990).

23. Fritz Heider, *The Psychology of Interpersonal Relations* (New York: Wiley, 1958).

24. E. E. Jones and K.E. Davis, "From Acts to Dispositions: The Attribution Process in Person Perception," in *Advances in Experimental Social Psychology*, ed. L. Berkowitz, (Orlando, FL: Academic Press, 1965).

25. Susan T. Fiske and Shelley E. Taylor, *Social Cognition* (New York: McGraw-Hill, 1991).

26. Roger Brown, *Social Psychology* (New York: The Free Press, 1986), 169.

27. Erving Goffman, *The Presentation of Self in Everyday Life*, (New York: Doubleday,1959), 22–23.

28. Goffman, *The Presentation*, 27.

29. Goffman in George Ritzer, *Modern Sociological Theory*, (New York: McGraw-Hill, 1996), 74.

30. Goffman, *The Presentation*, 38.

31. Erving Goffman, *Stigma: Notes on the Management of Spoiled Identity* (Englewood Cliffs, New Jersey: Prentice Hall, 1963).

32. George Ritzer, *Modern Sociological Theory*, 4th ed. (New York: McGraw-Hill, 1996), 220.

33. Goffman, *The Presentation*, 79.

34. Goffman, *The Presentation*, 83.

35. Goffman, *The Presentation*, 95.

36. Michel Foucault, *Discipline and Punish* (New York: Vintage Books, 1977), 19.

37. Foucault, *Discipline*, 48.

38. Foucault, *Discipline*, 49.

39. Foucault, *Discipline*, 49.

40. Anthony Giddens, *Emile Durkheim: Selected Writings* (New York: Cambridge University Press, 1972), 123.

41. Giddens, *Emile Durkheim*, 127.

42. Giddens, *Emile Durkheim*, 129.

43. Giddens, *Emile Durkheim*, 133.

44. Giddens, *Emile Durkheim*, 136.

45. Giddens, *Emile Durkheim*, 139.

46. Joe R. Feagin, Anthony M. Orum, and Gideon Sjoberg, *A Case for the Case Study* (Chapel Hill, NC: University of North Carolina Press, 1991), 1.

47. Robert E. Stake, "The Case Study Method in Social Inquiry" in *Case Study Method: Key Issues, Key Texts*, ed. Roger Gomm, Martyn Hammersley, and Peter Foster (London: Sage Publications, 2000), 24.

48. Elliot Liebow, *Tally's Corner: A Study of Negro Street Corner Men* (Boston: Little Brown, 1967).

49. William Foote Whyte, *Street Corner Society: The Social Structure of an Italian Slum* (Chicago: University of Chicago Press, 1955).

50. Erving Goffman, *Asylums: Essays on the Social Situation of Mental Patients and Other Inmates* (Chicago: Aldine Publishing Company, 1961).

51. Laud Humphreys, *Tearoom Trade: Impersonal Sex in Public Places* (New York: Aldine, 1975).

52. John Lofland and Lyn H. Lofland, *Analyzing Social Settings: A Guide to Qualitative Observation and Analysis*, 3rd ed. (Belmont, CA: Wadsworth, 1995), 16.

53. Lofland and Lofland, *Analyzing*, 17.

54. Earl Babbie, *The Practice of Social Research*, 8th ed. (Belmont, CA: Wadsworth, 1998), 290.

55. Babbie, *The Practice*, 290.

56. Steinar Kvale, *Interviews: An Introduction to Qualitative Research Interviewing* (Thousand Oaks, CA: Sage, 1996), 3.

57. Babbie, *The Practice*, 292.

58. John Lofland and Lyn H. Lofland, *Analyzing Social Settings: A Guide to Qualitative Observation and Analysis* (Belmont, CA: Wadsworth, 1995), 56.

59. Earl Babbie, *The Practice of Social Research* (Belmont, CA: Wadsworth, 1998), 292.

60. John Lofland and Lyn H. Lofland, *Analyzing Social Settings: A Guide to Qualitative Observation and Analysis* (Belmont, CA: Wadsworth, 1995), 56.

61. Patricia A. Adler and Peter Adler, *Membership Roles in Field Research* (Newbury Park, CA: Sage, 1987), 50.

62. Earl Babbie, *The Practice of Social Research* (Belmont, CA: Wadsworth, 1998).

63. William J. Bowers, "The Capital Jury Project: Rationale, Design, and Preview of Early Findings," *Indiana Law Journal* 70(1995): 1043–1102; Craig Haney, "Taking Capital Jurors Seriously," *Indiana Law Journal* 70(1995): 1223–1232; Hans Zeisel, "Race Bias in the Administration of the Death Penalty: The Florida Experience," *Harvard Law Review* 95(1981): 459–460; Austin Sarat, "Violence, Representation, and Responsibility in Capital Trials: The View from the Jury," *Indiana Law Journal* 70(1995): 1103–1135.

64. Haney, "Taking Capital," 1223–1232.

65. Haney, "Taking Capital," 1235.

66. Robert Emerson, Rachel Fretz, and Linda Shaw, *Writing Ethnographic Fieldnotes* (Chicago, IL: University of Chicago Press, 1995).

67. Howard S. Becker, "Whose Side Are We On?" *Social Problems* 14(1967): 239–247; Abraham Kaplan, *The Conduct of Inquiry* (San Francisco, CA: Chandler Publishing, 1964);

Alvin W. Gouldner, "The Sociologist as Partisan: Sociology and the Welfare State," *The American Sociologist* 3 (1968): 103–116.

68 Becker, "Whose Side," 245.

69. Becker, "Whose Side," 246.

70. Abraham Kaplan, *The Conduct of Inquiry* (San Francisco, CA: Chandler Publishing, 1964), 382.

CHAPTER FOUR

~

The Legal Fight

The difference in substance between first-degree murder and second-degree murder is that first-degree murder requires the additional element of premeditation.

The Legal Fight: First- versus Second-Degree Murder

It is important to understand that both sets of attorneys had different goals in this case. The prosecution, for example, was working to convict the defendant of first-degree murder so that they could seek the death penalty. The defense attorneys, on the other hand, wanted to obtain a second-degree murder conviction, which would remove death as a sentencing option. To that end, the defense attempted to plea bargain with the prosecution before the trial began; they sought a second-degree murder conviction and a sentence of life without the possibility of parole.

Title 18-3-102 of the Colorado Revised Statutes states that

A person commits the crime of murder in the first degree if: (a) After deliberation and with the intent to cause the death of a person other than himself, he causes the death of that person or of another person.

Title 18-3-103 of the Colorado Revised Statutes states that

A person commits the crime of murder in the second degree if the person knowingly causes the death of a person . . . murder in the second degree is a class 3 felony where the act causing the death was performed upon a sudden heat of passion, caused by a serious and highly provoking act of the intended victim, affecting the defendant sufficiently to excite an irresistible passion in a reasonable person; but, if between the provocation and the killing there is an interval sufficient for the voice of reason and humanity to be heard, the killing is a class 2 felony.

The Colorado Revised Statute goes on to state that "the difference in substance between first degree murder and second degree murder is that first degree murder requires the additional element of premeditation."[1]

Lawyers and Court Proceedings

Lawyers are the conduits through which all evidence that is presented at trial is conveyed. Lawyers are the first and the last to speak about the defendant. They determine the order of witnesses, the relevance of evidence presented to the jury, how the evidence and witnesses are linked together, the mood of the courtroom, the framework of the theory being presented, and the timing of exhibits. As such, lawyers choreograph a very complicated stage play, according to Goffman,[2] and are responsible for making sure that the audience (the jury) understands and interprets correctly the artistic view that is presented.

The jury, on the other hand, serves as a sometimes eager and oftentimes bored audience, but one in which participation serves a pivotal role in the performance because not only does the jury view the portrayal that is presented by lawyers who have rehearsed and organized the performance prior to the trial date, but the jury also renders a verdict in the end that places one interpretation of the drama in permanent record.

Three principal types of evidence are presented during the trial: material objects (props), testimony of witnesses, and rebuttal testimony of witnesses. Each side, in the current case, attempted to organize the presentation of evidence to their advantage. Both sets of attorneys used specific tactics and strategies during the trial that warrant preliminary discussion.

Attorney Tactics

Nonverbal Communication
There were two attorneys working for the defense and two for the state. The credibility of the attorneys was important. The lawyers dressed in suits and ties. Three of the attorneys were middle-aged white men. One attorney was a mixed-race, middle-aged man. The attorneys spoke loudly and used very

simple language. They showed deference and respect to the judge and disdain or impatience as well as cooperation and agreement to witnesses at various times. They harmonized their movements with each other. And they made sure that they directed all of their comments and gestures to the jury and judge.

Also, the demeanor of the lawyers set the mood for the trial and even added drama to an otherwise boring procedure. For example, attorneys would lean over the podium and peer at a witness with their mouths open in disbelief to something that the witness had uttered or they would abruptly interrupt the testimony of a witness with dismissive hand gestures that indicated that what the witness had said was irrelevant. Also, attorneys would themselves look bored or even shocked at statements made by witnesses and they would approach witnesses with respect or disdain in their countenance. Their demeanor when questioning witnesses, then, played an important role in conveying to the jury how they thought the jury should view the testimony of a particular witness.

The Use of Props

Erving Goffman discussed how people are interested in appearances and that they use props to accentuate their theatrical performances.[3] Props that the attorneys and witnesses used during the presentation of evidence were enlarged, colored, magnified, intensified, highlighted, and multiplied. In fact, the props were sometimes (intentionally) distracting. Sometimes it was difficult to listen to statements being made in the courtroom because a PET scan video (positron emission tomography—a technique used to examine brain function with glucose or oxygen consumption) was more interesting to view.

The jury watched several videos during the trial. The judges viewed additional videotapes during the penalty phase and were presented with a notebook of exhibits from the guilt phase that included autopsy photographs and crime scene photographs. Such props, though not always pleasant, were meant to capture the hearts and minds of the decision-makers in the case with great effect. The jury members and the judges paid increased attention to the proceedings when such props were used. For that reason, a concerted effort was made by the attorneys to use props even when they were unnecessary, rude (such as the half-naked, bloody picture of the victim slumped in the corner of the bedroom), and sometimes condescending (such as when the words of the confession were magnified and placed on large poster boards for the jury to see even though they already had a typed transcript in front of them. The prosecutor pointed to each word that the defendant uttered during one portion of the tape).

Incorporating the Defendant

Four male attorneys took part in the *Page* case and their treatment of the defendant was remarkable. Both sets of attorneys wandered freely around the room during the presentation of evidence addressing comments to either the judge or the jury, using props, and making statements about the defendant. But some of the attorneys referred to the defendant as "Mr. Page," or "Page" (usually the defense) while others referred to him as "the defendant" (usually the prosecution). Some of the attorneys looked directly at the defendant when they spoke about him while others averted their gaze. And some of the attorneys gestured sternly or pointed at the defendant while others waved at or stood next to him. This treatment indicated the position of the attorneys as to their interpretation of how the defendant should be viewed, i.e., touchable or untouchable.

Making It Understood: Language

Language used in the trial was diverse in its complexity. The lawyers and lay witnesses used very simple language during the trial, but the expert witnesses sometimes offered industry terms to explain something to the jury. Terms like "controls," "parietal lobe," "blood spatter," "cortex," "outliers," "myelination," and "statistical significance" were used, sometimes with little or no explanation, and the judge gave instructions to the jury that included terms like "reasonable doubt" and "speculative doubt," but he did not explain the difference between them. At times, this jargon was confusing, but there were other times when the language was not important because the jury, apparently, was not paying attention. At such times, the lawyers and the expert witnesses seemed more to be having a conversation between themselves than to be trying to get the jury to understand the testimony. Perhaps the testimony simply needed to be preserved on record for future use.

The Use of Credentials

Credentials of the speakers played an important role in defining the stories that were told in this trial. For example, before the attorneys could question expert witnesses who were called to testify, trial procedure required that they be accepted by the court as an "expert" in a specified field of study. Sometimes the witness's qualification went unchallenged. Other times, the qualification was complicated. All of the expert witnesses that were called to testify were eventually accepted in one way or another, but the objections that were raised by attorneys about the qualifications seemed important and oftentimes delayed the proceedings for several minutes. A battle of the experts ensued, then, that was (apparently) important to the portrayal of the defendant because the side with the better experts was expected to win. On the other hand, lay witnesses (family members and friends of the defendant and victim) did not have to be qualified by the court, but their demeanor, words, attitude, relationship to the victim or defendant, opinion of the victim or defendant, truthfulness, motive, and intent were sometimes forcefully challenged.

Themes

There were several themes that arose from the focused coding of the trial transcripts and my observation notes: the social distance between the defendant and the jury and between the jury and the victim, the humane versus subhuman portrayal of the defendant, and the jury's focus showed repeated patterns of occurrence throughout the proceedings.

Social distance is the "degree to which people are willing to accept and associate with those having different social characteristics."[4] The social distance between jury members and the defendant was manipulated by the attorneys presenting the case. In other words, the amount of social distance that *appeared* to exist between the jury and the defendant was probably quite different from the amount of social distance that *actually* existed between them. One set of attorneys worked to enlarge the distance. They portrayed the defendant as a subhuman, rabid animal who showed little remorse for the crime that he committed. But the other set of attorneys struggled to portray the defendant as a human being with severe emotional and mental problems (the result of child abuse and trauma), who made some terrible mistakes because of those problems. They seemed to argue that many normal people would behave as the defendant did, given similar life histories. As such, whether the jury could relate to the defendant was an important issue to be resolved during the trial. In fact, it would, later, determine the outcome of it.

The battle to define the defendant, then, became a battle to define the amount of social distance between the jury members and their experiences in life and the defendant and his experiences in life. Theoretically, the closer the jury could be made to feel in relation to the defendant, the less likely conviction was to occur, even though, in the current case, the physical evidence against the defendant was overwhelming. That is, regardless of social distance, the jury in the *Page* case could have convicted the defendant on the physical evidence alone, but the current study seeks to examine other factors (besides physical evidence) in jury decision-making that may influence guilt decisions in capital trials. Thus, the social distance between the jury and defendant in the current case may not be relevant, but it is included to establish that the main task for the attorneys was to attempt to decrease or increase the social distance between the defendant and the jury to win the case.

Also, the extent to which social distance could be placed between the jury members and the victim affected the distinction that the jury needed to make between first-degree and second-degree murder. That is, first-degree murder requires that the jury find that the defendant deliberated before he killed the victim, while second-degree murder requires that the defendant intended to harm the victim, but not necessarily to kill her. This distinction is important because a second-degree murder conviction would remove death as a sentencing option and likely leave the defendant with a chance to someday be released from prison. If the jurors felt that the defendant had acted unintentionally, accidentally, with mental defect, or out of rage, for example, the social distance between them and the defendant would be small—they would have to be able to relate to how the defendant was feeling at the time that he committed the murder.

Likewise, the mitigators presented by the defense and the aggravators presented by the prosecutors during the penalty phase represented the efforts of both sides to increase or decrease the social distance between the judges and the defendant. That is, the more empathy that could be aroused for the defendant during the penalty phase, the less likely the judges would have been to sentence the defendant to death. The mitigators (child abuse, lack of intelligence, brain damage) offered by the defense during the penalty phase were used to decrease the social distance between the defendant and the judges, that is, to help them to recognize his personal struggles. The prosecutors' list of aggravators (the crime was heinous, premeditated, and committed for pecuniary gain), on the other hand, were used to increase the social distance between the jury and the defendant so that they would refuse to accept his personal struggles and hold him criminally responsible for the murder because he is innately evil rather than dysfunctional.

The humanity of the defendant was always at issue, too. The prosecution vehemently denied that the defendant was capable of feeling disappointment, sadness, remorse, or fear. In fact, the prosecution denied that the defendant experienced tragedies in his lifetime (e.g., the murder of two of his best friends, child abuse, and rape). They further denied that these tragedies, even if they ever occurred, could have affected his growth and development. But the defense highlighted these things as factors in the development of the defendant's personality. The prosecution denied that a human being could act in the same way as the defendant—only an animal would engage in such behavior. But the defense argued that the defendant's actions and thoughts were reasonable under the circumstances—any person could act the same way if similarly situated. The prosecution even claimed that the defendant's actions were not the actions of a person who values freedom and humanity, but rather of a dumb deviant who simply chose one life path to follow over numerous others. The defense, on the other hand, suggested that the defendant was not aware of choices available to him because he was lost in despair.

The attorneys attempted to change the jury's focus numerous times throughout the trial. At times, the jury was asked to look only at the day of the crime and the events that took place in that time and space. At other times, the jury was asked to go back in time to another space where different conditions and different people played pivotal roles in the development of the events on the day of the crime. In other words, the jury was shown a very narrow view of what to consider in their deliberations *and* an enlarged or widened view of what to consider in their deliberations. The jury, however, was given a choice of which view to accept in much the same way that a photographer chooses to take a picture of an object using either a telephoto or a wide-angle lens. To be sure, both views were accurate, but only one could be used for the verdict.

Discussion of the victim (who she was and what she experienced) came in smaller portions of the trial than one might have expected—during the prosecution's case and the penalty phase. The victim only played a small role in the trial that resulted from her death: her death was the reason for the convention. Beyond that, the victim was rarely referred to during most portions of the trial. The presence of her family, however, was a constant reminder of the purpose of the trial. In absentia, the jury and the judges may not have paid as much attention to their grief.

In short, observation of the trial and analysis of the trial transcript raised issues about the important role that attorneys play in constructing an image of the defendant that lends itself to conviction or acquittal. The winning image has everything to do with the jury's focus, the amount of social distance that can be placed between the jury and the defendant, the amount of social distance that can be placed between the jury and the victim, the credibility afforded to witnesses, the language used to describe scientific information, the entertainment versus informational value of props, and the treatment of witnesses and the defendant by attorneys. For that reason, this chapter addresses three questions: (1) What are the questions that each side tried to answer? (2) What images of the defendant were constructed at trial? and (3) How might these images be related to the verdict?

Notes

1. *Colorado Revised Statutes*, Title 18-3-103, 755.
2. Erving Goffman, *The Presentation of Self in Everyday Life*, (New York: Doubleday, 1959).
3. Goffman, *The Presentation of Self in Everyday Life*.
4. Allan G. Johnson, *The Blackwell Dictionary of Sociology: A User's Guide to Sociological Language* (Cambridge, MA: Blackwell, 1995), 259.

CHAPTER FIVE

~

The Guilt Phase: How the Defense/ Prosecution Saw Their Mission

If you bring together brain damage of some sort, which impairs the ability to control your impulses and impairs judgment, and if you combine that with psychotic symptoms, particularly with paranoia, the belief that one is being threatened, the belief that you have to protect yourself, and a child with these vulnerabilities is abused, then you create a very, very violent individual.

The Guilt Phase: How the Prosecution Saw Its Mission

Who Did What: The Behavioral Dimension

The prosecution, like the defense, used its opening statement to raise the questions that it wanted to answer. Questions that the prosecution attempted to answer during the guilt phase of the trial were simple: Who did it, to whom, and why? These questions were summarized in opening statements and evidence of each was presented during the first part of the trial. The prosecution may have had an advantage at trial in that they were the first to present any evidence. Theirs was the first voice, the first version of the story, the first portrayal of the defendant, and the first theory of the crime that the jury heard. As such, the prosecution spent a great deal of time presenting its argument (in the form of an opening statement) so that the jury could get a clear view of what evidence was to follow.

The prosecution's case focused on the day of the crime and the events that transpired within the 24–48 hour period surrounding it. They concentrated on the defendant and the victim, the killing, and the physical evidence that pointed to the defendant's guilt. It was a persuasive story in that the defendant confessed, but the jury would, later, determine the validity of the evidence presented by the prosecution at trial and they did so within the confines of the jury room. That is, the jury listened to the prosecution's case having (supposedly) put all information from news media sources, all prejudices and stereotypes, and all preconceived notions about crime and criminality out of their minds. Only the words coming out of the prosecutor's mouth and the evidence that they presented in court were supposed to be considered. For example, the prosecution's opening statement clearly demonstrated that "who did it, to whom, and why" were the only important issues to be addressed. And, though the jury may not have been aware, the "to whom" question became increasingly important as the prosecutor's statement continued:

> Good morning, ladies and gentlemen. For the next several days you will hear about one of the most heinous and tragic crimes to ever happen in your community. You will hear firsthand how this defendant intentionally and deliberately robbed, raped, and killed Peyton Tuthill. You will hear that back in February of last year, Peyton Tuthill was 24 years old. She had recently graduated from the College of Charleston in Charleston, South Carolina. The evidence will show that Peyton was not from Denver, Colorado. She came out here with a friend of hers named Heather Nelson. They came out here on vacation in 1998 right after they graduated. You will hear that they liked the Denver area. They liked the mountains. They were somewhat young and adventurous so they decided that they would move out here. The evidence will show that Heather and Peyton went back home and that Peyton came out a few weeks later to start looking for a home for her and Heather Nelson.
>
> The evidence will show that Peyton Tuthill and Heather Nelson had met another person, a man by the name of Bryan Mullins. The evidence will show that Bryan Mullins was going to be their roommate as well. And Peyton searched for a house in Denver. The evidence will show that Peyton Tuthill and Bryan Mullins found a house; it was at 1637 Gaylord Street. It was a duplex. Heather moved out here a couple weeks later and the three of them settled into the modest three-bedroom duplex in central Denver. But unfortunately they did not know who their neighbors were. Because you will hear that two doors down from Ms. Tuthill, Mr. Mullins, and Ms. Nelson was the defendant. He was new to Denver too. But his roommates weren't college friends. His roommates were other members of a halfway house called the Stout Street Foundation. The evidence will show that the defendant was sentenced to Stout Street as part of a criminal sentence out of Prince George's County, Maryland.

The evidence will show on that fateful day, February 24th, 1999, or—yeah, 1999, Peyton, Heather and Bryan all left their house and they went to work. They all had jobs. You will hear that Peyton Tuthill was working for a temporary agency and they had her at Cherry Creek Mortgage. But this was a big day for Peyton Tuthill because she had a job interview for a permanent position with the Cystic Fibrosis Foundation. She was excited she had a job interview scheduled for later that morning.

The evidence will show that Peyton went to that interview for the Cystic Fibrosis Foundation that morning; she interviewed with a Leslie Parker. You will hear that Leslie Parker was very impressed with Peyton Tuthill. Found her to be the type of employee they were looking for. Leslie Parker on February 24th, 1999, offered her a job.

The evidence will show that Peyton Tuthill left that interview happy, contemplating her future and thinking about this new job offer that she had. Well, at the same time Peyton was considering her future this defendant was considering his as well. But he wasn't thinking about job offers. He was thinking about the next crime he was going to commit, because the defendant had been kicked out of Stout Street; dejected and told to leave, he was sitting around that day waiting for a bus ride back to Maryland thinking about the next crime he was going to commit. And you will hear at that point he devised a plan. A plan where he could go down the street and he would break into Peyton Tuthill's house and he would look for whatever he could find.

The evidence will show that he does—that the defendant does that. He walks down the street to Peyton Tuthill's empty house and breaks in through the back door. The evidence will show that the defendant immediately grabs a beer out of the refrigerator and arms himself with two knives, two knives. He starts walking around the house seeing what he can get in to.

Ladies and gentlemen, unfortunately and tragically, Peyton Tuthill decided to stop at her house after the interview and before she went back to work. You will hear that Peyton Tuthill pulls up to the front of the house, she walks in the front door unaware of the horror and the torture that await her. She sees the defendant. She screams. She tries to run up the stairs. She kicks and she fights but she is no match for this 300-pound intruder. He beats Peyton, he subdues her, and he ties her with a cord at the top of the stairs. You will hear that he then asks her where is the money, where is the money. He is told that her purse is in her car. The defendant then walks out of the house leaving the bound Peyton Tuthill in the house and goes to her car to retrieve the purse and the money that he wanted.

Ladies and gentlemen, you will hear that once the defendant is outside of the house and once the defendant has the purse he is not content, because you will hear this defendant goes back into the house to finish the job. The evidence will show that the defendant goes back into the house and takes this knife, this knife, ladies and gentlemen, and attacks Peyton Tuthill.

The evidence will show that Peyton Tuthill put up her hands to try to ward off the attack, but you will see and hear that she has cuts all over her hands from the fight that she put up. But again, she was no match for the defendant. And the defendant ultimately gets her, he subdues her, and he cuts her throat. But you will hear that Peyton Tuthill was violated and that a slashed throat does not kill her. She's not dead. And what does the defendant do then? He rapes her both vaginally and anally.

Ladies and gentlemen, at this point, Peyton Tuthill has had her home broken into, she has had her property taken, she has been robbed, she has had her throat cut, but this man is not done. He takes this knife and he plunges it into Peyton again and again and again and again. He stabs her multiple times puncturing her heart, puncturing her lung.

Ladies and gentlemen, at this point the defendant has violated Peyton Tuthill in every way that a human can. The lady dies. Once Peyton Tuthill is dead, the defendant coolly and intentionally begins his attempt at a cover-up. You will hear that he washes his hands in Peyton Tuthill's sink. You will hear that he takes the time to wash his clothes in Peyton Tuthill's washing machine while she is laying [sic] dead upstairs. The defendant discovers that the blood won't come out of the clothes, so this defendant takes his sweater off and takes this knife, takes the keys to Peyton Tuthill's vehicle, takes some other items and puts them in a trash bag and throws them in a dumpster behind the house. He then takes a shopping bag full of ill-gotten gains and casually walks back to Stout—when I say "street" I don't mean Stout Street Foundation Halfway House that's two doors down.

You will hear that he goes back to Stout Street, waits for his bus, gets on a bus for Maryland before anybody even knows that Peyton Tuthill is dead. Around 7:00 or 7:30 that evening one of Peyton Tuthill's roommates, Bryan Mullins, comes home. He walks in, he sees the back gate open, [and] that's not normal; he sees the lights are all off, [and] that's not normal; he sees that the back door is broken into. He immediately calls the police; he calls 911. The police respond. And they start going through the house like it's a routine burglary. You will hear that the police officer asked Bryan to walk in front because that's police procedure as they go through the house, and you will hear how Bryan walks up and finds his roommate dead.

Denver homicide detectives are called. Detective Dale Wallis, Sergeant Jon Priest are among the detectives that show up at the scene and they begin searching the house for clues trying to find out who committed this crime. Little do they know that the man that committed this heinous crime is heading down I-70 back to Maryland.

You will hear the detective or Sergeant at the time searches the dumpster behind the house and he sees in the dumpster a bag with a piece of molding that matches the molding from the door in the house. They look through the bag and they find the knife, they find Peyton Tuthill's car keys, and they also find the sweater that the defendant was wearing that day. And it has a tag in the bag but the tag has been torn off the sweater. The name on the tag is Gerald Simpson. The police now feel they have a lead. So they go down the street to the halfway house, because that's, I guess, where they start their investigation. They say, do you have a Gerald Simpson here? Well, yeah. The police go and they get Gerald Simpson. They start interviewing him; they talk to him. It turns out that Gerald Simpson had given his shirt to another Stout Street member named Daniel Stewart. The police ultimately talk to Mr. Stewart. Mr. Stewart is able to tell them that the shirt was stolen from him and is traced to the defendant Page. Other people that work and reside at Stout Street are interviewed as well and it turns out that the defendant Page only had that shirt, what was observed by many wearing the shirt on February 24th when Peyton Tuthill was killed.

At this point the defendant is now the center of the investigation. Sergeant Priest locates the defendant in Maryland. He flies out there. He flies out there so that he can get blood, hair, and saliva samples for some DNA testing. He goes out there and he talks to the defendant. He asks the defendant, do you know anything about this girl that was killed in Denver? The defendant says, "No, I don't know anything about it." Later during the interview, Sergeant asks him about—shows him pictures and things like that from the crime scene. The defendant denies everything.

Ultimately Sergeant confronts the defendant with the fact that they are going to get DNA samples from the defendant while they are there. And that DNA is going to be compared with the DNA found from the vaginal and anal swabs from Peyton Tuthill. DNA is extracted from the defendant. The defendant comes back to the interview room with Sergeant. Again, he confronts the defendant—Sergeant confronts him with evidence that he thinks will be developed in Denver. And the defendant says, "Okay, okay, I killed her."

The defendant then gives a chilling account of how he planned to break in to 1637 Gaylord Street. How he slashed her throat because he didn't like her screaming. And how he thought that might cause somebody to hear what was going on and might cause somebody to call the police. And you will hear how he intentionally and deliberately killed Peyton Tuthill so that he wouldn't get caught. That's why he killed her, so that he wouldn't get caught. You will hear that this rape and murder is intentional, purposeful, and motivated by his lust for violence and his desire to avoid apprehension.

Ladies and gentlemen, that is the evidence that you will hear in this case. You may also hear evidence that the defendant had a troubled childhood, problems in school, possibly abused. But you will not hear of any justification for what he did. You may also hear from psychiatrists, psychologists hired by the defendant to come in here and do, as they do all over the country, attempt to explain why the defendant did what he did. But you will not hear anybody say that this defendant is insane. This defendant knew what he was doing; this defendant did what he wanted to do. He accomplished his goal because he didn't get caught right away. He was eventually caught but he didn't get caught right away. That's the evidence that you will hear, ladies and gentlemen, and we will ask you to find him guilty of all charges.

It is clear from this opening statement that (1) Peyton Tuthill is dead, (2) the prosecutors believe that the police arrested the right person, and (3) the prosecutors believe that the defendant, Donta Page, killed her to avoid capture for a burglary and rape.

Prosecutors do not have to establish more than just their theory of who did it, to whom, and why, though. In fact, establishing a motive is just the icing on the proverbial cake when the physical evidence against a defendant is as incontrovertible as it was in this case. Nonetheless, the prosecutors went to great lengths to attempt to establish that the defendant not only committed the murder, but did it to procure money and that the monetary motive fit the personality of the defendant.

The Cognitive Dimension

There is, of course, no doubt that the defendant in the current case committed the murder. He confessed to the crime, giving a detailed confession about how he did it, and his DNA was found at the scene of the crime. The next task for the prosecution, however, was to show that the defendant premeditated and intended to kill the victim.

Premeditation and Intent

Premeditation refers to *conscious consideration and planning that precedes some act.* Intent is the *state of mind accompanying an act.*[1] In order to establish that the defendant intended the result of murder, then, the prosecution played the audiotaped confession for the jury and called witnesses to testify about how the crime was committed in an organized and vicious manner. Following are excerpts of the audiotaped confession that the defendant gave to Detective John Priest of the Denver Police Department. The audiotape was played for the jury during the prosecution's case:

> Priest: Okay. Wh-why don't you, in your own words, why don't you just tell me what occurred on, uh, the day of, uh, February 24th, 1999. That would've been the last day that you were in the Stout Street Center program. Do you remember that?
>
> Page: Yes.
>
> Priest: 'Kay. Why don't you tell me about that.

Page: That mornin' I was . . . well, that night I was told I had to leave. So they told me to come back that mornin'. And I came back that mornin' and they leave me sittin' on the bench. While I was sittin' on the bench, I was lookin' out the door an' I saw a lady come out her house, get into her car, both [sic] drive off. I didn't pay no attention to her at first, till I got over to the other . . . one o' the other buildings [sic]. They told we could leave if we wanted to. Just be back by a certain time. As I was walkin, leavin', thought to myself, I ain't got no money, I ain't have nothin', so it . . . it dawned on me that I seen that lady leave. So I went to the back door . . . couldn't get in so I went to the basement door, got in through that way, but there was no way into the house. So I went back upstairs, broke the back door, and went in. I went through the house lookin' for stuff I could probably sell to get money. An' while I was there, uhm, I grabbed . . . I opened up the drawer . . . saw some knives in there. I grabbed a knife. Put it on the desk . . . on the counter. Uh, I drank some beers or sumpin' [sic] while I was in there. Uhm, I was in the back, by the back door when I heard the front door. So I ran, I grabbed the, the knives, and she came in. As soon as she seen me, she looked at me and started yellin', so I tried to keep her quiet. An' sh-she just started freakin' an started to run upstairs, so I tried to grab her. She was kickin' me, so I'm tryin to grab 'er an' pull 'er back to me. She just kept kicking me, kept kicking m- . . . And then she ran upstairs some more. I chased 'er. I grabbed her. I tried to tie her hand wif' [sic], uhm, a iron, a cord o' the iron. She kept fightin', kept fightin'. Kept yellin', so I tried to grab her mouth an' keep 'er from yellin'. I . . . I just kept aksin [sic] her where the money at, where the money at. An' she kept sayin' she didn't have none, but then she just started yellin' all over again. An', uhm, she just kept zappin' [sic], fightin' me, fightin' me, kicking me, so I tried to cut 'er throat. She . . . she still kept yellin' an' she grabbed the knife. I snatched it from her. An' by this time, she was turnin' over, so she just kept yellin', kept yellin'. An' I stabbed her in the . . . in the chest. After that, I just went downstairs. Tried to wash the clothes I had on. Went out to her truck, grabbed her purse, came back in. Went through her purse, got what I could get. Took the stuff out the washin' machine, threw it in a . . . a trash bag. Took it an' threw it in the . . . trash can out back. Then I went back to the foundation . . . to Stout Street.

    *   *   *   *   *   *

Priest: What was goin' through your mind when all this is happenin'? What were you thinkin' about?

Page: Jus' tryin' to keep her quiet so I can get outta there. An' jus' get away. 'Cause she's dead.

Priest: And the reason you stabbed her was why?

Page: She . . . she jus' . . . uh, I d- . . . I don't know, jus' . . . . that was the fir- . . . first thing that came to my mind.

Priest: Why'd you stop stabbin' her?

Page: After I did it I looked at her . . . I, I was like, oh, my God, an' hopped up. Jus' ran.

*   *   *   *   *   *

Priest: Did you do anything else while you were in the bedroom with her?

Page: No.

Priest: You're sure about that?

Page: Yeah.

Priest: You didn't try to have sex with her?

Page: (Pause) Yeah.

Priest: Yeah, you did?

Page: Yeah.

Priest: Tell me about that.

Page: (Long pause) (Whispering) I don't know. I jus' . . . I'm [sic] (long pause) I don't know (sic) (whispering).

Priest: Were you angry with her?

Page: (No verbal response)

Priest: Were you mad at her for screamin' . . . not shuttin' up?

Page: I wan't [sic] mad. I was jus' scared. I wasn't mad. I was jus' scared an' I thought she would be quiet, but she didn't. I wan't [sic] I didn't, uh, I don't know. In a way this . . . [sic] (whispering).

Priest: Did you have sex with her before you stabbed her or after you stabbed her?

Page: Before.

Priest: Did she say anything to you while that was goin' on?

Page: No. She jus' kep' screamin'.

Priest: Did she try to stop ya?

Page: Yeah. She grabbed me; she had stopped kickin' by then [sic] . . .

Priest: Do you remember if you ejaculated?

Page: Uh, yeah, I think I did.

Priest: (Pause) How many times did you have sex with her?

Page: Once.

Priest: Just one time?

Page: (No verbal response)

Priest: (Long pause) Were you holdin' a knife on 'er while you were doin' that?

Page: Well, the knife was . . . I like dropped it because she was fighting.

Priest: Was she tied up then?

Page: No, she was . . . she wasn't tied up till after when I was tryin' ta [sic] get away.

*   *   *   *   *   *

Priest: (Pause) Did you have any problems while you were having sex with her?
Page: What do you mean?
Priest: Any trouble gettin' the job done?
Page: (Long pause) Huh-uh. I don't think so [sic].

*   *   *   *   *   *

Priest: How many times did you stab her; do you remember?
Page: (Long pause) I think it was like twice.
Priest: Could it have been more?
Page: (Pause) I don't think it was more than that.

*   *   *   *   *   *

Priest: So the reason you didn't leave was you didn't want her callin' the police, right?
Page: Yeah.
Priest: And the only way you knew to get her to stop was to stab her? Is that right?
Page: I just' . . . I jus' . . . I jus' popped man. I jus' popped in my head [sic]. You know [sic].
Priest: Did you tell anybody about this?
Page: No.
Priest: This is the first time you're tellin' anybody about this?
Page: Yeah.

After attempting to establish that the defendant premeditated and intended to kill the victim, the prosecution moved on to trying to establish the motive for the crime.

Motive: Why He Did It

Motive refers to *something, especially willful desire, that leads one to act*.[2] As such, the prosecution, during their opening statement and following the taped confession being played for the jury, reiterated its belief that the defendant cut the victim's throat to keep her quiet so that the police would not be alerted to the crime that he was committing.

The prosecution further argued that the crime was committed for pecuniary gain, which would later become one of the aggravators offered during the penalty phase of the trial, because the defendant stole coins that he found on the dresser. In fact, the prosecutor called a witness, Jon Fisher, during the guilt phase of the trial to testify that coins were found at the bottom of a shopping bag that the defendant was carrying when he got out of the van that took him from Stout Street to the bus station. Mr. Jon Paul Fisher was a resident of the Stout Street Foundation and it was his job to transport Stout Street residents to various daily appointments:

Prosecutor:	And did anything happen when you dropped Mr. Page out at the bus station?
Fisher:	In pulling one of his bags of clothes out of the van it had tore open and some change had come out.
Prosecutor:	Where did that take place?
Fisher:	Right at the van. It was like just coming out of the door of the van at the bus, Greyhound Bus station.
Prosecutor:	Did that strike you as unusual?
Fisher:	Well, yeah, because we're not allowed to have money.
Prosecutor:	When you say, "We're not allowed to have money," who are you referring to?
Fisher:	The Stout Street Foundation residents.
Prosecutor:	Okay. If you are a resident in Stout Street you can't have money?
Fisher:	No.

Clearly, the testimony of Mr. Fisher was meant to establish that the defendant had money despite rules of the Stout Street program that forbade residents from having it. Not only was the defendant in violation of the rules of the program, but also where the money came from became an issue supporting the motive of pecuniary gain. Establishing that he had money also placed him at the scene of the crime where a Lerner shopping bag and a large number of coins (apparently for laundry) had been taken. At this point, the prosecutor was attempting to establish that the defendant was the person who committed the crime, that the victim was killed during the commission of a burglary of her house (felony murder), and that the defendant struggled with the victim in order to avoid detection for the burglary and rape.

The prosecution's case did not end with establishing the guilt, intent, and motive of the defendant. In addition, it seems the prosecutors' job was to construct an image of the defendant that was conducive to their interpretation of the crime as heinous and deliberate (first-degree murder). In order to do that, they had to attack any belief that the jurors might have held of the crime having been accidental, for example, or the result of sickness or mental defect. Instead, the jurors needed to believe that the killer was cold-blooded and remorseless—a person without any sense of responsibility or concern for other people. If the prosecutor failed to portray the defendant in such a light, the social distance between the jury and the defendant would be decreased in the sense that his social characteristics would be accepted or, at least, understood. The prosecutor used fear of crime, the perfection and vulnerability of the victim, and stereotypes to accomplish this task.

During the trial, the prosecutor used numerous photographs of the crime scene to establish that the crime was very bloody, including photographs of the victim lying dead in the corner of the bedroom in a pool of her own blood. They showed several objects to the jury that had been taken from the house as evidence including the bloody bedsheet, the knife, the towels that were discovered in the dumpster, and the iron cord that had been used to tie the victim's hands. They implied that the defendant was a large, lazy man who had no intention of doing anything good with his life. They referred to the neighborhood where the crime occurred as a nice place to live because the neighborhood had grass and trees and it was located near a city park—a place to walk your dog. As such, the prosecution struck fear into the hearts of the jurors by not only talking about the defendant as a convicted felon with no feelings who had been released into their community without notification, but also by mentioning that the place where it happened was typical of the clean, quiet suburbs in which they themselves probably lived.

Although she was not discussed at length, an image of the victim was presented at trial. Peyton Tuthill lived the American dream—she had graduated from college after having joined a sorority, had a boyfriend, was well liked by her coworkers and roommates, made plans to go to graduate school, had visited Europe, and was visited and telephoned by her family members frequently. During the trial, several smiling and happy photographs of her were shown to the jury, photographs that depicted a very popular, pretty girl who had a soft spot for stray animals and a willingness to do charity work. Her family attended every day of the trial and unabashedly showed outrage and grief over the death of their loved one. Her mother was frail when she testified during the penalty phase and Peyton's boyfriend and roommates sobbed uncontrollably when they took the stand. The entire family wore huge buttons on their clothes that bore a graduation picture of the victim that was taken about one year prior to her death. By all accounts, it was clear that the victim's life had been full of promise and that it was tragic for it to have been cut short. Here, the prosecution tried to minimize the social distance between the jury and the victim; that is, she is "one of us."

Stereotypes:
Knowing the Individual by Knowing Similar People

Stereotypes are conventional, highly simplified, and often negative ways of looking at groups of people and their behavior.[3] Oftentimes, stereotypical thinking happens subconsciously—so deeply embedded in the psyche that people do not even know when they are relying on stereotypes to make judgments. In the current case, the stereotype of criminality was used to establish that the defendant was guilty of the crime, had the requisite motive, and was, therefore, a dangerous person to let live in society. Such stereotypes were raised with his appearance, e.g., "she is no match for this 300-pound intruder," and his voice, expressions, and choice of words during the taped confession:

Prosecutor: Sergeant, during your interview with Mr. Page did he ever cry?
Sergeant: No.
Prosecutor: Did he ever tell you that he was sorry for what he did?
Sergeant: No.
Prosecutor: Did he ever at any time show any remorse for killing and raping Peyton Tuthill?
Defense: Objection, speculation.
The Court: Overruled. You may answer.
Sergeant: No.

And the prosecution also used his prior criminal record:

He was thinking about the next crime he was going to commit, because the defendant had been kicked out of Stout Street; dejected and told to leave, he was sitting around that day waiting for a bus ride back to Maryland thinking about the next crime he was going to commit. (prosecutor's opening statement above)

To be sure, there were times when stereotypes were alluded to as an indicator of his dangerousness because stereotypes often surface when people are asked to use their common sense. The jury was asked twice in the prosecution's closing statement to resort to "common sense" to determine whether the defendant committed the crime deliberately:

Use your common sense and judgment. In just a few minutes the defense is going to have the opportunity to talk to you. And I anticipate that they are going to argue that every bad thing that happened to Mr. Page during the course of his life came together in a particular moment in time, that moment being after he had cut Ms. Tuthill's throat but failed to silence her. So then something snapped in his mind and he decided to plunge the knife in her chest four times from two different angles. But as you listen to that story ask yourself the following question: *Why is his entire life story relevant to your deliberations?* If what he told Sergeant and from what we know from the proof at the scene of the crime shows that the defendant Page did deliberate inside that house.

And later,

And finally, like I said, use your common sense, step back after two weeks of testimony, step back and ask yourselves, can you explain what the defendant did in Peyton Tuthill's home on February 24th of 1999 with a few little blue spots [referring to colored spots on the PET scan video that indicated that the defendant's brain was functioning abnormally]?

The defense never asked the jury to use its common sense, but rather insisted that the jury use only reason to draw its conclusions. If reasonable is defined as *a fair, proper, or moderate judgment under the circumstances*,[4] common sense does not qualify. Also, the prosecution directly attacked the defense's argument that the defendant's life history is relevant to the discussion of culpability. When the prosecution asked whether his entire life story was relevant to the jury's deliberations, they implied that the jury should view the defendant's circumstances in a vacuum. Stated another way, the prosecution may have been attempting to draw a cookie-cutter analogy to the defendant: that is, why look at the entirety of circumstances when the defendant looks like, acts like, and talks like a stereotypical criminal?

The Guilt Phase: How the Defense Saw Its Mission

Defense attorneys have a different responsibility than that of the prosecution. Their job is to counter the argument of deliberate and intentional bad acts with an argument about the culpability for those acts. That is, the defense never suggested that the defendant didn't commit the crime, but rather that the requisite intent was lacking because the defendant is not a normal adult. If culpability is defined as *blameworthiness*,[5] the defense attorneys were attempting to show the jury that the blame for the killing could be shared by other people and social forces in the environment because people are influenced by their environment. In this way, the defense acted as a team of social scientists gathering data about social forces that have been shown to influence human behavior (poverty, discrimination, welfare, and emotional states like hopelessness).

Who Did What: The Behavioral Dimension

In the current case, the question of *who else* might share responsibility for the behavior that the defendant displayed in the victim's house that day was important to answer as well as the question of *who else* might have created the anger, fear, lack of judgment, lack of intelligence, lack of self-control, and overall dysfunction in the defendant because the defense conceded early in the trial that the defendant had committed the crime. As such, the defense built their case on what steps could have been taken to avoid the situation that caused the defendant to explode in the victim's house that day. Their goal was to remove the possibility of a death sentence by working towards proving that a second-degree murder conviction was appropriate under the circumstances. At issue, therefore, was the cognitive state of the defendant.

The Cognitive Dimension

Much of the defense's case used testimony of lay witnesses who were asked to fill in the details of the defendant's life. This was a tedious task to accomplish because various aspects of the defendant's life were relevant while numerous others were not. For example, it was important to establish that the defendant had been the victim of horrible child abuse because that would show that the defendant was violent through no fault of his own—rather that violence had been a part of his everyday life from the beginning, especially with regard to maintaining control in a situation: that's how people relate to each other where he's from, where only the strong survive.

Factors Diminishing Premeditation and Intent

Mitigating circumstances refer to *a fact or situation that does not justify or excuse a wrongful act or offense but that reduces the degree of culpability and thus may reduce the damages.*[6] Criminal culpability requires a showing that the person acted purposely, knowingly, recklessly, or negligently with respect to each material element of the crime. As such, the defense attorneys introduced evidence of the existence of two mitigating factors in the commission of the crime for which the defendant was charged: (1) physical and sexual abuse, and (2) neurological impairment as a result of the abuse.

The defense called three lay witnesses to testify that the defendant had suffered severe physical, sexual, and emotional abuse as a child, including neglect. The defendant's grandmother, ex-girlfriend, and cousin sometimes witnessed the abuse and at other times simply described the effect that the abuse seemed to have on the defendant.

Linda Page, the defendant's grandmother, testified extensively about beatings she witnessed that the defendant received from his mother (Patricia

Page) and a rape incident that occurred in her apartment building. The defendant was raped by Wayne Franklin, his babysitter, when he was ten years old. The defendant was treated at Howard University Hospital for an anal fissure as a result of the rape, but Linda did not report the rape to police. Wayne Franklin died of AIDS in May of 1987. Following are excerpts from the trial transcript of testimony that Linda Page provided during the trial. Her testimony was elicited to show that the defendant had experienced grave hardships during his development that affected his personality and helped shape his view of the world as a physical struggle for survival. With this testimony, the defense attempted to portray the defendant as a victim of his environment, a social failure, and a generally disturbed human being.

Defense: Throughout the time between two-and-a-half and four years old, did you start to ever see her [the defendant's mother] do anything more than shake the defendant in order to discipline him?

Linda Page: Yes.

Defense: Can you tell the jury what was done and how it changed.

Linda Page: When she would get angry, whatever was there she would hit him with it and she would beat him with a belt and it would leave welts and blood coming, you know, the wounds, places where she had hit him. And he couldn't protect himself because he was a young child.

*   *   *   *   *   *

Linda Page: She would beat him and tell him not to wet the bed. And I think the beating caused him to wet the bed longer, you know. He was much older where he should have stopped when he was five or six but he just had a nervous condition and he wet the bed until he was about 11 years old.

*   *   *   *   *   *

Linda Page: Like if I would see a mark on him I would ask him how did that happen. And he would say, "Well, my momma got angry with me and she hit me with a belt and then it went into an extension cord."

Defense: Was the extension cord used often?

Linda Page: Yes, many times. He had welts on his body from the extension cord and the belt.

Defense: When you say welts, what do they look like?

Linda Page: It would be swollen up with blood coming out of it.

Defense: How large would they be?

Linda Page:	About like my finger here (indicating).
Defense:	And where would these welts be on his body?
Linda Page:	On his back, his leg, and on his bottom or wherever.
Defense:	What would you do with these welts?
Linda Page:	I wouldn't do anything. I would just hug him and talk with him and tell him to be good.

*   *   *   *   *   *

Defense:	Was there a time after Mr. Franklin [neighbor and babysitter] had taken care of the defendant where he, the defendant, was needed to be taken to the hospital for some bleeding?
Linda Page:	Yes.
Defense:	What part of his body was bleeding?
Linda Page:	His rectum.
Defense:	Were you home at the time that he was taken to the hospital?
Linda Page:	No, I wasn't.
Defense:	Where were you?
Linda Page:	I was at work.
Defense:	Did you find out about it after you got home from work?
Linda Page:	Yes.
Defense:	Had the defendant been suffering from something before he was taken to the hospital that you knew about that would cause the bleeding?
Linda Page:	No.
Defense:	When he got back from the emergency room, did you take care of him?
Linda Page:	Yes.
Defense:	Approximately a week—well, was he ever taken back to the hospital for any follow-up?
Linda Page:	No, he wasn't.
Defense:	Approximately a week after the defendant went to the hospital for the bleeding, did he tell you what happened to cause him—
Prosecution:	Objection.
Defense:	—to bleed in the emergency room?

(Conference at the bench)

The Court:	Lay further foundation. I will overrule the hearsay objection and allow you to proceed.
Defense:	(By Mr. Castle) Ma'am, talking about this time a week after he went to the hospital, when the defendant came to you how was he acting?
Linda Page:	Shy.
Defense:	Shy?

Linda Page:	Shy. Like he had something that he wanted to tell me.
Defense:	Was he looking at you in the eye, looking down? Where was he looking?
Linda Page:	He was looking down.
Defense:	Could you tell whether he was upset or not?
Linda Page:	Yes, he was upset.
Defense:	Did he tell you why he was upset?
Linda Page:	Yes, yes.
Prosecution:	Your Honor, object for the same reasons stated.
The Court:	The objection is overruled; go ahead.
Linda Page:	Yes.
Defense:	(By Mr. Castle) What did he tell you?
Linda Page:	That Wayne had molested him.
Defense:	And when you say "molested," did he tell you how that happened?
Linda Page:	He said that he was playing with him and he put his penis behind him.
Defense:	Behind the defendant?
Linda Page:	Yes. Yes, in his rectum.
Defense:	What did you do about that?
Linda Page:	I confronted Wayne about it.
Defense:	Did you call the police?
Linda Page:	No, I didn't. I didn't call the police.
Defense:	Without getting into what Wayne said, did you move the defendant out of that apartment building?
Linda Page:	No, I didn't.
Defense:	Why didn't you move the defendant out of the apartment building, and why didn't you call the police?
Linda Page:	Well, number one, the reason I didn't move because I really didn't have the money to move. But—and number two, I think I was more hurt because I had took Wayne as a true friend of mine. And when the defendant told me what he had did to him, I didn't trust him no more.
Defense:	Did you let Mr. Franklin take care of the defendant again after that?
Linda Page:	No, I did not.
Defense:	Did you get help for the defendant so that he could talk to someone about it, maybe a counselor or a therapist or somebody like that?
Linda Page:	No, I did not.

Erica Penny, the defendant's high school girlfriend, testified about the defendant's reaction to his mother's beatings and various other behaviors she observed that made her worry about his mental state and overall welfare. With her testimony, the defense attempted to show that his environment outside of his home was untenable, too. His family wasn't the only group of people who treated him poorly, in other words; his classmates also mistreated him. And the violence and dysfunction that the defendant experienced at home was indicative of the type of lifestyle that the people in his neighborhood experienced. Overall, the defense argued that the defendant's adolescent experience was chaotic and that the defendant reacted to the chaos in a violent and self-destructive way.

Defense: Did you see him do things around the house like chores?

Penny: He would wash dishes while his mom was at work. Babysit the little brother. Literally clean the house from top to bottom. And when they gets home, it's like that wasn't good enough. And she would just go off again and start arguing about little things. If the shirt was on the floor that he didn't see, she would go off about that.

Defense: How would he react to those?

Penny: He would just stand there and take it, basically. It was her argument, and not really saying much. Just ask her what she asked him, a question like do you realize that you left these? I don't know it was there. He would look at her with like a blank face, like I don't believe she's doing this to me again.

Defense: Overall, in your opinion, how did his mom treat him at the times you saw him interact?

Penny: Like she didn't want him around.

    *   *   *   *   *   *

Defense: Okay. Was there ever a time that he tried to force himself on you sexually?

Penny: Yes.

Defense: Can you tell us, first of all, what happened there.

Penny: It was when he came back from where he was staying in Maryland. We were in my room and we were laying [sic] in bed watching television and he made a phone call to somebody. And I didn't like the fact that he called someone from my home, for one, because we just, you know, got back together and we were spending quality time. So while I'm laying [sic] there, he got on top of me. And I'm like, we are not doing this, get off of me. And all of a sudden it's like I notice his eyes change and he looks at himself, and I'm like get off me, get off me. He actually looks at me again, and he got up and he said I'm going to leave. And I said, I think you better. And like days after that I wouldn't talk to him and, when I finally did, I told him what I felt took place. And he said, no, I didn't. And I said, yes, you did. And he said, I don't remember that. And I'm like, okay.

Defense: Did he seem to be kidding with you when he said he didn't remember that?

Penny: He was dead serious. He was not playing. The way his voice was, you can tell when he would kid and when he was really serious about something. And he said, why didn't you tell me after the fact. And I'm like, I told you no. And he was like, I don't remember doing that. And he was like, if I did, I apologize.

Defense: Okay. Did you ever see anything else like that when you thought he looked different or acted different?

Penny: Once when we were at his grandmother's house she had just moved to Maryland. And he was in the bathroom and I was ready to go. And I went upstairs in the bathroom and he had a gun pointed to his face playing with the trigger. And I'm like, okay, can you take me home now. And he looked at me like he didn't know who I was, and I'm like waiting a minute. He was playing with the trigger with the gun pointing to his face.

Defense: Demonstrate this.

Penny: The barrel is here, and the trigger is here. And he is like tapping on it. I'm like, what is he doing. I'm like, I'm not going to be here for fear something is going to happen and I don't know how to explain it. I didn't know what was going on with him. I left. When I talked to him again, he said, why did you leave. And I said, because I had to go. And he was like, well, why did you leave. And I explained to him what I saw. And he was like, are you sure? I'm like, I'm sure, you don't remember doing that? I'm like, I don't want to stay in this. That kind of spooked me out. And so from like that point on, I didn't talk to him for a couple of months.

The defendant's cousin, Frederick (Freddy) Witherspoon, age forty-one, grew up with the defendant's mother and the defendant in Rock Hill, South Carolina. He testified about Patricia Page's temperament and the defendant's mood swings, which started at the age of thirteen. Sometimes, the defendant would be happy, but at other times, he would leave home and stay away for days and weeks at a time without telling anyone where he was, according to Witherspoon. His grandmother discovered that he had been sleeping in abandoned buildings with no heat, water, or toilet facilities during some winter and summer months. Mr. Witherspoon's testimony augmented the testimony of Linda Page and Erica Penny in that the defense attempted to show that the abuse that the defendant suffered was ongoing and long-lasting, beginning in his childhood and continuing in adolescence. Mr. Witherspoon also filled in some of the details about the defendant's mother that were conducive to portraying the defendant as a victim of child abuse; that is, Patricia Page was a mean person who had also experienced terrible abuse.

Defense:	Would you say over the years you have gotten to know Patricia Page pretty well?
Witherspoon:	I think so, yes.
Defense:	Can you describe her to us.
Witherspoon:	Well, like I say, she was kind of a hotheaded kind of person. She was really crazy. She does have an attitude.
Defense:	Did you notice that growing up?
Witherspoon:	Yeah.
Defense:	Did you notice that throughout life?
Witherspoon:	Oh, yes.
Defense:	When you say she is aggressive, what kinds of things would you see to support that?
Witherspoon:	Well, like I say, she can't take—like if you say something to her, and that's not what she wants to hear, she is going to tell you, that's for sure.
Defense:	She is going to what?
Witherspoon:	She is going to tell you. She will come at you with something. She will get loud with you. Possibly you end up in a fight with her.
Defense:	Growing up, did you know her to be in fights?
Witherspoon:	Oh, yeah.
Defense:	How often?
Prosecution:	Your Honor, I'm going to object at this point on relevance.
Defense:	I think her general demeanor is quite relevant here. He is talking about her demeanor when she was a child.
The Court:	Objection sustained.
Defense:	Have you—from what you know of her growing up, does she, as an adult, has she changed or does she act the same?
Witherspoon:	Pretty much the same, you know, pretty much.

  *   *   *   *   *   *

Defense:	Was there a time the defendant was sent to Rock Hill, South Carolina?
Witherspoon:	Like we had—we have some type of event going on, and I had finally got a whiff that he had been leaving home without permission and staying gone like the weekend.
Defense:	How old was he?

Witherspoon:	At that time he was 13. And I finally got a chance to get to talk to him, brought him in front of the house and talked to him. And I was letting him know, though, you decide to leave home let somebody know, don't just up and leave.
Defense:	Were you yelling at him or anything?
Witherspoon:	No, I was just talking to him. Like I say, he broke down crying, you know. Like I say, I didn't really know why. I just told him, that was just pretty much it.
Defense:	Did he ever tell you what he was crying about?
Witherspoon:	No, no.

Such testimony was intended to serve the additional task of bringing the jury closer to the defendant (decreasing the social distance between them and the defendant). That is, the humanity of the defendant became apparent when his grandmother testified in flesh and blood, clutching damp tissues as she cried on the stand while explaining how the defendant had to clean up his own blood from the whippings he received from his mother, for example. Certainly, the fact that the defendant's own mother refused to testify on his behalf notified the jury of her lack of concern or indifference to the situation that her son was facing.

In addition, a different motive for the crime began to develop from the testimony of the defendant's family: It became possible to entertain the notion of a crime of passion or temporary insanity—an act of extreme desperation, hopelessness, and despair that necessitates a second-degree murder conviction. Combined with a history of environmental violence, periodic homelessness, and a lack of familial support, then, it became possible to view the entire episode as a random act of unintentional or negligent violence (second-degree murder) rather than premeditated (or first-degree) murder. This is not an isolated incident. In fact, Hazel May, in studying the social construction of murder, asserts that

> That innocent woman walking along the road, it's nothing to do with her whatsoever. And the man who murdered her is building up and building up and building up until that day something triggers him and it's vomited over her, everything that happened to him since the moment he was born, she becomes the tragic recipient of the lot.[7]

These issues were raised during the defense's opening statement and reinforced with the testimony of expert witnesses who explained the impact of brain damage (specifically frontal lobe damage) on the behavior of individuals and on the relationship between child abuse and later violence.

Neurological Impairment

Several expert witnesses testified about the relationship between child abuse and later violence, that is, that child abuse can result in physical and emotional problems, specifically neurological impairment, that prevents the impaired person from acting rationally or reasonably in some situations.

Dr. Dorothy Otnow-Lewis, a Yale-educated psychiatrist, was called by the defense to testify about her examination of the defendant which included an analysis of his life history, an analysis of his brain function, his intelligence, and his inability to control his emotions. Her testimony was intended to show scientific evidence of the relationship between child abuse and later violence, which the defense argued was a catalyst to the defendant's current predicament—a crime of passion and negligence (second-degree murder) rather than premeditation and intent (first-degree murder). Her testimony was also meant to help show that the social welfare system does not always work for children in impoverished communities—that there are serious problems with the diagnoses, treatment, and placement of abused children in urban cities so that many of the children, including the defendant, never get the help that they need. Consequently, blame can be shared with the larger society for some violent crimes.

Defense: The first board [display] is titled "Medical History." If you could tell the jury, first of all, with respect to the first item, why that's important in your analysis and what it indicates to you as a psychiatrist.

Lewis: Oh, the first item tells you that the defendant's mother made two attempts to abort him. And it's important for two reasons: One is it tells you her attitude toward the infant. So it tells you the kind of—of world that he was going to come into. But it's also very important from the point of view of development. Because to the best of my knowledge, his mom got no prenatal care except maybe a couple weeks before his birth when she was treated for gonorrhea. But she did reportedly take some kind of potion to try to abort him. And as— as we all know, even smoking, even drinking can be harmful to a fetus. What this potion was, it's potential harm, we can only imagine. But that's important for the two reasons that it tells you a mother's attitude and it also tells you about a possible injury to the fetus.

* * * * * *

Lewis: Well, when infants have injury to their head, as you all know, the skull is much softer in an infant than it is in an adult. And, well, even the slightest injury to the child, injuries like just shaking a child, can cause little hemorrhages to the brain. When you get scars that you could see to this day, you know they were serious injuries and they affected his brain. There—there is no way of falling out of the top of a bunk bed and hitting your head and you would have that knot, if you were a newborn, that would not affect your brain.

*   *   *   *   *   *

Lewis: When he was three he was taken to Children's Hospital and this was, I believe, in Washington. And it was because—it had been noted—I believe it had been noted in day care that he was—he was not well nourished. That he wasn't growing properly. And so his grandmother took him to Children's Hospital for an assessment. And what was interesting was the grandmother said that she put food in his mouth and he would just keep it in his cheek and he wouldn't eat it. He was already acting peculiarly at three years of age. This also sounds very much like what pediatricians call failure to thrive. And children who are horribly abused don't eat properly; they don't—they are malnourished. And so this is yet more evidence of the kind of emotional abuse that he was experiencing.

*   *   *   *   *   *

Lewis: At ten years of age, here the record is—it's—it's—he was brought to the Howard University Emergency Room because of rectal bleeding. And what they found was a tear in the anus. And this is—the common cause of this kind of—of injury is sexual abuse or sodomy. And indeed, they did a culture for gonococcus, for gonorrhea. And the family was told to bring the defendant back; however, to the best of my knowledge, there was no follow-up.

*   *   *   *   *   *

Defense: Let me bring you down to the first red bulleted item at three years old. Could you tell the jury about that, and what the significance of that is in the development of the child.

Lewis: Well, these data, again, come from—from the defendant's grandmother. They—the defendant was extremely protective of his mother and said, some things it was better not to know and not to talk about. And—however, beating a child to the extent that—that apparently this woman totally lost it and just beat him and beat him and beat him, this—and also at a certain point she started to punch him in the face and punch him in the head. And I don't need to spell out what that does to the brain. But there is data now that also tells us what that type of mothering does to the brain and then to behavior. I'm sure you have all heard the term attachment and attachment behavior. Attachment behavior is—it's the behavior that infants show to relieve stress. And in—in babies, with secure attachment, if a stranger comes into the room or if you wanted to take the baby away from the mother, the baby turns to the mother for comfort, and this is a secure attachment. And there are various less secure, ambivalent attachments in mothers and children with more or less difficult situations or experiences. However, in children who are raised by incredibly rejecting, psychiatrically ill, abusive mothers, you get something called disorganized attachment, where the child freezes and doesn't know what to do, and sometimes walks toward the mother backwards or behaves in odd ways. And the reason that this matters is—I'm talking about behaviors that are occurring in the first and second years of life. The reason that this really matters a whole lot is that during these first two years of life, the brain is growing at an incredibly rapid rate. So that by the time a child is two, his brain is about 90 percent of the size that it will be when he is an adult. That's why kids look so huge, big heads, compared to the rest of us. However, nature has—has created us in such a way that many, many more connections are made in the growing brain than we ultimately will need. And during these first one, two, three years of life, a lot of connections are being broken off. Certain cells are dying and other connections are being made. Presumably, in a healthy mother/child relationship, these are connections that have to do with affection and with attachment and with—this is part of a normal development. In—we know this more really from animal research than just from child behavior—

*　　　*　　　*　　　*　　　*　　　*

Defense:　Doctor, the next bulleted item I want you to look at and I want you to try to address a number of points. After this had happened at ten years old, were you able to see either in the records that you saw or in the interviews that were conducted, that the defendant's behavior started to change in a different way than he had exhibited prior to that?

Lewis:　Certainly. He—he was more withdrawn. He was more depressed. He was—he would run away and stay in cold, unheated, empty buildings, on his own. And his function had deteriorated rapidly.

*　　　*　　　*　　　*　　　*　　　*

Defense:　Next I want to switch to when he turns fourteen. Was there any information you were able to glean from the records or interviews with the witnesses that indicated that the defendant's—Page's behavior began to change at that time for the worse?

Lewis:　Well, it was deteriorating, at least subsequent to age ten. That he had always been peculiar and withdrawn and described as kind of spacing in school and not being with it. But it became more peculiar, and around fourteen his grandmother reported that—well, she said he didn't make sense a lot of the time when he talked. And she said that he would hoard food, he would hide food, he would hide food under his bed and keep dirty dishes under his bed. But, in addition to this, he stopped bathing. And he stopped changing his clothes. And if she got him new clothes he gave them away to other people. And apparently, he smelled bad. And the other kids at school teased him or didn't want to go near him. What she describes, I have seen and heard reports of in extremely depressed adults. It's a pointed kind of description that he was experiencing this degree of depression that—with no hygiene. It was peculiar behaviors at fourteen.

Defense: Doctor, if you go down to the next bulleted item, did something else happen at the age of fourteen which indicated to you that Mr. Page had some more significant problems?

Lewis: Yes. At—at age fourteen he was accused of fondling an eight-year-old girl. And he was actually sent for a psychiatric evaluation at Children's Hospital.

Defense: Was there—

Lewis: I guess his behaviors and controls were deteriorating.

Defense: When you talk about this evaluation at Children's Hospital, were there records about that?

Lewis: Yes, there were some records.

Defense: Were either the mother or grandmother even able to recall that event?

Lewis: It's peculiar, because the records tell you that—if my memory serves me, that both the mother and the grandmother brought him and participated in this and knew about it. And yet when they were asked about it, they had no memory of bringing him.

*   *   *   *   *   *

Defense: Doctor, I now want to talk to you [about] what happened up in the bedroom. How would you characterize what happened in that room from what you could tell from the evidence and from the statements made by Mr. Page in his confession? What happened in that bedroom, was it any different between the before period and after period?

Lewis: Oh, I think it was very different. I don't think that when he went in to this apartment that he had any intention of hurting anyone. In fact, no one was supposed to be there. He did want to cover his tracks. He wrapped beer bottles with paper towels and he took out knives, as he said to me, to protect himself in case somebody attacked him. But he—when this woman came in, apparently she was extremely frightened, as anybody would be, and she began to yell and yell and yell. And at that point he apparently snapped. His memory of this is impaired and he gives confusing statements to the police. Not statements that in any way exonerate him, they are just confused. I mean he doesn't tell two different stories in order to get you to like him better, but he just puts things out of order. And first he—apparently he didn't seem to remember the rape at all. And I think to this day he does not remember any anal attack on this woman. He was in a sort of frenzy. And I actually came back to Colorado to talk with him about the—about the event, because it was so puzzling. And he didn't know why he had done it. But as he was talking to me, he said—he said to me something like she was yelling and yelling and yelling. And the next thing he said was my mother yelled at me. My mother wanted to kill me. Now, I don't know whether this is a leap; I wasn't there and I didn't see it. But something snapped and he—he behaved in a kind of reflex way rather than a premeditative sort of fashion.

Clearly, Dr. Lewis's testimony painted a picture of someone who was raised in a dysfunctional setting. The defendant suffered physical and sexual abuse that was not tended to, he exhibited signs of being out of control, he molested a young girl, and he committed a murder, years later, in a confused state reminiscent of the kind of turmoil he faced at home with his abusive mother. In conclusion, Dr. Lewis testified that

Given our statistics in this country in terms of abuse, that most abused children do not grow up and become violent. However, what we have found, again and again, is that if you bring together brain damage of some sort, which impairs the ability to control your impulses and impairs judgment, and if you combine that with psychotic symptoms, particularly with paranoia, the belief that one is being threatened, the belief that you have to protect yourself, and a child with these vulnerabilities is abused, then you create a very, very violent individual. And the more serious the psychiatric and the more serious the neurologic impairment, if that child is abused, the more violent that individual becomes.

In sum, it seemed from her testimony that the defendant was worthy of sympathy, not only for the torturous abuse that he had endured throughout his life, but also for the fact that he had not "snapped" and killed someone sooner. Again, the absence of the defendant's mother in the courtroom signified overall neglect, particularly because during this testimony her abuse of the defendant was being discussed. The prosecution's motive claims were, thus, being attacked by the testimony of Dr. Lewis and two additional expert witnesses, Dr. Johnathan Pincus and Dr. Charles Opsahl, who were called to testify that the defendant is not a normal adult and therefore worthy of mercy.

Dr. Johnathan Pincus, chief of neurology at Georgetown Medical School in Washington, D.C., testified that the defendant demonstrated abnormal brain function on several neurologic exams that he performed on the defendant for the purpose of testifying in the case. The defense called Dr. Pincus to provide additional scientific evidence that people with certain kinds of brain injuries sometimes act violently and irrationally. His testimony helped the defense show that the defendant is not just a mean person, but rather someone with emotional problems who needs to be in a safe and controlled environment. Even though Dr. Pincus suggested that the defendant was dangerous, he also said that the defendant is manageable, which, later, helped the defense argue for life imprisonment without parole instead of the death penalty. Finally, Dr. Pincus offered an expert opinion on the treatment that the defendant received previously, that is, that it did not work and that it may have exacerbated his condition.

Defense: Doctor, we've heard a bit over the last few days about the role of the frontal lobes in your behavior. Can you tell the jury a little bit about what happens if those frontal lobes are damaged while you're going through this process of myelination. What—what—what—what happens?

Pincus: Well, first of all, they are the most sensitive parts of the brain from two perspectives: One is they haven't developed yet. And, therefore, their development isn't set yet. And so damage is more likely to be manifested in—in them. The other thing is that head injuries, shaking injuries, banging injuries are going to be—show up in the frontal part of the frontal lobes because that's right up against the bone. The brain is like jelly, in a very, very hard container, the bone. And when the brain gets hit, it hits up against the—the bone and it gets damaged. The same thing is true of the undersurface of the brain and the temporal lobe tips. Is that—it—that those acceleration/deceleration injuries are going to—let's just say you—you get hit as an acceleration/deceleration, say you were in a car or whatever it happens to be, you fall, you hit your head, those are the parts of brain that become affected. Most likely to be affected. The way they are affected is that—well, first of all, that can be hemorrhages, an actual damage to the tissue that leads to—to bleeding.

But there is another way too, and that is that the axons, the nerve cell processes get twisted and get disrupted microscopically and cause concussion. I mean that a concussion is a behavioral change that occurs after an injury that lasts for a period of time and then im—improves.

*　　　*　　　*　　　*　　　*　　　*

Defense: Doctor, is there a—is there another neurologic component when a child gets injuries from intentional child abuse that's aside from just the physical damage?

Pincus: Yes. There are—there are two ways that a child is damaged: One is through the physical injury of the brain, and the other, more insidiously, is what the child learns as the result of his physical abuse. I mean, what does an infant do? An infant needs to be fed, an infant needs to be changed, [and] an infant needs to be clothed and held and comforted. And how does the infant signal that he wants all those things? He cries. And what you do is you pick up the child and comfort it and feed it and change it and you walk with it and manifest parental love, basically. But what if the child is treated differently than that? What if the response to the crying of an infant is to take the infant and shake the infant until it stops crying? Well, aside from the physical injury to the brain, you can change the child's emotional responsivity. You can change what—what the child knows is—is—is going to come as the result of crying. Maybe the child won't cry. It might just lie around inert and not move much.

*　　　*　　　*　　　*　　　*　　　*

Pincus: The front of the brain—the frontal lobes are not responsible for those things, but are responsible for attention, judgment, insight, motivation, drive, initiative, the ability to check yourself and say no, don't say that, no, don't do that, it wouldn't be wise. This is not what I want to accomplish. Take advantage of—change your plan in order to—to take advantage of circumstances. Change your plan in order to avoid adverse circumstances. Those are the kinds of—judgment. Those are the kind of things that the frontal lobe provides when it's fully developed. And when it's damaged, those things are affected. They are very difficult to test for in an objective manner. That—that—that is specifically for the frontal lobe and sensitive to diseases of the frontal lobe. For example, you go to a stockbroker and one of them says don't invest in this stock, and the other one says do invest in this stock. One is going to be right. Is the one that's wrong damaged? Maybe, but how would you know? You won't know unless you have reference to other things.

*   *   *   *   *   *

Defense: Doctor, you had talked earlier about some of the difficulties in measuring deficits in the frontal lobe portion of the brain. In this case, did you do a—an exam of Mr. Page—

Pincus: Yes.

Defense: —to determine whether he had any deficits in that portion of his brain?

Pincus: Yes. And I found only two abnormalities—well, three abnormalities on examination. One was he had a thing called a Wartenberg reflex in the right hand. When people have severe motor disability because of post—posterior frontal lobe damage or damage to the tracks that lead from the posterior part of the frontal lobe, they may develop what's called cortical thumbs, and maybe—their thumbs may be inside their fist and holding their hands in this position. Newborn babies do that, and it's normal. But if adults do it, of course, it's not normal.

Defense: Going back to Mr. Page's matter, you—you talked about the right Wartenberg. What else did you find that was abnormal?

Pincus: Well, he wasn't able to hold his hands—his fingers steadily when I asked him to extend his hands and hold them steady. He wasn't able to do what I'm doing now. Instead of that his fingers jerked up and down and he wasn't able to hold still. Those are called choreiform movements, c-h-o-r-e-i-f-o-r-m, choreiform movements. And that reflects something wrong with the basal ganglia, which are gray-matter areas deep in the brain that modify motor movement.

At any rate, he had this subcortical damage and—and cortico-spinal tract involvement on the left side of his brain. From that—and the only other thing that was abnormal was when I asked him to read paragraphs: there are certain standard paragraphs that are grade-appropriate, at eighth- or ninth-grade level, and he was able to read them quite well. And then when I asked him to repeat what he had just read, the way I do that test is I say I want you to read this out loud and then give me the card back again and tell me what you just said. And what he would do is he would incompletely remember what he had just read, and then confabulate, make up— put in elements that were not there, not in the paragraph. And that—that suggests a memory deficit or attentional deficit that he was trying to cover up by adding things. He was trying to appear normal.

Defense: Now, Doctor, when you—you indicate that he had the trouble with the shaking of the hands and the thumb—

Pincus: Not shaking, jerking.

Defense: Or jerking. And the thumb underneath and the insertion of paragraphs, does that tell us anything more than the fact that those three things are problematic in his life or can we extrapolate from that that there might be other behavioral problems that come out of that?

Pincus: I don't think that—that—that provides a very firm basis for saying that there is brain damage of the kind that would lead to the kind of crime that we are—we're discussing. And it's true that many people who have choreiform-movement disorders have an impuls—impulsivity problem. That—that—that is true.

*　　　　*　　　　*　　　　*　　　　*　　　　*

Defense: Okay. Perhaps I'll go to something else, or we will take up the rest of the day with that. Doctor, when you do—when you did a neurological exam on Mr. Page, did you check out his body?

Pincus: Yes.

Defense: And was there anything remarkable that you saw on his body?

Pincus: He had horrible scars all over his back and his arms and his thighs. And had been sustained in—it looked like it had been sustained in a whipping. And we have a history that he was whipped with a—an extension cord and that the whippings drew blood. And that these were delivered virtually daily, and last for minutes or so each, sometimes up to an hour. And they were delivered by a mother who was out of control and who couldn't be dissuaded from doing that by her own mother. And his response to that was to curl up into a little ball, or to try to run away, and to beg and to plead, and stop it, I won't do it again, please, please. But they would continue until the mother got tired or the mood had passed.

Defense: Doctor, the—the location and nature of these scars, could you tell if they were self-inflicted in recent months?

Pincus: No, they were not self-inflicted and they were not in recent months. They were old scars and they were the kinds of scars that are seen in people who have been whipped.

Defense: And you have seen people that have been whipped?

Pincus: Yes, many.

Defense: Doctor, were you able to count?

Pincus: There were 17 that I counted. That did not include scars on the forearms, where there were many others on hands, knees, and below, for which he could provide more benign explanations, football injury, that kind of stuff, bicycle. But the ones on the back and the flanks and the back of the thighs, and the shoulders, neck, there is—those are—looked like the kind of injuries that are delivered by somebody who is being beaten with something that cuts the skin. We have a history that he was beaten with something that cuts the skin, and that the skin was cut. So I don't think you really need to have a great deal of faith in order to put the connection between those two.

Defense: Doctor, when you were doing your physical exam of him before you looked at his back and his flanks, did you tell him that you were going to look for scars or for evidence of physical—

Pincus: No.

Defense: —abuse?

Pincus: No. As I said, I'm going to examine your back; that's part of the examination. The doctor wants to look at your back, chest, whatever.

Defense: Doctor, taking a look at all the evidence that you saw, whether it be the physical exam of Mr. Page, the records, the PET scan, the MRI, the EEG results, everything, do you have an opinion within a reasonable degree of medical certainty as to whether Mr. Page suffers from a brain injury?

Pincus: Yes.

Defense: What is that?

Pincus: I think he does. I think that it's most likely that his—the orbitofrontal cortex is not working properly and that the reason that it's not working properly is because of the traumatic brain injury that was sustained sometime in childhood.

Defense: Does everyone with traumatic brain injury commit crimes?

Pincus: Certainly not.

Defense: How about violent crimes?

Pincus: Certainly not. But there is a—a greater likelihood that someone with frontal brain injury will commit violent—will be a violent aggressive.

From the testimony of Dr. Pincus, the defense attempted to make clear the fact that the defendant suffered from brain damage that influenced his behavior. As such, they hoped to make it possible for the jury to begin viewing the murder as unintentional because Dr. Pincus asserted that people with frontal lobe damage oftentimes are not capable of making plans and sticking to them, particularly in stressful situations—they act impulsively when they get confused. Dr. Pincus proved to be one of the most credible defense witnesses, according to jurors (see chapter 8). Not only did the jury pay increased attention to him when he testified, but they made notes of his explanations often in their notebooks when he spoke. Some of the jurors even outwardly practiced the movements along with him when he demonstrated how he administered the neurological exams to the defendant, that is, arm and hand movements.

Also, Dr. Pincus's testimony about the existence of scars on the defendant's body was validating in that previously, the prosecutor had implied that the family and the defendant had lied about or exaggerated the extent of the abuse he suffered as a child. Photographs of the defendant's body (torso, back, legs, and arms) were entered into evidence to show the placement and size of the scars on his body and another expert witness, a dermatologist, later testified about how scars are formed on the body and which kinds of scars never go away. The dermatologist counted 53 significant scars in peculiar places on his body that would not have been caused by horsing around or playing football, for example, because sports equipment or clothing would have protected his skin. In other words, Dr. Pincus's testimony paved the way for the defense to prove that the defendant had bled when he was beaten as a child and that he was beaten with extension cords and other objects that left peculiarly shaped marks on his body.

Dr. Charles Opsahl, chief psychologist at the Yale University of Health Sciences in Connecticut, testified to the existence of brain damage, specifically frontal lobe damage on the PET scan of the defendant's brain, and how such damage manifests in behavior. His testimony was elicited to augment the scientific evidence of brain damage that had already been presented by the defense. In fact, Dr. Opsahl's work validated the conclusions drawn by Dr. Lewis and Dr. Pincus about the existence of brain damage. The defense offered the testimony of these three notable scientists to show that the defendant should be viewed with sympathy because he has brain damage as a result of abuse and has lived a traumatic life.

Defense: Now, we will get to the details here in a little while, but, based on your evaluation, did you come to a conclusion of whether the defendant suffered from brain damage?

Opsahl: Yes, I did.

Defense: What was that conclusion?

Opsahl: He certainly suffers from brain damage.

Defense: Given that, is it still possible to tell from the damage that you observed what—what the damage is consistent with in terms of what part of the brain is damaged?

Opsahl: Yes, the—in terms of the overall testing, the—these results are consistent with damage to the areas of the brain, in particular, that deal with memory and abstract reasoning, which would be the temporal lobes and the frontal lobes. Those would be the two major areas, or both, temporal and frontal lobes is where the localization would be.

This additional expert testimony attempted to widen the jury's attention to include social factors in the defendant's life that contributed to his delinquency. It wasn't *all* his fault; in other words, his brain damage influenced at least some of the circumstances that led to the killing and any one person (jury member) may have acted the same way if he or she had the same brain damage and experiences. Also, the humanity of the defendant was uncovered in the testimony that allowed good or humane aspects of the defendant's personality to surface such as chores that he did for his mother and the times that he cried in front of his cousin for no apparent reason. A foundation for second-degree murder instead of first-degree murder had, thus, been laid.

Motive: Why He did It

Importantly, the defense attorneys attempted to forward a different motive for the crime than that argued by the prosecution. Instead of a cold-blooded killer who simply wanted to rob a house to get money, the defendant became a frightened, emotionally and physically scarred, vulnerable young man who was trying to protect himself from further abuse; that is, he had not intended or premeditated the murder, but had reacted violently to the threat of detection. Indeed, he viewed the victim as an attacker who was capable of harming him the way his mother did when she yelled at him and beat him and threatened to call the police on him. When the defense put witnesses on the stand to testify about how a person with frontal lobe damage is unable to control his emotions, switch plans, make clear decisions, and generally act rationally under intense circumstances, it became possible for the murder to be viewed as unintentional. The fact that the defendant tried to wash his clothes in the victim's washer, that he left biological evidence all over the house (including fingerprints, saliva, and semen), and that he walked out into the backyard to dispose of some materials in broad daylight were stupid things to do, in other words, particularly for a calculating murderer. In fact, the defense argued that the murder was more the result of panic and stupidity than an act of premeditation.

"Snapping" and the Lack of Motive

The defense's case, including expert witness testimony on the relationship between child abuse and later violence, attempted to portray the defendant as more of a "troubled youth" who never got the help that he needed to control his emotions and live normally. To be sure, he was referred to mental health experts numerous times throughout his adolescence. In fact, several reports from mental health experts were submitted to the court to prove that he had been under the care of or at least evaluated by psychologists and psychiatrists.

These reports were entered as evidence even though the experts who evaluated the defendant and wrote the reports did not testify. Such reports sought to demonstrate the troubled nature of the defendant from a very young age, including allusions to his future dangerousness. For example, a psychological evaluation of the defendant by a Washington Assessment and Therapy Services therapist (Cornelia Sweezy) where he was referred by the D.C. Superior Court for psychological evaluation following his arrests in 1991 stated (in part) that

> Donta came to live with her [his grandmother] because he said that his mother was "too hard on him" . . . . He was polite, cooperative and helpful throughout the testing session. Donta tended to be very quiet and seldom smiled. . . . Ms. Page appeared angry and excited. She immediately launched into criticism of him, stating that he needs help, is a problem, and is not doing anything to straighten himself out. Ms. Page said that she is tired of his lack of cooperation, his continued friendship with the boys who got him in trouble, his laziness around the house, his lying, and his poor work habits in school. . . . Donta seemed angry and sullen, but did not attempt to state his views, apparently overwhelmed by his grandmother's very aggressive outpouring of criticism. . . . Ms. Page rapidly described Donta's faults and insisted that she "would not have it." When Donta attempted to respond, she cut him off by saying that this disrespect and backtalk was just what she was talking about . . . she overwhelmed both Donta's attempt to explain about the shoes [his grandmother said that he was wearing her shoes] and the examiner's request that she allow Donta to state his ideas. During the time that Donta and Ms. Page were seen together, Donta was never able to assert himself or express his opinions. Donta was interviewed alone before the testing session began. He stated that he cannot talk to his grandmother and leaves the house to avoid her criticism . . . he said that . . . his arrests have resulted in tension and disagreement. . . . He repeatedly pointed out that all of the teenage boys who live near him or go to school with him get into trouble.

It was clear from the social welfare reports that the defendant was a person of low intelligence, incapable of planning a murder to completion. In fact, numerous social welfare reports were admitted into evidence that mentioned his below-average mental ability as well as his emotional problems.

Ms. Sweezy reported that Donta scored in the "low-average" on some verbal skills and he scored "low" on arithmetic and verbal comprehension which indicate "gaps in his academic progress." His concrete thinking and mental skills were lacking, too. Her report also said that he works very slowly and may need extra time for written work and mathematical computation.

With regard to his emotional and social abilities, Ms. Sweezy stated (in part) that

Donta's responses to projective questioning and personality inventory indicate that he is aware of many unpleasant feelings (anger, depression, oppositional attitudes) and worries that he cannot control his anger. . . . He vacillates in his attitude toward women, believing that they are bossy, but also warmer and friendlier than men. Donta is very distrustful of, and expresses paranoid feelings regarding, the police. He is often depressed, lonely, and nervous, and reports feelings of unreality. . . . He reports feelings of helplessness and lack of control. . . . He is concerned by "bad thoughts," sadness, feelings of self-consciousness, loneliness, and wishes to escape. One questionable area is his willingness to control his anger, since he repeatedly states that the only way to cope in this society is through fighting. Despite this attitude, Donta expressed the desire to change and willingness to participate in therapy.

Ms. Sweezy concluded that "he appears at risk for further involvement with antisocial activity unless his anger, depression and insecurity are addressed through therapy and assistance in school." Remedial math with tutoring and involvement in a mentoring program with an adult male were recommended. The defendant was sixteen years old at the time of Ms. Sweezy's evaluation.

Inability to Plan and Premeditate

A timeline of the defendant's life which included dates of arrests, criminal activity, and therapy sessions with mental health experts was admitted into evidence by the defense, too. The timeline sought to demonstrate that the defendant had witnessed and been the target of numerous violent attacks in his neighborhood including being shot in the right hand as he was walking down the street. Some of the bullet fragments were left in his hand when he sought treatment at Howard University Hospital and the hospital report noted that he had suffered from high blood pressure since the age of nine. The defendant's friend, Ricky Williams, was murdered in October of that year. Following Ricky's death, the defendant told his probation officer that he was "assaulted yesterday and remains in fear for his life at this time." The probation officer's report also states that the defendant reported being shot at five times between October 4 and October 19. Ricky Williams was murdered on October 9, 1992.

In 1993, the defendant was seen at St. Elizabeth's Youth Forensic Unit for a psychiatric evaluation where he was diagnosed with "Dysthymia and a tendency towards Dependent Personality Disorder." Dr. Milton Engel, who examined and diagnosed the defendant at St. Elizabeth's, stated:

when Donta goes to visit his mother, which he wants to do, the meetings often end up poorly in that Donta is seeking supplies either in the form of acknowledgment, encouragement, or literally some food or support and Ms. Barco

(Patricia Page) offers none. . . . Donta has changed schools several times. . . . In recent years he has not done well in school, having to repeat the second, eighth, and ninth grades. He worked at the Mayor Summer Youth Program at the WUDC Radio Station in 1990 and said that he liked it . . . . He was a quiet, cooperative, not unruly and slightly subdued youngster throughout the interview. . . . Donta was not effusive, spoke in short sentences with few words, but did not communicate with the interviewer and was available despite being guarded and saying little spontaneously. He is a somber, slightly apathetic youngster who does appear to be somewhat indifferent, passive, and dependent. . . . There was little range to his emotions, but I think this is due to his chronic sense of being in an unsafe environment. . . . He said when he was five years old, he remembers falling out of a car. I thought this memory was a symbol for him of his general sense of not being well-cared for and insufficiently supervised as a child. . . . He did add spontaneously toward the end of the interview that he "likes science" because he enjoys "finding out how things work." I thought this was a very hopeful sign and a very honest one. She [Linda Page on the phone] said that it was disheartening to watch Donta go time after time to visit his mother hoping that she would be sympathetic and caring, and yet each time to find that she essentially rejected him, spent little time with him and in grandmother's words "gave him nothing."

In recommending Donta for residential treatment, Dr. Engel reported that

Donta is a youngster who is caught in an earlier phase of development still trying to form an attachment with his mother and figure out why his father was not part of his life. . . . He is also a youngster who needs further help with developing more adequate controls over his impulses. At a residential treatment center he can be evaluated for the possibility of adding medication to his therapeutic regimen which might address both his fear of losing control and his depressed feelings. At the present time, I think the prognosis for his community adjustment is not great, but I do not see him as a threat to the community, but rather see him as more in danger both because of his size and because of his psychological problems.

Dr. Engel's report was admitted into evidence, but he did not testify at trial.

A behavioral consult from George Washington University Pediatrics division dated July 29, 1993, reported that the defendant had a history of failure to comply, that is, "was seen sporadically by mental health—had some no shows as well—also referred to D.C. Youth Initiative Project but patient did not follow through." The practitioner stressed (to his mother and grandmother) the importance of keeping appointments in order to address behavior problems. Approximately three weeks later, the defendant was referred by the Juvenile Branch of the Social Services Division of the Superior Court of the District of Columbia for a psychological evaluation with Dr. Beverly A. Parker-Lewis at St.

Elizabeth's Hospital for the purpose of "determining the appropriateness of a residential facility placement." Dr. Parker-Lewis did not testify in the trial, but her report was admitted into evidence. In part, her report stated that

> Donta described his early childhood as "alright. It was fun. I got to do whatever I wanted to do." He continued to state that he could throw clothes all over his grandmother's house. "I knew I could get away with more things at my grandmother's. She's too easy." Since birth, Donta has moved back and forth between his grandmother and mother's homes . . . he lived with his grandmother while his mother was in California. She [Pat] was concerned because Donta was left on his own while Ms. Page [his grandmother] worked twelve-hour days. . . . All parties interviewed denied any form of abuse in the family. At the present time, Donta is repeating tenth grade at Cardoza High School. He has repeated grades one, seven, and eight. . . . He dislikes some of the teachers. "They tell you what to do all the time, even when you ain't in their classes." . . . He was absent from school at least twice a week because he overslept.

Dr. Parker-Lewis administered a set of exams on her third meeting with the defendant that allowed her to conclude that he "falls within the Average range of intellectual abilities," that he is "functioning intellectually at a level equal to or better than approximately 42 percent of adults the same age," and that "Donta demonstrated average skills for reading, low average skills for math, and borderline skills for written language."

On other tests that require the test-taker to draw pictures, Dr. Parker-Lewis observed that

> His manner of drawing supports feelings of insecurity and inadequacy and an erratic personality. He may tend to be suspicious and highly anxious. . . . His renderings indicate generalized discontent with feelings of inferiority, ineffectiveness, inadequacy, and insecurity. He may tend to display excessive defensiveness with low self-esteem. Ego structure is weak and ego strength is low. . . . His perception of himself and his environment is weak. Emotional and social development are immature. There appears to be some conflict or concern regarding sexual issues, especially with women. It is highly likely that he will use his physical size and strength to assert his masculinity and control in a situation.

More questioning resulted in insightful responses about his father and his fears:

> Relationships appeared to be the focus of his responses. He expressed concern about his father. (I want to know) "who my father is." (My father) "is a punk." There also seems to be a great fear of being left alone. (My greatest fear) "is that of losing my family." (My greatest worry is) "That I will be rejected." Insecurity is suggested by the response, (Boys) "are the better sex." . . . He often

exhibits an exaggerated identification with the traditional masculine role which may place an overemphasis on strength, toughness, and dominance.

In conclusion, Dr. Parker-Lewis stated that

> Donta is chronologically a young man, but emotionally a child. He presents with behaviors which emphasize his size as a mechanism for stressing power and maintaining control in situations. Feelings of insecurity, inadequacy, impotence, ineffectiveness, and anxiety are significant factors in his behavior although his behavior and size do not easily allow one to see this. . . . Even though there are significant emotional and relationship problems in Donta's life, he seems to have little remorse for and understanding of his problems. He knows he is out of control, but is making no effort to make changes in his behaviors. He seems to enjoy the fact that he can make others uncomfortable and control situations just because of his size. While this examiner has little concern that the defendant will harm anyone, it is more likely that harm will come to him.

Residential treatment, tutoring, and individual therapy to work out his family issues were recommended by Dr. Parker-Lewis to the court. Following this assessment, the defendant was recommended for residential treatment at Bowling Brook Home for Boys, in Middleburg, Maryland. At the time, he was living with his grandmother, Linda Page, and her male companion. Subsequently, the defendant was admitted to Bowling Brook in April of 1994 (just after his eighteenth birthday) with the expected release date of February 11, 1995. His progress reports at Bowling Brook rated him "fair to poor" (on July 21, 1994), "satisfactory" (on October 21, 1994), and "satisfactory progress, improvement most noticeably in self-esteem" (on January 20, 1995). In January, right before he was released from Bowling Brook, the defendant scored 340 Verbal and 340 Math on the SAT. He was released from Bowling Brook on January 31, 1995. Shortly after being released, he received his G.E.D. His final grades from Bowling Brook were one A and four Bs.

A more detailed version of the defendant's life was presented by the defense, then, that explained the defendant's paranoia, feelings of being unsafe and out of control, desperation, and isolation (*prior* to the murder of Peyton Tuthill). As such, the defense turned the picture of the defendant around to resemble more of a "troubled youth" image than the one of a savage beast that had previously been constructed by the prosecution.

Perpetual Cycle of Violence

Some of the defendant's family members were shown to have been sympathetic to him at times even though terrible mistakes in his upbringing had apparently been made. It was clear that the defendant's family belonged to the lower socioeconomic class and resided in impoverished areas of Washington, D.C., and South Carolina where violence, abuse, and neglect were common. It was also clear that testifying in court was an uncomfortable and embarrassing experience for the family because their secrets were being exposed to strangers. One topic of extreme sensitivity seemed to be the defendant's father.

Family members relayed to investigators (but not to the jury because the court decided not to receive such testimony) that the defendant was born as a result of rape by a retarded man named Ronald when his mother was fifteen. The defendant's father was never discussed in the family and inquiries about him to the mother, Patricia Page, were met with physical and verbal attacks. The defendant, therefore, never knew anything about his father except through rumors that said he was a very violent man towards women; that is, Patricia Page was not the first nor the last woman that Ronald had raped in Rock Hill, South Carolina, and his close relatives still reside in the area where Ronald lives. Also, the defendant's mother tried to abort the defendant, twice, by drinking a concoction of fluids that the family called "voo doo potion." Dr. Lewis testified that these stories were relayed to her by the defendant's family even though the court decided not to receive medical evidence of the attempted abortions or the rape.

This information was used to expose the human frailty of the defendant and his family, opening new ways to view the defendant's behavior in light of circumstances that, on the surface, may have been overlooked. To be sure, Linda Page, Freddy Witherspoon, and Erica Penny were clean, appropriately dressed, articulate individuals, but their testimony divulged a great deal of pain in their lives, not only as the victims of abuse, violence, and neglect, but also as witnesses to the abuse of others. Their voices lowered when they spoke about beatings and rapes and shootings and other violent episodes they had witnessed; their demeanor softened when the defendant was alluded to in such discussions. In fact, Freddy Witherspoon became physically upset, holding back tears, when he relayed the story of his cousin crying, and Erica Penny cried softly as she spoke of the violence that had occurred in her and the defendant's neighborhood and school, including the stabbing of a classmate and a fire set in the hallway of their school.

Low IQ + Lack of Self-Control + Cycle of Violence = Murderer

The defense attorneys hoped that it would become possible for the jurors to view the defendant and his situation as tragic, involuntary, hopeless, and with collective responsibility because the social services and juvenile programs (community service, educational, and therapeutic) to which he was referred were either ignored by his family (they did not take him to the follow-up appointments) or simply failed to divert his path. The fact that the Stout Street Foundation simply kicked the defendant out on the street the night before the killing (with no food, clothes, or money) also served as a way to view the defendant—the attorneys hoped—as a victim of circumstance because he had been forced to sleep on the street twenty-four hours before the killing occurred. Using hindsight, then, a clear path of destruction was forged not only by the defendant, but also by some of the social forces in his environment that influenced his behavior. The jury's task, then, was to determine whether those factors were relevant during the commission of the crime.

Notes

1. Bryan A. Garner, *Black's Law Dictionary*, 7th ed. (St. Paul, MN: West Group, 1999).

2. Garner, *Black's Law Dictionary*.

3. Allan G. Johnson, *The Blackwell Dictionary of Sociology: A User's Guide to Sociological Language* (Cambridge, MA: Blackwell, 1995).

4. Garner, *Black's Law Dictionary*.

5. Garner, *Black's Law Dictionary*.

6. Garner, *Black's Law Dictionary*.

7. Hazel May, "Who Killed Whom: Victimization and Culpability in the Social Construction of Murder," *British Journal of Sociology* 50 (1999): 503.

~

CHAPTER SIX

The Penalty Phase:
The Prosecution's/Defense's Mission

He needs to be punished severely but not killed.

The Penalty Phase: How the Prosecution Saw Its Mission

The Four-Step Process

In Colorado, the decision of whether to put a person to death for a capital offense is made by a panel of three judges. The decision was put in the hands of judges by a legislature who believed that more death penalty convictions would result from removing the sentencing task from juries. Juries had demonstrated reluctance in the past to use capital punishment. In fact, before 1994 when the legislation was introduced, juries in Denver County had sentenced one in nine capital defendants to death in the previous twenty years. Thus, in 1995 Colorado decided to impanel judges to decide whether death should be imposed upon capital defendants.[1]

As such, judges are selected "from a computer-based random number generator from the then-sitting district court judges of the region wherein the charge was filed," according to a University of Colorado Law Review article researched by Robin Lutz during the *Page* trial. "In order to impose a death sentence, the finding must be unanimous."[2] To date, three (out of seven) death penalty defendants have received the death penalty in Colorado with this process in place, including Francisco Martinez, William Neal, and George Woldt. The other four defendants received life sentences.

According to the article researched by Lutz:

> Colorado mandates a four-step analysis for sentencing in capital murder cases. This process is clearly set forth in *People v. Tenneson* and the sentencing statute [Colo. Rev. Stat. Section 16-11-103 (2000)] and has been repeatedly reaffirmed by the Colorado Supreme Court. The first step of the process is for the sentencing body "to determine if at least one of the statutory aggravating factors exists." Second, if one of the aggravating factors is proven beyond a reasonable doubt, the sentencing body must consider "whether any mitigating factors exist." Mitigating factors do not need to be proven beyond a reasonable doubt; in fact, no burden of proof is required for "proving or disproving mitigating factors." In the third step, the sentencing body must determine whether the mitigating factors "outweigh" the aggravating factor(s) proven in the case. Lastly, during the fourth step, the panel decides "whether the defendant should be sentenced to death or to life imprisonment." This fourth step has been interpreted to be an opportunity for the sentencing body to "consider all relevant evidence without necessarily giving special consideration to statutory aggravators or mitigators." At this stage, both the prosecutor and the defendant may present all admissible evidence "that the court deems relevant to the nature of the crime, and the character, background, and history of the defendant.[3]

All seven of the sentencing panels that have convened in Colorado to decide a death penalty sentence have strictly followed this procedure. However, the Supreme Court ruled on June 24, 2002,[4] that sentencing by judges in capital cases is unconstitutional. As such, three of the current Colorado death row inmates' sentences (George Woldt, William "Cody" Neal, and Frank Martinez) will be converted to life imprisonment without the possibility of parole.

Statutory Aggravators

An aggravating circumstance in Colorado is defined as *a fact or situation that increases the degree of liability or culpability for a tortious or criminal act*.[5] There is a long list of statutory aggravators that can be argued in a capital trial, but in the current case, the prosecution argued that four aggravators existed: (1) the crime was heinous, which means that it was *shockingly atrocious or odious*, (2) the crime was committed for pecuniary gain, which means that the crime was committed *to gain money or something having monetary value*, (3) the crime was premeditated, which means that *conscious consideration and planning preceded the act*, and (4) the crime was committed *in the commission of another felony (felony murder)*. During the penalty phase, the focus of the prosecution's case shifted to a discussion of the aggravators introduced at the guilt phase of the trial. To prove that they existed, the prosecution called expert and lay witnesses to testify that the victim suffered a great deal during the murder, that the defendant is not a good candidate for prison (future dangerousness), and that the abuse that the defense alleges to have occurred during his childhood was not as bad as the defense alleged, that is, the implausibility of the "abuse excuse."

Aggravator One: Heinousness

The prosecution's case began with a depiction of the crime as heinous. The first homicide detective to arrive on the scene on the night of the murder was called to testify about what he found at the crime scene, including the amount of blood and the placement of objects in the house that showed that a struggle had taken place. He also displayed to the panel the bloody sheet from the bed where the victim was stabbed. As he pointed out various portions of the bloody sheet that depicted the victim's struggle, the prosecutor attempted to ask the detective about how brutal he thought the crime had been. The defense's objection to such "expert" testimony was sustained. The prosecutor moved on to showing the panel the crime scene walk-through video, which played for about forty minutes and the audiotaped confession, which played for about twenty minutes.

Dr. Thomas Henry, Denver coroner, went through the autopsy photographs explaining the wounds on the victim's body in graphic detail, especially the wounds that killed her. On display, the victim's body looked like a scientific specimen rather than a dead person as the coroner pointed to the bruising in her vaginal and anal area and explained how trauma to those portions of her body probably occurred. The jury in the guilt phase had not seen the autopsy photos that were presented to the judges, but they had viewed the crime scene photos that were taken by police. The autopsy pictures showed very violent entry and exit wounds on the victim's body—her flesh was torn and mutilated in the vaginal and anal area. According to the prosecution, the defensive wounds on the victim's limbs and torso were consistent with a very long and hard struggle for survival.

The defense made a motion that the "court rule as a matter of law" that the prosecution had not proven that the crime was heinous. Judge Meyer said the panel would take the matter under consideration. Later, the motion was denied. According to the defense, evidence that the murder was "especially cruel, heinous, or depraved" was lacking. The court disagreed.

Importantly, the panel did decide, during the prosecution's case, to hear evidence of the "proportionality review" of death penalty sentencing in Colorado. Proportionality review refers to *an appellate court's analysis of whether a death sentence is arbitrary or capricious by comparing the case in which it was imposed with similar cases in which the death penalty was approved or disapproved.*[6] Previously, the defense, in a pretrial motion, had asked the panel to consider evidence that blacks in Colorado, specifically Denver, are disproportionately sentenced to death where murder and sexual assault occurred. The defense brought fifteen Denver cases to the panel's attention where the death penalty was not sought in such cases and most of those defendants were white. Specifically, the supplemental exhibit stated that several studies conducted for the purpose of examining racial disparities in death penalty sentencing "concluded that non-white defendants faced an increased risk in receiving the death penalty" and "the studies also concluded that in cases where the victim was white, the defendant faced an increased risk of receiving the death penalty." The panel agreed to consider the fifteen cases and to rule on the proportionality issue at a later date. Ultimately, the proportionality evidence influenced the judges' sentencing decision. In fact, it was "based primarily on a proportionality review of the other Colorado cases in which the death penalty had been imposed," according to the sentencing order which also mentioned that "such a review assists in the weighty determination of whether the death sentence, if applied in this case, can be applied with fairness and consistency."

Aggravator Two: Pecuniary Gain

The prosecution also argued that the crime was committed for "pecuniary gain." The defendant had taken coins from a dresser and a Lerner shopping bag from the crime scene when he left. He had also taken some clothes and a camera, which were later found in the dumpster behind the house where the killing occurred. The stolen objects were linked to him by several witnesses, including the roommates of the victim, who testified that the objects were missing, and a resident of the Stout Street Foundation who testified that he saw the defendant with the shopping bag and the coins. Thus, the following issues were discussed between the prosecutor and the judges: Did the defendant go into the house to murder? Did the defendant go into the house to get money? Did the defendant murder the victim in order to get the money? The verbal exchange between the prosecutor and the judges on these issues lent itself towards an interpretation of pecuniary gain that favored the defense, that is, that the defendant did *not* go into the house to murder, but he *did* go into the house to get money. The issue of whether the defendant murdered the victim *in order to* get money was resolved at the end of step one of the process. The court denied the aggravator, effectively suggesting that he *did not* murder the victim *in order to* get money.

Aggravator Three: Premeditation and a Pattern of Criminality

Premeditation means that the crime was committed with *conscious consideration and planning that preceded the act*,[7] or with the intention of killing the victim, particularly after deliberation. The prosecution introduced evidence that the defendant had planned crimes before. In fact, they called a former resident of the Stout Street Foundation to testify that, as a friend of the defendant, he had witnessed the defendant's preparation for a robbery of a convenience store.

Lawrence Owens testified for the prosecution that he had become a client of the Stout Street Foundation because it was a free drug rehabilitation program. He said that he had suffered from drug addiction for many years. Mr. Owens had attended the "games" with the defendant on the night that the defendant was expelled from the program. The purpose of the "games," according to Mr. Owens, was to "talk about people's shortcomings." He relayed that earlier in their stay at the Stout Street Center, he and the defendant had been walking down the street when the defendant suddenly pulled out a gun and told Mr. Owens to go away because "he was going to rob some place to get some money." Mr. Owens did not know if the defendant had really done what he said he was going to do because Mr. Owens walked off in a different direction from the defendant when he told him to. Apparently, the defendant had not wanted Mr. Owens to be involved in the crime. Mr. Owens was also on the bus with the defendant when they returned to the East Coast following the defendant's expulsion from the Stout Street program. Mr. Owens was testifying having just been released from prison on a felony conviction for second-degree robbery.

Mr. Owens's testimony was, in part, damaging to the defense's contention that the defendant only acted violently when he was attacked because the testimony showed that the defendant robbed stores on a whim sometimes and that he was fully willing to break the law to obtain money and weapons and clothing or food. But Mr. Owens testimony also showed that the defendant was, indeed, capable of making friends, of caring for those friends (by not wanting Owens to be involved in the robbery), and in holding on to those friendships over a period of years because it was clear from Mr. Owens's testimony that he did not want to testify for the prosecution and his demeanor on the stand showed that he held strong feelings about his friendship with the defendant. The fact that Mr. Owens testified for the prosecution having just been released from prison on a felony conviction, however, probably influenced the credibility that the judges afforded him and his depiction of the defendant. But the prosecution was interested in showing a pattern of violent criminality within which the defendant engaged freely. To that end, they also questioned a victim of another one of his violent crimes.

Ms. Josephine Gill, a Maryland store owner, testified that the defendant had robbed her. He hit her in the face, broke her jaw (which required five years of treatment), and demanded money from the register. When she could not get money from the register, he demanded her purse. He showed her a knife, too, and hit her on the head with the handle of it. The robbery was videotaped and the video was shown to the panel of judges. The courtroom fell silent during the showing of the videotape—it was very violent.

Clearly, the defendant was capable of harming others to get what he wanted and the prosecution was successful in establishing that not all of his violence stemmed from unsolicited attacks, such as when someone tried to shoot him on the street. At this point, during the penalty phase, then, the defense was crippled by visual evidence of the defendant's criminality and what the prosecution argued was remorseless behavior. To that end, the visual effects, such as the bloody sheet and the videotaped robbery were extremely interesting to the judges. Most of them perched on their seats and donned eyeglasses or sat up straight in their chairs in order to view the prop.

Aggravator Four: Felony Murder

The judges deliberated on the issue of whether the defendant murdered the victim during the commission of another felony (robbing the house) and ruled affirmatively on the aggravator. There is no record of their deliberations or any indication as to why they ruled this way during step one of the penalty phase—although the answer may seem obvious. This is the only aggravator that the judges agreed to affirm, in that, the other aggravators (pecuniary gain, heinousness, and premeditation) were denied. As a result, the panel of judges agreed to move to step two of the process, which requires the defense to show evidence of mitigators during the commission of the crime.

Other Factors to Consider

There were three additional factors that the prosecution brought before the court to consider with regard to sentencing the defendant. Their view was that the defendant posed a future danger to society, that victim impact statements should be heard, and that the "abuse excuse" was implausible.

Future Dangerousness

Testimony from the prosecution that was intended to damage the defense's contention that the defendant was a good candidate for prison came in the form of behavior reports that the prosecution's lead investigator procured from the Maryland prison where the defendant had been incarcerated before his parole in 1998. The investigator produced a lengthy progress report from the prison that showed several infractions including, but not limited to (1) the defendant had tied his bedsheet into a long rope that was found in his cell, (2) the defendant had left a "dummy" in his bed so that he could be out of his cell (when he was not supposed to be) to watch a football game (he was apprehended in the television room a short time later) and (3) a gun (without bullets) was found in the defendant's cell. The progress report was admitted into evidence. The defendant had admitted to each of these infractions when he was caught for them, but the testimony severely damaged the defense's ability to present the defendant as a good candidate for incarceration. Instead, the reports strengthened the prosecution's argument about future dangerousness, that is, that the defendant is likely to try to escape from prison if the judges sentence him to life without the possibility of parole.

Victim Impact Statements

The prosecution was allowed to present additional evidence of the victim's character and background that would help the judges determine whether the defendant's life was worth saving. For that reason, during step four of the process, the prosecution seized the opportunity to present victim impact statements to the panel of judges. Testimony from the victim's mother, grandmother, and friends was received by the court. During these statements, very little questioning went on. Instead, the witnesses were clearly given leeway as to how long or how emotional to make their statements. Questions from the prosecutor were used to amplify or clarify the statements that were made by the witnesses, but the tone of the trial changed significantly in that the witnesses seemed to control the proceeding during their testimony.

This change may have been an indication of the court's sympathy for the loss of the victim in their lives. But it could also be interpreted as a sign of irrelevance. Perhaps, the victim impact statements were received because it would seem harsh to appear not to care about how the victim's family felt, but during the testimony, the judges did not seem particularly interested in the tears, and the music, and the anecdotes about the victim. I noted judges looking out the windows of the courtroom, cleaning their eyeglasses, perching their chins on their hands, and looking sad. In other words, their behavior showed sadness and sympathy, but they were not riveted by the displays. They certainly did not seem as engrossed in the family's statements as they were in the autopsy photographs. The prosecution used the victim impact statements to persuade the judges that the crime was heinous.

Heather Nelson, one of the victim's roommates, testified about the victim's mother. She said that Pat Tuthill had been a "well-put-together woman" before this happened. "Now," according to Heather, "she doesn't put on makeup" and "she wonders if she'll make it." The victim's mother only works sporadically now, too, whereas she used to work consistently. The victim's grandfather, who Peyton affectionately called "Pa-Pa," is also "shook-up," she said. "He cries and he's . . . messed up."

Cory Chyr, the victim's boyfriend, testified that he had met the victim in October of 1998 at a sports bar called the "Sports Column" located in downtown Denver. He portrayed the victim as "kind and caring" and said that their relationship developed quickly—they had talked about marriage. Mr. Chyr said that he had gone to Florida with Peyton to meet her family and said that she was the "love of my life." He cried openly as he relayed that Peyton talked to her mother almost every day on the telephone. When asked how the murder had affected Pat, the victim's mother, he said, "A piece has been ripped from her soul." Mr. Chyr did not look at the defendant at all during his testimony and he sat with his fists clenched and his mouth closed through most of the trial. The defense did not cross-examine Mr. Chyr.

The victim's grandmother, Betty Rugkowski, testified that she called Peyton "Stephanie" because that was the name that they had originally chosen for her. The prosecutor handed several baby pictures of Peyton to her and she took a few deep breaths as she flipped through them, clenching a pretty pink handkerchief in one hand as she moved the pictures with the other. "She loved animals . . . she was always picking up strays," she said. All of the family members were wearing big buttons with Peyton's picture on them. The grandmother seemed proud of hers as she removed it and held it in her hands as she spoke. Betty played an active role in Peyton's life having attended her first communion, graduations, and birthday parties, among other significant life events. She even bought her a refrigerator full of food when she visited her at college because "her refrigerator was kind of bare." Pat, the victim's mother, "doesn't eat, looks horrible, doesn't sleep," and often says, "Mom, I just want my daughter back."

The victim's mother asked the judges if she could stand at the witness stand to speak because she has "difficulty speaking when she sits." The prosecutor waited patiently at the podium for her to look up and smile at him, apparently signaling that she was ready to begin. She talked about the day of the murder: That day at work, she had a fleeting thought, "What would you do if something ever happened to Peyton—she's so far away." But she went on with her work that day having put the thought out of her mind. The defendant held his head low and he did not move during her testimony. He seemed to be listening intently to every word she said.

The prosecutor asked Ms. Tuthill to flip through some baby pictures of Peyton. As she flipped through the pictures, she talked about how she handled all of the funeral arrangements for her daughter and would not let anyone help her. This, she did as a means of taking control of the situation. Sometime after the funeral, she was given Peyton's belongings from the night of the murder and she recounted how the watch that she had been wearing had been a special present to Peyton from her. Ms. Tuthill had worn the watch ever since it was returned to her. She also talked about a bracelet and a cross necklace that Peyton was wearing and showed it to the panel of judges as she spoke about how much they had meant to Peyton.

A video of Peyton's life was shown to the panel of judges during Ms. Tuthill's testimony. The video was a collection of photographs of Peyton that had been put to music by people of Pat Tuthill's acquaintance. The judges watched the video intently and Ms. Tuthill stood and shook and cried as she leaned in closely to the video monitor never taking her eyes off the screen for a moment. The defendant sat motionless in the midst of the victim's mother's despair. All of the songs from the video, including "The Rose," "How Do I Live Without You," "My Heart Will Go On" (theme to *Titanic*), brought tears to everyone's eyes. A five-minute recess was taken following Ms. Tuthill's testimony.

The Implausibility of the "Abuse Excuse"

Testimony from Dr. Patti Rosequist, a pediatrician who specializes in child abuse and neglect, was offered by the prosecution. Dr. Rosequist was asked by the prosecution to examine the defendant's body and to give an "expert" opinion on the scarring she found as to whether it probably resulted from abuse or from other forms of injury. The defense "voir dired" Dr. Rosequist at the beginning of her testimony and asked that she be qualified as an expert on "child scarring," instead of adult scarring because she had no experience with examining adults for scarring at all. Dr. Rosequist was qualified as a "pediatrician" in general.

Dr. Rosequist's testimony began with her description of her inspection of the defendant's body: she conducted the examination in a conference room of the jail where the overhead lighting was poor. She did not bring an additional light to aid in the examination. (The defense questioned her about the lighting sources and established that the lighting was poor and quoted literature that states that African-American skin needs to be examined under additional light because of the various skin hues that may be present.) It appeared from her testimony that she had attempted to locate *big* scars on the defendant's body, but not to examine his body for *all* of its various skin color variations and scars. She took pictures of what she called "significant findings," and her pictures were given to the judges for their review.

In the pictures, the defendant was standing in his underwear in the conference room of the Denver County Jail. The camera was aimed at his face, his back, the backs of his thighs and calves, his shoulders, his chest and stomach, the front of his legs, and the sides of both of his arms. Dr. Rosequist's opinion was that she "suspected" abuse, but that she could not "diagnose" it.

The defense also asked Dr. Rosequist if a nine-month-old child in general has the physical strength to climb out of a moving car window. Dr. Rosequist replied "it could be." (During the guilt phase, the defense's expert, Dr. Dorothy Otnow-Lewis, had suggested that a nine-month-old child does not have the physical strength to *climb* out of a moving car window. Instead, the doctor suggested that the defendant was *thrown* out of the window when he was about nine months old, according to hospital records that indicated that he had been admitted to the emergency room for a large gash on the front side of his forehead after falling from a moving car. Dr. Johnathan Pincus, a defense expert, agreed with Dr. Lewis's contention that the defendant had been *thrown* out of the car because he lacked the physical strength to climb).

It is clear from the testimony of Dr. Rosequist that the prosecution attempted to establish that the defendant was not abused because her testimony directly contradicted the defense's claim that the defendant was severely abused as evidenced by the presence of old scars. Marvin B. Scott and Stanford M. Lyman address this issue in a famous article titled "Accounts."[8] In it, the authors refer to the re-negotiation of an actor's identity as "altercasting" because, in the current case, the prosecution attempted to confer a *particular kind* of role (that of a child who was clumsy) on the defendant, rather than the one that the defendant and the defense attorneys conferred upon him (that of an abused child). The account, "a statement made by a social actor to explain unanticipated or untoward behavior,"[9] that the defense gave of the defendant's actions was recast as an "excuse" that the jury could choose whether to honor or not. And "excuses based on accidents [in this case, conduct for which responsibility is mitigated because humans cannot control all motor responses] are thus most likely to be honored precisely because they do not occur all the time or for the most part to the actor in question."[10]

The defense, on the other hand, forwarded a "justification" for the defendant's untoward conduct, which, according to Scott and Lyman, is "a selected . . . arrangement of facts that highlight an extremely dismal past, and thus explains the individual's present state."[11] The defense hoped that the jurors would honor the set of facts presented to them as a "justification" rather than as an "excuse" because, according to Scott and Lyman, honoring the account as a "justification" would result in a second-degree murder conviction, while honoring the account as an "excuse" would result in a first-degree murder conviction.

The Penalty Phase: How the Defense Saw Its Mission

Mitigating Circumstances

The defense countered the prosecution's arguments of aggravation with arguments for mitigation, that is, *facts that did not justify or excuse the act but that reduced the degree of culpability of the defendant.*[12] As will be recalled from chapter 2, prior to *Lockett v. Ohio,*[13] in Ohio the sentencing judge was "not permitted to consider the defendant's character, prior record, age, lack of specific intent to cause death, and her relatively minor part in the crime"[14] before sentencing the petitioner (who was convicted of aiding and abetting a robbery which caused the death of a person) to death. In that opinion, the court held that "the limited range of mitigating circumstances [history, character, and condition of the defendant] which may be considered by the sentencer under the Ohio statute is incompatible with the Eighth and Fourteenth Amendments" because the constitution requires that "a death penalty statute must not preclude consideration of relevant mitigating factors."[15]

Mitigators in *Colorado v. Page*

Defense attorneys argued that the defendant did not deserve the death penalty for four reasons: (1) the defendant was severely abused as a child, which resulted in brain damage that influenced his behavior, (2) the defendant's family history is so dysfunctional and abusive that the defendant never learned how to live normally, (3) the defendant does not pose a future danger to society, and (4) current Colorado death row inmates' crimes were more aggravated. To prove that mitigation existed, the defense attorneys presented academic research and the testimony of more famous experts like Dr. Carol Jenny of the Kempe Children's Center, introduced evidence of the defendant's fitness for prison in the form of prison records, and called the defendant's family to testify about his abusive childhood in more detail.

Mitigator One: Child Abuse

Dr. David Lisak testified by phone about the relationship between abuse of boys and later violence. Dr. Lisak, an associate professor of psychology at the University of Massachusetts in Boston, has published a great deal of literature on the topic. Judge Meyer administered the "oath" to Dr. Lisak via speakerphone in the courtroom. The prosecution's objection to Dr. Lisak's testimony, on the grounds that he had not examined the defendant personally, was overruled and Dr. Lisak went on to state that the link between child abuse and later violence is "widely accepted." Further, he stated that the more forms of abuse suffered in childhood (physical, sexual, neglect), the greater the likelihood of later violence. Also, the age of onset (earlier = worse), the relationship of the abuser to the child (closer = more damage), the frequency of the abuse, and the absence of a caring, consistent adult role model all combine to increase the likelihood of later violence.

The defense moved for admittance of numerous articles about child abuse, the connection between child abuse and violence, and brain damage. The prosecution objected vigorously to the admittance of the articles on the grounds that they were irrelevant, but the judges discussed it and received the articles into evidence.

Dr. David Johnson from the Colorado State Hospital was called to testify (for the defense this time) that (1) he did not find signs of "malingering" (faking) from the defendant during his stay at the hospital, (2) that he did not think that the crime the defendant committed was premeditated, (3) that the defendant expressed remorse about the crime, and (4) that the defendant had a tendency to blame others for his own problems, but that he was taking responsibility for the crime that he committed in this case. Dr. Johnson reiterated that the defendant had taken part in all of the therapy sessions that were offered at the hospital during his stay including attending sessions on anger management, relaxation, games and recreation, and community therapy. The defendant attended all of these sessions voluntarily. Just as a letter to Dr. Johnson from the defendant (that the doctor had found in a file just before leaving Pueblo to testify in this trial—the attorneys did not know about it) was being admitted into evidence, Dr. Johnson was abruptly halted from continuing to speak by the panel of judges. He had begun to talk about other Colorado death row inmates that he had evaluated and who seemed more "pitiless" than the defendant.

The prosecution's cross-examination of Dr. Johnson suggested that the defendant had expressed remorse at "getting caught" rather than for the murder. "He picked up a knife as soon as he went into the house," the prosecutor said. One judge interrupted and questioned whether that act amounted to deliberation and the subsequent discussion between the prosecutor and the judges seemed to result in an interpretation of the act as deliberation, but not premeditation; that is, he acted out of fear and anger, but he did not intend the result that occurred.

Dr. Pincus also testified by telephone during the penalty phase of the trial. His testimony, as in the guilt phase, focused on the defendant's ability to "conform his behavior." Dr. Pincus insisted that the defendant's "capacity to conform his behavior was impaired due to frontal lobe disease that the PET scan showed." As such, the defendant was unable to control his impulses when he was under a great deal of stress. Dr. Pincus went on to say that the defendant's "uncivilized behavior is due to disease that he finds convincing" and that he should "be in an environment where his behavior can be controlled if he gets out of hand and where his routine is the same every day." Dr. Pincus's testimony established that he had worked with over 150 murderers and that in most cases, they had been victims of what some would call abuse, but what Dr. Pincus calls "torture."

Upon cross-examination, Dr. Pincus asserted that although the defendant poses a risk of offending again, it could be managed in prison. One judge asked: "What behavior was the defendant unable to modify?" Dr. Pincus responded that the crimes for which the defendant was currently being charged and some of those for which he had previously been charged were "stupid and poorly planned." For example, the fact that the defendant tried to wash his clothes in the victim's washing machine before leaving the crime scene was stupid and one of the robberies that he attempted in Maryland involved him physically picking up a cash register and walking out of the store and down the street with it. The defendant fidgeted and whispered to one of his attorneys when he heard his actions being called "stupid." Dr. Pincus's last comment, "he needs to be punished severely but not killed," was stricken from the record.

Dr. Karynne Duncan, a dermatologist from the University of Colorado Health Sciences Center and Hospital, testified about the scars on the defendant's body. The defense offered her testimony as proof that the defendant had been beaten so severely as a child that scarring from the beatings was still noticeable. Dr. Duncan is the assistant chief of medicine at the hospital and she completed her residency at Yale University. Following her unchallenged qualification as an expert in the field of dermatology by the defense, Dr. Duncan described the procedures she used to examine the defendant's skin: she used a flashlight to go over every part of his body. She defined a scar as "the result of a wound healing" and documented that she found fifty-three "scars" other than those that would normally appear on an adult male such as stretch marks. In addition, she found nineteen "hyper-pigments." Overall, Dr. Duncan said that what she found was "definitely an excess of scars for men his age." In fact, she was "struck" by the "number of scars and the placement of them where we do not normally see scars from accidents or falling." Such scars, she said, are "consistent with electric cord literature." The judges questioned Dr. Duncan about "how many of the fifty-three scars are from child abuse?" Dr. Duncan's response was that the six loop-shaped scars and the double lined scars were probably from child abuse. She was not certain about the other scars that she found on the defendant's body.

The defense's star witness, Dr. Carol Jenny, testified about the connection between physical and sexual child abuse and later violence. Dr. Jenny is director of the Kempe Children's Center (a Denver-based child abuse prevention and treatment organization) and a Dartmouth Medical School graduate. The defense offered her testimony as a superior opinion on the relationship between child abuse and later violence; that is, her experience and expertise far outweighed that of the previous defense witnesses who testified. She began by stating that the effects of child abuse tend to be violence and low self-esteem. "Trauma," she said "has been shown to change the chemistry of children's brains." In fact, it can even "kill neurons," but it depends on the age, extent, and duration of the abuse. Children manifest aggressive, troublesome behaviors, particularly "sexual acting out," as a result of the abuse and it can be very devastating, according to Dr. Jenny, because the abuse is often secret.

Dr. Jenny went on to say that how the family reacts to reports of abuse is extremely important to the child's later development. For example, if the parent gets angry and tries to protect the child, the children are better able to recover. In her opinion, beatings with cords are "particularly brutal and painful." With regard to the records she examined about the defendant's anal fissure, Dr. Jenny said that it was "worrisome that the fissure was inside and outside . . . fondling or touching wouldn't cause that kind of tearing." Furthermore, she said the reaction from the defendant's grandmother was "very inadequate" and it would likely give the defendant the impression that his safety was not important. Moreover, there were "so many points in the record where you can see that if someone had acted responsibly, it wouldn't have come to this tragic end." Lashing out at people, according to Dr. Jenny, is how these kids cope with stress.

The recovery rate for these kids is not good, either, according to Dr. Jenny: "one-third do very well, one-third think about it and it still effects them, and one-third do poorly." In fact, she mentioned that some studies have shown that 30 percent of federal prison inmates report physical and sexual abuse. When asked why no one had documented or reported the defendant's abuse, Dr. Jenny stated that it was probably due to "totally overwhelmed social services in Washington, D.C."; that is, their effectiveness of response was almost nonexistent and very little preventive care is offered. Dr. Jenny also stated that "many things reduced his chance for success . . . poverty, abuse, neglect, he was often left alone, and no one sought follow-up treatment for his problems."

Mitigator Two: Horrible Family Background
Frederick Witherspoon testified again about Patricia Page's (defendant's mother) relationship with the defendant and with the defendant's father. He

said that Pat had not known her own father (the defendant's grandfather), that Pat was only sixteen when the defendant was born, that the defendant's father was much older than Pat, and that the defendant's father was married at the time that he impregnated Pat. The defendant's father was never involved with the defendant either, according to "Freddy." Frederick's testimony served to focus the panel's attention on the cyclical effect of abuse in the Page family, that is, that the defendant's mother had suffered from abuse and had, in turn, abused the defendant. The defense hoped to show the panel of judges that the defendant was not, therefore, a cold-blooded murderer, but rather a victim of circumstance who had very little control over his emotions and no positive role model in his life. The prosecution, on the other hand, attempted to establish that Pat and Linda Page were hard workers and provided for their families. Their questioning of Freddy suggested that Pat was more of a "disciplinarian" with her children than an abuser. Freddy's testimony never wavered in conveying that Pat went too far in "disciplining" the defendant.

I took the stand, following Frederick's testimony, as a defense investigator to discuss information that I had collected about Washington, D.C., during the early 1990s when the defendant was growing up there. I was questioned about the neighborhood where the defendant lived because I had attended Howard University in the same area in 1989 and 1992–1995. I told the judges about the "terrible" environmental conditions of the area that included gunfire, police sirens, street arrests, prostitutes, vagrants, graffiti, fights, threats, trash, congestion, and noise where the defendant lived. The judges seemed unimpressed with my portrayal of the defendant's neighborhood, but decided to receive several copies of Census Bureau Statistics that I had found that described the economic and crime conditions of Washington, D.C., during that time, particularly the median household income of single parents, murder rates, unemployment rates, incarceration rates by race, graduation rates by race and age, and public school expenditures.

Mitigator Three: Future Non-Dangerousness
The defense attempted to have a report of an interview that I conducted with Sergeant Darryl Brown, a shift supervisor at the Denver County Jail, entered into evidence. The report detailed a conversation between myself and Sergeant Brown where Sergeant Brown stated that "he had no knowledge of any disciplinary actions taken against Mr. Page in the jail and that he had never had to correct Mr. Page in any way since he became aware of Mr. Page's presence." In fact, the defendant was a member of the Inmate Council of Building 8, which means he served as a "representative to address

administrative concerns affecting building 8," according to Sergeant Brown. He went on to say that

> If he had a violent history inside the jail it would be unlikely he would be considered for Inmate Council because it would require additional precautionary measures . . . he'd be placed under a different classification code which would require him to be housed in a special management building known as building 6.

The prosecution objected to the admission of my report and the panel decided not to receive it, but said that Sergeant Brown could appear personally to give testimony if he wanted to. I was given the assignment of subpoenaing Sergeant Brown, but before the process could be completed, the defense decided against it and moved for the admission of the defendant's records from the Denver County Jail, which were received. The defendant had had no disciplinary action taken against him in the Denver County Jail for the two years that he was incarcerated there. The defense offered this evidence as proof that the defendant was a good candidate for prison undermining the prosecution's attempt to characterize the defendant as a future danger to society.

Mitgator Four: Proportionality

As previously mentioned, proportionality review refers to *an appellate court's analysis of whether a death sentence is arbitrary or capricious by comparing the case in which it was imposed with similar cases in which the death penalty was approved or disapproved.*[16] For that reason, the defense argued that compared to the six individuals who then sat on Colorado's death row, the crime committed by the defendant was "run of the mill" because in every one of those cases, six or seven aggravators had been proven to exist and with little or no argument for mitigation. In one of those cases, for example, the victim was held captive and physically tortured for several days before finally being killed. In fact, in that case, the victim's anus had been cut with a knife and she had been sodomized with a broom handle. Also, most of the current death row inmates had more than one victim.

Notes

1. Roxane J. Perusso, "And Then There Were Three: Colorado's New Death Penalty Sentencing Statute," *University of Colorado Law Review* 68(1997): 189–227.

2. Robin Lutz, "Experimenting with Death: An Examination of Colorado's Use of the Three-Judge Panel in Capital Sentencing," *University of Colorado LawReview* 73(2002): 231.

3. Lutz, "Experimenting with Death," 248.

4. *Ring v. Arizona*, 536 U.S. 584 (2002).

5. Bryan A. Garner, *Black's Law Dictionary*, 7th ed. (St. Paul, MN West Group, 1999).

6. Garner, *Black's Law Dictionary*.

7. Garner, *Black's Law Dictionary*.

8. Marvin B. Scott and Stanford M. Lyman, "Accounts," *American Sociological Review* 33(1968): 46–62.

9. Scott and Lyman, "Accounts," 46.

10. Scott and Lyman, "Accounts," 48.

11. Scott and Lyman, "Accounts," 52.

12. Garner, *Black's Law Dictionary*.

13. *Lockett v. Ohio*, 434 U.S. 889 (1977).

14. *Lockett v. Ohio*, 434 U.S. 889 (1977), 597.

15. *Lockett v. Ohio*, 434 U.S. 889 (1977), 608.

16. Garner, *Black's Law Dictionary*

CHAPTER SEVEN

Who Is the Defendant?
The Prosecution's/Defense's Answer

Nobody took the time to ask why but rather who. I've been asking for help for years. Nobody cares until I hurt someone, then they wanted to give me medicine, but when I went home nothing until I got in trouble again.

"Who Is This Defendant?" The Prosecution's Answer

The images of the defendant that the prosecution attempted to construct at trial were negative, to say the least. Three specific categories of negativity were elicited from witnesses that testified for the prosecution that portrayed the defendant as a monster-like creature with innate savage tendencies. To be sure, the prosecution went to great lengths to establish that the defendant is (1) deviant and evil, (2) uncaring and unremorseful, and (3) motivated by selfish concerns, but also that his negative lifestyle was the result of the defendant's rational choice. It was clear from the beginning that the prosecution placed no value at all on the defendant's life experiences in shaping him, that they regarded as ridiculous the notion that childhood abuse had anything to do with an adult's behavior, and that adults always do what they want to do when they get to be a certain age. For that reason, the prosecution made every attempt to discredit the defense's witnesses and they did so, in part, with witness testimony.

Deviant and Evil
The prosecution portrayed the defendant as an unscrupulous person—someone who is unprincipled, immoral, unethical, and corrupt. There were sev-

eral references made to his conduct in adolescence that pointed to his lack of commitment to the norms of society. Examples of such deviance included dropping out of school, ignoring his mother's and grandmother's advice, talking back to teachers, involving himself in drugs and criminality, and running away from home.

There were additional references to his attitude as unscrupulous and his behavior as deviant in the sense that he often used curse words to express his rage, he displayed defensiveness with therapists who attempted to help him, and he talked back to teachers in his school when they demanded answers from him about his behavior (absences, homework, inattention in class, and so forth), among others. Such references to his attitude were discussed between prosecutors and their witnesses as simple insolence—he didn't like being told what to do or being made to follow the rules. Dr. Johnson, from the Colorado State Mental Hospital, for example, said as much:

Prosecution:	Okay. Did he obey the rules?
Johnson:	Some of them.
Prosecution:	Okay. Did you ever have an occasion to discipline him for violating a house rule?
Johnson:	Yes.
Prosecution:	And how did he react when you did that?
Johnson:	Kind of like he didn't care.
Johnson:	It's very typical case when they get into trouble at the state hospital, they very seldom quickly take responsibility or quickly acknowledge what they have done wrong. Now, in his case, he basically thought that going into his—having to stay in his room for the duration of the yard activity was unfair. And even though that was the standard rule and procedure on the ward, and even though he had done that before, on that particular occasion, he simply didn't want to do it and he had great difficulty acknowledging that not following the rules was wrong.
Prosecutor:	That denial, did you at all interpret that as some sign of psychosis?
Johnson:	Not at all.

Therapists and social workers that were called to testify for the defense were cross-examined by the prosecution as to what the defendant's behavior meant. For example, one doctor who said that the defendant was "paranoid" was questioned about that term and was forced to disagree with the statement that the defendant "just didn't like her," as an alternative explanation for the defensiveness. Not only was paranoia ruled out as a possible influential force in dictating the defendant's reactions to people because of his abusive childhood, but also the prosecution insisted that suspicion of people was not at issue—only the fact that he deliberately killed Peyton Tuthill. In other words, any explanation of *why* the defendant did what he did in the Tuthill home was earnestly fought by the prosecution so that, in their view, only a deviant who decided to murder in order to avoid detection for a burglary remained.

Inability to Feel Like We Do: Uncaring and Unremorseful

The prosecution also portrayed the defendant as someone devoid of human concern. The fact that he didn't cry during the confession showed a lack of remorse, according to the prosecution, and they highlighted the fact that none of the therapists' reports that were entered into evidence described the defendant as "sorry" for what he did. In fact, the defendant never seemed to say that he was sorry for anything. Instead, the defendant had a tendency to run away and hide when he knew that he was in trouble. The prosecution suggested that such avoidance behavior acknowledged his understanding of right and wrong—he ran away to avoid taking responsibility for his actions.

Sometimes the prosecution portrayed the defendant as a predator who was looking for another crime to commit or for another person to harm. They talked about the defendant's violent criminal past where he threatened people with weapons, hit people with his fist, and threatened to kill people at various times.

In addressing the issue of familial support, the prosecution alleged that the defendant didn't need it—he was able to provide food, clothing, and shelter for himself even when his family failed to do so; his drug dealing allowed him to make enough money to buy clothes and food, and he often stayed with friends when his family kicked him out. Also, he at least had the love and support of his grandmother on a periodic basis and, according to the prosecution, that served as a sufficient amount of familial support when he was growing up.

It is important to note that the prosecutors never looked at the defendant when they talked about him. Sometimes they gestured at him from across the room, but the physical distance between them and the defendant remained great. This may have served as an indication of his defect—the lack of concern that he had shown to others is the lack of concern that he deserved to be shown at present.

Irresponsible, Greedy, and Selfish

Only a selfish person could commit the kinds of crimes that the defendant committed, according to the prosecution, because an unselfish person would consider the effect that his arrest and possible execution would have on his mother, brothers, and grandmother. But the prosecution did not offer a solid reason why the defendant was so selfish, only that the defendant acted out of immediate needs for attention and money—that is the reason why he molested women and the reason why he robbed stores. The defendant was not interested in finding legitimate employment or going to school or in abiding by the laws of the state because he had too much fun committing crimes, hanging out, and shirking responsibility. Not only was the defendant interested in shirking responsibility in his youth, but he was also, apparently, willing to shirk responsibility in adulthood because he didn't abide by the rules of the Stout Street Foundation, which led to his dismissal and subsequent incarceration. The prosecution, then, laid a foundation of laziness that was primarily motivated by selfish concerns. Instead of trying to become a better person, in other words, the defendant chose to rob stores. Instead of going to school, the defendant chose to buy weapons and sell drugs. Instead of helping to support his mother and brothers, the defendant chose to live with friends and buy clothes with his money. A desire for fun and excess, according to the prosecution, is the typical mind-set of criminals like the defendant.

Interestingly, the prosecution alleged that the defendant *chose* to commit criminal acts and to become a street person, and that he did so knowingly and consciously, that is, having weighed the consequences of his actions. Even at the age of 14 when the defendant molested an eight-year-old girl and ran away, he was thinking like an adult with the full knowledge of the consequences of his actions, according to the prosecution. His decision to seek immediate self-gratification, in other words, was carefully weighed against alternative lifestyle options. The prosecution, in their closing statement, suggested that the defendant could have cleaned up his act, gotten help for his problems, and become a successful adult while acknowledging that the abuse, lack of intelligence, brain damage, neglect, and criminal activity had been preserved in social records:

> Prosecutor: Let's talk a little bit about the defendant, Donta Page. Mr. Page did not have an ideal childhood. He did not have a father figure. He did not have a mother who gave him the attention that a mother should. He may have been sexually abused once. He may have been physically abused as a child. And if that's true, none of those are the defendant's fault. But by the same token, none of those things excuses what he did to Peyton Tuthill. Does the fact that someone is abused as a child give that person the right to kill someone? Does the fact that someone may have been physically abused as a child give that person the right to sodomize a helpless woman? There are few people in life who are dealt a perfect

hand. But despite not getting a perfect hand, people make do. They work hard. They try to improve themselves. They try to make their circumstances better. They follow the rules of society and they follow the laws that people have passed to govern conduct. And absolutely nothing that you have heard suggests that Donta Page could not do that if he wanted to. Donta Page is smart. He's strong. The Stout Street people told you that when he's in these therapy sessions he could provide good insight into other people's problems. Other people are able to take those types of talents and make something good come of them. But Donta Page grew up and he decided that he wasn't going to make something good come of his talents. He didn't apply himself in high school. He hung out with the wrong crowd. He got into delinquency problems. And he never let his grandmother help him to become a better person, although she tried.

In short, the images portrayed of the defendant by the prosecution reveal three things: (1) that the defendant fits many of the stereotypes that society holds about criminals—he's poor, smart but lazy, mean, and selfish, (2) that the defendant never tried to do better, and (3) that his actions are now and have always been the result of rational choice. As such, the defendant was portrayed as unable to rehabilitate, incorrigible, and unworthy of taxpayer money to keep him alive. Such a portrayal, according to the prosecution, lends itself not only to a first-degree guilty verdict, but also to a sentence of death.

"Who Is This Defendant?" The Defense's Answer

Worthy of Mercy

A very different view of the defendant was offered by the defense, one that rendered the defendant worthy of mercy. The defendant is not an animal, in other words, but rather a human being who does not know (because he has not been shown) how to live a compassionate life. His life has been a struggle for survival from the beginning: he was born to a mother who did not want him; he was severely beaten by her for wetting the bed and for having a learning disability, among other irrational reasons; he was thrown out of the house numerous times and he was never given a sufficient amount of clothes or food or comfort and support. Consequently, the defendant turned to selling drugs and robbing stores to meet his basic needs. But, when he started committing crimes, he got arrested and his mother continued to beat him, so in desperation, he ran away. The defendant never really had a chance to improve his conditions or himself because his life was in constant turmoil—he never even had a quiet place to read or study and never received a pair of eye-glasses or the high blood pressure medicine that he needed.

The defendant is a victim of his own life, in other words. He was given numerous opportunities to get help for his learning disability and his emotional problems, but his family never took him to the appointments. They never even followed up on the medical appointment that was made to supervise his recovery from rape at the age of ten. Besides, the defendant lived in a very violent, impoverished community where murder and homelessness and despair were common. One author calls life under such conditions the poverty deprivation syndrome.

The Poverty Deprivation Syndrome

Charles R. See argues that the death penalty is wrong because too many young black men are caught in a cycle of poverty, deprivation, shame, hopelessness, and despair that eclipses their chances for survival and subsequent success.[1] He calls the state of affairs the "poverty deprivation syndrome" and lists several factors that contribute to its prevalence including dysfunctional families, inadequate schools, violent neighborhoods, and a lack of religious faith. Such situations wreak havoc on a young black man's emotional, physical, and spiritual well-being such that he cannot grow, develop, and prosper as easily as other children do. For example, witnessing the violent murder of a friend shakes the confidence of a young boy in terms of whether he will live past his current age. In addition, having to walk past prostitutes who offer to provide sexual favors to him or a homeless person asking for money while the child is on his way to school demonstrates that the world is not full of success stories. In fact, most of the people he comes in contact with are failures by American standards.

Even the view of drug addicts slumped in doorways and trash in the street contributes to a view of the world as unfair, particularly when the junkies that the boy has to step over to get into his building look like him in terms of race and gender. Combined with the beatings he received from his mother and the teasing that he received from other kids at school, Page along with these adolescents was less likely to be successful in the pursuit of the American Dream. In fact, such an experience is likely to negatively affect the way that a young man views his life chances.

The poverty deprivation syndrome affects children of low and high intelligence, according to See. Young people with low and high motivation levels, and those with big and small physical stature, are affected, too. It is a curse brought on by structural problems in society that have little or nothing to do with the individual child's ability. Such children sometimes end up on death row for heinous crimes that demonstrate the abnormality of the child's experience. And to that cry for help, society responds thusly:

> You did willfully and knowingly be born into poverty. You did conspire to have dysfunctional parents. With malice and forethought you did undermine the effectiveness of your schools. With cunning and guile you did under-fund the housing authority where you reside. You did with purpose and intent allow yourself to be hungry and cold and sexually abused and physically battered. And on one day in your struggle to survive, in the midst of the confusion you know life to be, you did commit a capital offense. We a jury of your "peers," although not having suffered any of these hardships, do hereby find you guilty without mitigation and do sentence you to die by the hands of the state. Next case please.[2]

The defense's closing statement illustrated the affect of the poverty deprivation syndrome on the defendant, Donta Page:

The Court: Now ready for the closing argument for the defendant, Mr. Castle.

Mr. Castle: Thank you, Your Honor.

> It will be a long time, if ever, before any of us will forget the image of Peyton Tuthill in that bedroom, or the image of a six-year-old boy wiping the blood of his body from wounds that his mother inflicted. It will be a long time, perhaps never, before any of us can forget the sounds of Peyton Tuthill's screaming in the last few minutes of her life, or the bleeding of a little boy asking his mother to please leave him alone because he'll never do it again. It will be a long time, perhaps never, before any of us will be able to forget the indignity of the rape of Peyton Tuthill, or the indignity of a ten-year-old boy being raped in the only place he ever felt safe. These are the lasting images of this trial. We can't look at one without thinking about the other. It's been three weeks that we've all been here in this case, and we heard a lot of evidence. And any discussion of the evidence must start with what happened to this young woman. She was a woman that had everything before her. She didn't deserve this in any fashion and nor does her family. The horror is everyone's nightmare. As a parent I can't imagine what her family is going through. And I don't want any of my comments here to in any way suggest that what happened to her is at all excused by anything that we've presented or anything that I say, because there's no excuse for what happened to her in that house. There is none. And we have not attempted to give you one.

Pictures we saw were horrible, but we had to see them to understand exactly what happened in that house and exactly how it happened. We had eighty-one of those pictures in that book that will tell you a story that happened to Ms. Tuthill by Donta Page.

It's my job, however, to also give you some pictures of what happened in his life, because without those pictures we can't understand what happened here. And if you think for one moment that we made this up as suggested a few minutes ago that Mr. Canney and I have made this story up and told Linda Page what to say and how to act in this courtroom then please tune me out right now. But I don't think that any of you believe that, nor anyone in this courtroom does. Donta Page was born to a mother who didn't want him. But that happens on a daily occasion in this country. And once those mothers hold that little baby in their arms they feel motherly love and they bathe their children in love, but not Donta Page. His mother bathed him in resentment and in anger. And when that little baby would cry that was an assault upon her and so she would shake him. And we saw how Linda Page would show us about the shaking. We don't know much about those first two years because the defendant was left with his mother alone, no grandmother around to sometimes intercede or give him a safe haven. But we do know that when the grandmother finally does see how her grandchild was being treated, she sees that the mother of this child, the only parent that he ever knew, would punch him and hit him and not love him or care for him. And that cannot be miss—or understated. Because between the times of the beatings we also have to understand what was not provided to this young boy. And that was any of the things that we know we need to live and survive and to grow and to be good human beings to be part of our society. I remember Juror Williams telling us that—she's not with us in the jury, but I remember her telling us how her grand—her mother who had—they finally found out she had a mental illness, and they were able to look back in her past and be able to point to points in her life and be able to connect the dots to be able to lead up to the mental illness that they finally saw and was diagnosed. And what she said you had to look between those dots to be able to really understand the picture. Folks, I can only give you those dots. But I think all of us know what happened between those dots in the Donta Page's life was probably worse than we were able to get out of Linda Page.

But we do know that by the time he was five or six the punches and the hittings turned to the use of weapons. And that's the only thing that you can call using electrical cords in the violent way that Linda Page [sic] used them, and for five to ten minutes at a time. And if you can get an idea of how long that is, that's how long I've been talking. That's how long a little boy was beaten with a cord or any other object that was close by. He wasn't doing things out of the ordinary. This was done because he wet his pants, or because he didn't get out of the bathtub in time or pick up his toys. Folks, I don't have a picture to show you, but I think in our hearts we know the fear that that child experienced and the horror that he had to live. It's a horror that I can't imagine, no more than I can imagine the horror that happened in that house. But we have to imagine because our goal here is to understand what's going on in Mr. Page's brain, in his thoughts. And we can't ignore the thoughts that a six-year-old child has to have when he's being whipped to the extent that he has to go wipe his own blood off his body.

Next snapshot we have is the first month in first grade when other children are excited about being a big kid. The first time they get to be a big kid. First grade is the time that we learn to read. It's when you learn to write. It's when you learn how to deal with other kids. It's the time that is literally the time that you need to begin your process of growing up. And what happens in the first month of his first grade? His teacher notices not that there is a little problem, but what she titles severe emotional disturbance in a six-year-old child. That's before he was in trouble with the law. It's one of the 19 times professionals, not his family members, professionals said that the defendant Page needed to be checked out.

What also happened in first grade? His teacher notices that his performance isn't up to speed with the other kids. He's testing fine, but his performance isn't good. And so she thinks that he has a learning disability. And folks, learning disability isn't why we're here. But what was the family's reaction to finding out about the learning disability? It was the same reaction that was taken for him wetting his pants or crying too loud or not picking up his toys; he was beaten for it and whipped.

To understand Donta Page's mind you have to understand the terror and the fear that that causes in a little boy. We heard in opening statement that Donta Page's life was a story about his lust for violence and a thirst for evil. I can tell you from the pictures that I saw of his life up to the age of six he lusted for the care of a parent and thirsted for the love that he never got. If that's evil, I miss the mark.

The next picture we have, the next dot that we can find in Donta Page's life was when he's ten years old. And yes, you know, he did have a place that he could go to get away from his mother and her tirades and her demeaning nature of him and her beatings and lack of care. It was the grandmother's house. But at age ten that safe haven was lost when he went there after his mother left to California without him. And at the age of ten, the one safe haven he had was a place where he was raped. And we only have evidence of one rape, that's true, only one, but you have to understand that to understand Donta Page's mind because it's not a thirst for evil. This is a young man who had some major bad things happen to him and there is no way to deny it.

The third part of our trial that dealt with experts. And you know what, I kind of agree with the prosecution, they really didn't tell us anything that we don't know in our hearts and in our souls. And that's that what happened to this kid is why he is here, and it shouldn't have gone the way it did. And maybe he should have been able to overcome the things that happened in his life, but he didn't. Before I talk about the experts I need to say this. Take a look at the shifting sands that have happened in this case. In jury selection it was that abuse is not an excuse. We agree with that. We have always agreed with that. When it came time to confronting Donta Page's grandmother, the sands shifted to Donta Page deserved the abuse. And now the sands shift again to it never happened. In a courtroom we have the duty to bring out the truth between the parties. And you know what, if you're going to accuse Linda Page of lying, do it when she's on the stand. That's what courage is about. That's what honesty is about. And if you're going to come into a courtroom and accuse a woman like Linda Page, do it to her face. We certainly did it with Dr. Martell.

And then the shifting sands about the sexual abuse. Because remember the first time it came up the question was, Well, this doesn't say anything about sexual abuse. But when they found out that GC culture meant gonorrhea culture on the rectum of a ten-year-old boy it then became, "Well, I guess it happened or possibly could happen, but you know, it wasn't that important." It is easy for those who have been given everything in life to discount the horrors that happen to those who have not. I want to talk a little bit about the experts.

First of all, folks, and I don't know if you can see this, I will talk about it anyway. You heard from Dr. Raine. Now Dr. Raine, as opposed to all the other witnesses, this is the second time he ever testified. Second time. He refused pay for his testimony because of the importance of the matter. And his opinion was that Donta Page suffered from brain damage. Now, you know we can pick and choose pieces of what was happening here and try to misrepresent what Dr. Raine's testimony was about, but use your own collective memories. Did he say he saw no artifacts, as just represented, or did he say he saw few. He said I don't know what Dr. Wu was talking about. Lawyers can say things but that's not the evidence. The evidence is what you all heard. Then we heard—and folks, use your own judgment, does anyone here think that Dr. Raine was being elusive or trying to lie to us? I don't think so. Check out his resume. He's a Ph.D. and he spent his life trying to figure out what causes violence. If that doesn't give you the expertise to be able to testify in court, a law degree certainly doesn't. Dr. Opsahl, chief psychologist at Yale Hospital. Why do you bring that up? Do you think he's going to risk his career to testify for a man he never met, Donta Page? I don't think so. He has testified, I think, a dozen times, although it may have been 20. I can't remember exactly. Use your own memory. He doesn't find a lot of impairment. Why do I say that? Because the prosecution just got up and accused the defense of manufacturing a defense in this case, manufacturing abuse and brain impairment. Well, if we did that, we did a darn poor job because we forgot to tell Dr. Opsahl to show a lot of impairment and make up facts in his file. But he did find some impairment. And his clinical opinion, remember he treats people as opposed to Dr. Martell and Dr. Kassover now. He treats people. And his opinion was that he suffered from brain damage. No amount of picking a portion of a document and not showing the rest of it to you can change that opinion.

Then we talk to Dr. Lewis. Once again; I want you to take a look through those resumes because what you will notice is that Dr. Lewis has spent her life trying to find out the causes of violent crime so that we can make the world a better place. And she lectures about that. Not to defense lawyers, but to judges, to DAs, to social workers, to people whose jobs it is to try to make the world a better place. That's what her life is. And no amount of mischaracterizing and picking little facts in someone's life can change it. Look in that record; look in her resume. Testifying is not what her life is about. Her life is trying to make the world a better place. She can't give us an opinion about whether Donta Page deliberated. Once again, the defense in its attempt to manufacture a defense, I guess, has fallen a little short. We forgot to tell her to lie about that. Dr. Pincus, the chief of neurology at Georgetown. Somebody who the chief prosecutor in this entire country goes for help to. That's who the chief prosecutor goes to for help when she had problems. He comes in here and tells us that Donta Page had brain damage. And you know what, once again, if you read one portion of his report to the jury and ignore the final part, you can try to mislead this jury. I ask them right now to read the final part in their final closing of what Dr. Pincus said because that is what his conclusion was. He says, once again, well, he is not a forensic scar expert, but there isn't such a thing folks. And he saw the scars on his back. And I will talk about that later. We offered for them to look at our client. I'm not going to make him take his shirt off and his pants off in front of this jury. That would be the final indignity of this young man. But Dr. Pincus isn't going to risk his entire career and make up scars that didn't exist. And once again, that was the shifting sands in this case. Because I think at one point maybe they weren't all that serious of a scar. Then I think they were recent scars. And now I think they aren't scars. But once again, it doesn't make sense to you that Dr. Pincus is going to risk his career, one that's not based on testifying, it's based on treating people, trying to help people and make the world a better place. Is he going to risk that to be able to say a young man he had never met has scars on his back and has brain damage?

Dr. Johnson. I believe that Dr. Johnson is being honest with us. I think he was trying his hardest. But there's some things that we need to take into consideration looking at Dr. Johnson's testimony. First of all, he believes the defendant Page has an antisocial personality disorder. What is that? That is a psychological term for evil, folks, okay. That's what you want to call it. But they had a big term for it. What it is, he is saying that Dr.—that Donta Page is evil. But also listen to what else Dr. Johnson told us. Dr. Johnson feels that the lower socioeconomic groups, in other words, poor people, have a higher rate of antisocial personality disorder than other people in society. You know what, that's wrong. Poor people aren't any more evil than rich people or middle class. Perhaps the diagnosis is wrong. What else did Dr. Johnson tell us? He didn't even know that you had to rule out head injury before you could come up with this diagnosis. He had to look in the book with Mr. Canney up there. "Oh, I didn't realize that." He's unfamiliar with the new developments in the field of neuroscience, which I can understand because he's been down at the hospital for a while. But the bottom line when you come into court you should be prepared. But even with all that, he still told you on cross-examination that he can't tell you whether Donta Page deliberated. And he said, and I quote, "No one knows what's going on in his head at this time." And that was when he was talking about what happened in that room.

Dr. Kassover was hired in approximately 200 cases in the last ten years, both sides of the equation. Wanted to let us know how much he was fair by telling us he's tickled when he finds more impairment in a person than the other experts had found. He doesn't write. He doesn't do research. He didn't evaluate Donta Page. But still he has no opinion about whether he deliberated. Dr. Mayberg. Once again, I think she's an honest expert. She's trying her best to tell us what she thinks. But folks, if she's objective, listen to the way that she talked. What did she say? She disagrees with Dr. Wu and Dr. Raine and also believes the computer miscalculated significant differences in the wrong place. In other words, she was saying, "Well, the computer thinks that's brain but it's really not brain." Now, folks, think about this for a minute. She is looking at a PET scan. We all know these PET scans; they are not a structural image of brains. It's not structures. We heard that time and time again, probably ad nauseam. What did we hear from the one expert that talked about the structure. Dr. Simon. Dr. Simon said there wasn't any irregularity in the brain. Dr. Mayberg assumes an irregularity where none exists. She also shows us these pictures which are not in evidence that she knows were misleading because they hadn't been warped or whatever it's called, morphing, warping. And once again, she makes—she doesn't look at this kind of image. She uses a different kind of PET scan altogether, and she does it once a week compared to Dr. Wu who does it on a daily basis is wrong. And she makes assumptions about his protocol and his procedure without even trying to find out what they are. But once again, she doesn't give us evidence about whether he deliberated or not. And she refuses, interestingly enough, our offer to do another PET scan, a neurologic exam or a physical exam. And why do I bring that up? You know it's easy to come in and criticize other people's work. Why don't you do it yourself. I mean, at least that's the school I come from. Given an opportunity, do it. And if your PET scan showed it was outside the brain, that the irregularities were there, then come in and tell us the other people are wrong. It's a lot easier to go around the country and find in all the cases that you testify that everybody else is wrong. Every other expert in the country is wrong and you are right without trying it yourself.

And finally we get to Dr. Martell. The star forensic witness in this case, the one that they saved for last. Dr. Martell is a bad person. He lies. Now folks, not being board certified doesn't matter. I don't care too much about that. But going around the country lying about it until you're caught is a sign of dishonesty that can't be tolerated. These things are too important, too important. And it just doesn't stop at that. There was so many things that Dr. Martell has in his history that were brought out that you can't put any stock in this individual. Anybody who would secretly tape record a colleague. I mean, that's disgusting. It's immoral. Even if there were not a specific ethics rule against it. Although I doubt it. But that was their star witness. The doctors, what do they tell us? Can any of them tell us that Donta Page deliberated? Think about what they said. They were very careful. I think he had the capacity to, but they can't give an opinion on whether he did or didn't. These are the people whose job it is to look at that.

I want to talk to you a little bit about the law because we have to. It is pretty confusing. If you think the testimony of the experts was confusing, wait until you read the law. This is my version of where I think things intersect. Folks, not all criminal conduct is committed by people that have any kind of mental illness. In fact, I think it is safe to say that the vast majority has nothing to do with mental illness. And I think the experts talked about that. Mental illness. The vast majority of people with mental illness don't commit crimes. All the experts talked about that. But there are times when they intersect. And what do we do with that? The law starts to look at that and the instructions talk about it. And there's two ways that they talk about it. One is this thing that we call insanity. And insanity is a very specific definition. And what insanity does, if someone is insane the law says they're not responsible. Now, we have told you that Donta Page is responsible for what happened here. So you have to ask yourself why have we been hearing about insanity? Because the law says that before we can talk about anything else about the intersection between mental illness and criminal conduct, it has to be under the umbrella of insanity. Folks, I don't think that exists. We never have. What exists is right here. Folks, you look in the instructions and what it says is if someone has mental illness, whether it is neurologic, psychologic, his background, his life, neuropsychological, if they have that mental illness and it's stopped, and you didn't deliberate, you popped, you exploded. That's what we call insanity that shows no responsibility at all.

But it means that you're guilty but to a different level than those who have that evilness, that lust for violence, that thrust for evil, that makes them different.

Folks, we have one crime in this case that the defense is contending, and that is first-degree murder (after deliberation). "Deliberation," that term is only used in one crime in all the crimes in the books. And it's that one crime of first-degree murder (after deliberation). There are two kinds of first-degree murder. They're both equally important. They're both equally as serious. And they are the worst crimes that anyone can commit under our laws. But first-degree murder (after deliberation) is a little different. And the reason it is, is because what we say is that in order to convict someone of that crime, we have to find something special. What we have to say is that the person killed another human being after they reflected on it and after they used judgment. And although Dr. Martell will tell us that all decisions are use—are through the use of reflection and judgment, that's just not the case, because that's what marks regular first-degree murder from first-degree murder (after deliberation). It has to do with a special quality in an individual. A person who knows what they're doing but also sits there and reflects on it and still says, "Yes, I want to murder." That's what the law says. And it says it rightfully because we have to put those people in a little special class aside from the others. And none of the experts can tell us that Donta Page deliberated in this case. And the reason is, folks, think about it, it's hard for any of us to believe what happened to one human being can do to another. To convict Donta Page of first-degree murder (after deliberation) you have to believe beyond a reasonable doubt that he had that level of evilness in his soul that said that after he thought about it and after he reflected upon it and after he used his judgment that he decided to kill.

Donta Page, contrary to what the prosecution has said from the beginning, is not using abuse as an excuse. He is taking responsibility. He wants—we're asking to be convicted of first-degree murder (felony murder), first degree sexual assault, first-degree burglary, and aggravated robbery. You, as the jury, are the conscience of our community. Our laws decided that we would take 12 people from all walks of life and put them as the conscious of the community in a jury. And your verdict is the voice of the community in this case. And we're asking that you speak loudly about Donta Page's responsibility here through your verdicts. But we're also asking for you to speak loudly about the life in which he was bred. We're asking you to speak loudly that no one deserves abuse. And we're asking you to speak loudly that in a case of this magnitude you shouldn't bring in a witness like Dr. Martell. And most of all, we're asking you to speak loudly about hope instead of anger. Because if we're ever going to stop this cycle of violence it is going to be because we act out of hope and not purely out of anger. And that's a hard thing for us to ask you to do. I'm going to stop now. But before we stop, Mr. Canney is going to read once again to you the letter that none of us knew existed until Dr. Johnson talked to us about it, and those are the words of the defendant Page. Mr. Canney?

Mr. Canney: "Dr. Johnson, I'm sorry but I'm not very good with words. I never felt comfortable with speaking what I feel. Dr. J, I'm just writing to say thank you for not judging me before you got the chance to talk to me. Because no matter what people say that was not me that day. Donta likes to walk in the park, go fishing, watch birds, that type of stuff. I know it sounds crazy, but that's who I am. For whatever reason the Court sent me here, I don't care because I know it won't matter in the end. All they see is a black man that killed a white woman. Nobody took the time to ask why but rather who. I've been asking for help for years. Nobody cares until I hurt someone, then they wanted to give me medicine, but when I went home nothing until I got in trouble again. My lawyer came to see me Friday. I told him I was going to do this. He said it was not a good idea, but I don't care. Dr. Johnson, I don't know what will happen with me, but I know I'm going to jail. I'm sorry for what I did and I have to pay for it. I'm just worried that if the courts spare my life, will they do it again, because what if it happens again I won't get another chance. I mean, my first night here I slept the whole night because I felt I was somewhere that if I zapped out someone knew what was wrong with me and could help. But then I thought about who sent me here and why. In jail nobody is going to care why or help. Dr. Johnson, I don't see what I really have to live for. I have been asking for help for years, nobody cared. I told people about what happens to me. Nobody cared. Not until it happens, then I get the finger pointed at me. People act like they're shocked. What type of life is that? My mother beat the fuck out of me. All my life nobody helped me. No teachers, no doctors, no one. But I'm supposed to take the medication to keep me alive so that they can kill me. I don't think so. If I die it will be better than dying by someone else's hands. I'm twenty-four years old. I never had a chance to live. Now it's over. Thank you, Doctor, for taking the

time to read this. I'm sorry. It's the only way I can say what I was
feeling, Donta Page."

The Court: Thank you, Mr. Castle, Mr. Canney.

A Troubled Youth

In sum, the defense constructed an image of the defendant as a troubled
youth who never got the help that he needed to become a productive citizen. The defense's case focused on presenting credible witnesses that testified
about the existence of brain damage and the affect of that damage on the defendant's behavior. They thwarted attempts to portray the defendant as innately evil with attacks on the stereotypical nature of such characterizations.
They attacked rebuttal witness testimony that suggested that only an in-
significant amount of brain damage existed and replaced it with a portrait of
a young boy who grew up in isolation and terror: the victim of poverty, hate,
child abuse, violence, desperation, and turmoil. To be sure, the defendant
was not always violent. It was only in desperate situations when his violence
erupted, according to the defense. In fact, several witnesses and mental
health evaluations reported that the defendant often cooperated and "just
took it" when other people abused him.

Additionally, the defense approached the defendant during trial and
looked at him with concern when they discussed his situation. The physical
distance between the defendant and the defense attorneys was sometimes
small: they would lean over and put their arm over the defendant's shoulders
to whisper something in his ear during the trial, and they would lean close to
him when he had something to say to them. Such behaviors were predictable
in that the defense attorneys were expected to have a closer relationship with
the defendant than the prosecutors because he was their client, but something about their treatment of him also told the jury that he was a human being with feelings and emotions who deserved to be informed about what was
going on in the courtroom. He was not untouchable either—someone who
could infect people with a murder virus if physical contact with him was
made, for example. The defense attorneys treated the defendant humanely,
which demonstrated their compassion for him and his predicament. In addition, their humane treatment demonstrated their willingness to fight hard to
convey their compassion for him to the jury.

The Importance of Images to the Verdict

From the data available, then, it appears as though both the prosecution and
defense of a capital defendant depends entirely upon the case presented by

lawyers: what they say and do—including eliciting testimony from witnesses—is all that the jurors have to rely on in making their decision. Information that jurors and judges gather outside of the courtroom is not supposed
to be considered. That places an enormous burden on the attorneys to perform well. That is, if either side fails to present facts that can persuade a jury
or panel of judges that their view of the defendant and the crime is true, they
will lose the case.

But, through no fault of their own, the jury may simply decide to believe
one version of events or decide to tune out certain evidence whether it is important or not. To be sure, there were times during the *Page* trial when jurors
were sleeping, daydreaming, grooming themselves, or doodling in the notebooks that the court had given to them. I observed such behaviors frequently.
Juries are comprised of people, in other words. Their personalities, tempera-
ments, prejudices, beliefs, and values simply convene in a room to deliberate
about the actions of the defendant when the case presented by attorneys is
turned over to them. As such, there is much room for error. It may be that
the most cost-efficient, convenient, or normal case wins at trial. That is, it
may be that the prosecutor has an easier time convincing a jury that the defendant is guilty when the defendant confesses, his DNA is found at the
crime scene, and the defendant has a prior record of violent criminality. During such cases, the jury may sleep more often, listen less attentively, and take
fewer notes, for example, because the outcome appears inevitable. But it is
precisely at such times when the images of capital defendants are related to
the verdict: they may, in fact, predetermine the outcome. For that reason, the
data above can be discussed in light of several relationships: specifically, how
might the images presented by attorneys be related to the verdict that the
jury renders?

An Even Playing Field

Some literature suggests that an adversarial imbalance abides between prosecutors and defense attorneys in that district attorneys have many more resources available to them during investigation and preparation for trial than
defense attorneys. As a result, district attorneys are able to hire more expert
witnesses, pay for more travel, do more investigation, pay for more assistance
with administrative tasks, and prepare better props or exhibits.

District attorneys make the decision as to whether to seek an indictment
for capital murder, which means that they are able to carefully weigh the eco-
nomics of the decision to indict before actually filing the motion. District attorneys oftentimes have full-time, paid investigators on staff with their office,
which means that they do not have to take the time and energy to indepen-

dently hire them as defense attorneys do. And district attorneys oftentimes have the full cooperation of police personnel and other law enforcement officials (correctional officers, marshals, sheriffs, and so forth) who work for the state and share the same interest in obtaining convictions as the district attorneys do. For that reason, law enforcement officials may be less cooperative with defense attorneys in preparing their cases, and, as seen in the current case, their appearances on the stand for the defense may come across as hostile or non-responsive. Such hostility may give the impression that the law enforcement officials have already convicted the defendant and the jury may be persuaded to go along with that conclusion because they put faith and confidence in the judgment of law enforcement officials who work with criminals every day.[3]

These circumstances place district attorneys in an advantageous position over defense attorneys at trial because if their cases are better prepared, if their witnesses are less hostile and more credible, and if their props are more interesting, jury members may side with district attorneys because of their showmanship rather than because of the accuracy or rationality of their case. An adversarial imbalance, then, contributes to the overall impression jurors get of the accuracy of the image being constructed by the set of attorneys with the advantage, usually the district attorney.

This is not an independent observation, but rather a well-documented fact. The cost of an indictment for capital murder can be enormous.[4] Thus, a death penalty case that goes forward has already been allotted a certain amount of money for the prosecutors who are assigned to the case, whereas the defense attorneys, who are oftentimes public defenders, are not privy to such allotments.

The cost of hiring expert witnesses like psychiatrists, medical examiners, and forensic scientists (who are sometimes paid $500 per hour or $1,000 per day to testify), for example, can also be enormous as well as the travel expenses for those experts and lay witnesses like family members and friends. "Altogether, defense expert witnesses alone can easily cost more than $40,000 in capital cases."[5] Certainly, defense attorneys are limited in their ability to pay those fees and travel expenses when capital defendants go to trial and while prosecutors are oftentimes also limited, defense attorneys who are public defenders are more often limited than prosecutors because of the economics. More witnesses are usually called in capital cases than in non-capital cases, too.[6]

Public defenders are expensive. In North Carolina, for example, in 1991–1992, the average cost of a public defender was $42,000 per case and in Maryland in 1982, the average cost of defense counsel was estimated to range from $50,000 to $75,000 per capital case.[7] Coupled with all of the salaries of court personnel who are involved in a capital case (judges, court reporters, deputy court clerks, bailiffs, and so forth), the cost of a capital trial can mount quickly. In fact, "court costs are estimated to be 3.5 times greater in capital cases than they are in other felony cases."[8] These factors, however, are weighed prior to the district attorney's decision to seek an indictment for capital murder. Defense attorneys who are hired to defend a capital defendant do not have the luxury of predetermining the cost and deciding whether to participate in the case, particularly if they work for the public defender's office.

Even though the right to counsel was guaranteed in *Gideon v. Wainwright*[9] that decision in no way guaranteed the right to good counsel, not even in capital trials.[10] To be sure, the Supreme Court of the United States has revisited the issue of competent counsel numerous times since the 1932 *Scottsboro* decision, which held that capital defendants have a right to court-appointed counsel in state court. But the *Burdine v. Texas* (1995)[11] decision was upheld by the Supreme Court declaring that an attorney who only spoke nine words during the penalty phase of the trial, failed to present evidence of the defendant's mental illness, and waived closing argument during the penalty phase of his capital trial did *not* render him ineffective. As such, it is clear not only that the competence of attorneys is important to the outcome of a capital trial, but that ineffective assistance of counsel is extremely difficult to prove.

In the current case, both sets of attorneys seemed extremely competent, and though the defense attorneys were court-appointed, they were able to mount a defense that was rumored to have cost over $1 million by the end of the penalty phase. Randy Canney and Jim Castle engaged several additional attorneys (including one of their wives), one paralegal, two investigators, and several administrative assistants in preparation for trial. They employed nine expert witnesses and paid the travel expenses of five lay witnesses to appear on the defendant's behalf. At no time during the trial did they appear sleepy, lazy, inattentive, or confused. In fact, their performance was spectacular compared to the lackluster enthusiasm of the district attorneys, Philip Brimmer and Henry Cooper (who began the trial with a full confession, DNA evidence, and a prior felony record on the defendant). In the current case, then, it seems an adversarial balance was maintained.

Fear of the Defendant versus Fear of Those We Think Are Similar to Him
It is difficult to prove that a person is using stereotypes to make decisions about people. But it is important to acknowledge that stereotypes exist and that they play a crucial role in determining what people believe about other

people. Some literature has suggested that stereotypes are easy ways to cate-gorize people so that the brain can be freed up to think about other things.[12] Further, this research suggests that stereotypes are so deeply embedded in the human psyche that we do not even know when we are using them to make character evaluations, unless and until it is specifically brought to our atten-tion.[13] In the current case, then, how do we know that the jury did not con-vict the defendant based more on the fact that he is a black man with a prior criminal record than because of the confession he gave to the crime? How do we know that if the defendant had not confessed, and if no evidence of the defendant's prior record or of the defendant's DNA had been introduced, that the jury would not have looked across the room at him and decided that he was a future danger to society anyway? There is no way to know. But it is clear that with regard to jury decision-making, mistakes happen. At this writ-ing, 210 prison inmates have been exonerated of the crimes for which they were sentenced to incarceration and released from prison—all of the exon-erations were procured with DNA evidence.[14] Juries convicted those people. And, apparently, the evidence presented at trial was overwhelming, that is, beyond a reasonable doubt, which is the standard of judgment in capital cases. How many of those 210 jury decisions were based on stereotypes?

In the current case, one stereotype of violent criminality was affirmed: the defendant, a black man, raped and murdered a white woman. He confessed to the crime and he had a prior record of violent criminality, which helped the jury decide to convict him. But that is not always the case. In some cases, circumstantial evidence is used to connect a capital defendant with a crime. Eyewitness testimony, including identification of suspects, for example, is of-tentimes relied upon to convict capital defendants. Such witnesses may later recant their testimony, but such recantation has not always resulted in re-versals of conviction. Acknowledgement of the existence of stereotypes, as suggested by Jody Armour,[15] may help reduce the effects of stereotypes on jury decision-making because, if there is no way to tell that stereotypes in-deed play a role in jury decisions, there is also no way to tell if they don't.

Since jury deliberations require thought, oftentimes led by commonsensi-cal evaluations, such deliberations are subject to stereotype-driven conclu-sions. The images constructed by attorneys of a capital defendant are clearly meant to appeal to the jury's common sense or at least to what they already know about human beings and their behavior: there are no classes offered to potential jurors before the trial starts to teach them about human behavior from a sociological or psychological perspective. For that reason, jurors are virtually *required* to use the knowledge they already possess of human beings and behavior to reach a verdict. If stereotypes are defined as *conventional*, *highly simplified, and often negative ways of looking at groups of people and their behavior*,[16] jury deliberations may simply involve the comparison of the stereotypes of one juror with the stereotypes of 11 other jurors until a consensus about the appropriate stereotype to apply is reached, particularly if physical evidence that links the defendant to the crime is lacking.

Reducing Uncertainty: Questioning Guided Discretion

Guided discretion does not work.[17] Juries continue to allow prior-record evidence and their views about the future dangerousness of a defendant, among other irrelevant details, to affect their verdicts. They also continue to make premature decisions about guilt, sometimes even before all of the evidence has been presented at trial.[18] As a result, mistakes in jury verdicts are being uncovered. Guided discretion statutes, which are suppose to rid the capital trial process of arbitrariness and capriciousness in death sentencing, have failed to dissuade jurors from doing what they want to do with a capital defendant. After all, no one supervises their deliberations to make sure that they apply their discretion appropriately. The images constructed of a capital defendant at trial include statements or implied references to his character, the likelihood of his rehabilitation, and his worth to society, particularly during the penalty phase. If the image that the judges believe suggests that the defendant has an evil disposition and that he is, therefore, worthless to society, execution can be viewed as an appropriate punishment. On the other hand, if the defendant's life can be viewed in some way as valuable and worthy of rehabilitative effort, incarceration may result. Either way, the images portrayed of the defendant bring together a number of character evaluations of the defendant that render him either worthy of mercy or death. These images are constructed by attorneys at trial who argue that aggravators or mitigators exist to a lesser or greater degree.

In the current case, the prosecutors argued that the crime was committed heinously, deliberately, and for pecuniary gain. They constructed the image of a cold-blooded, selfish killer to prove that the aggravators existed. They raised issues about the defendant's willingness to be changed or rehabilitated by claiming that he ignored previous opportunities that had been presented to him for rehabilitation. They introduced evidence of previous bad behavior in prison to show that the defendant was incorrigible and not able to be controlled in prison. They talked about how the defendant enjoyed his lifestyle and had no desire to change even though opportunities to change had been made available to him. Such characterizations were offered to show that the defendant is worthless and unworthy of mercy, and that the state would be wasting its money to keep him alive in prison.

The defense attorneys, however, offered a different point of view. They showed the defendant to be a good, but not perfect, candidate for prison because he had done well in prison before; that is, he held a job, earned the privilege of serving on inmate council, took G.E.D. classes, and received no disciplinary actions for several long periods of time, for example. They showed the defendant to have been the victim of circumstance rather than just a performer of rational choice. That is, the defendant was driven by desperation, confusion, and fear to commit the crime of murder, not just recently but also from the beginning of his involvement with crime.

Guided discretion statutes require that such aggravators and mitigators be incorporated into jurors' and judges' deliberations to prevent arbitrariness and capriciousness in death sentencing. But the image of the defendant that the jury and judges believe is the view of the defendant that will determine the verdict and punishment. Apparently, there is no room for both views of the defendant to be combined: jurors and judges are required to choose one or the other. The image presented by the most credible attorneys or the most articulate attorneys or the set of attorneys with the most interesting props, for example, could be the image that the jury decides to accept. Guided discretion statutes do not supervise the deliberations of juries to insure that they are not persuaded by irrelevant factors. Instead, guided discretion is simply offered to them in hopes that they will remember and heed the advice of the legislature.

Notes

1. Charles R. See, "The Poverty Deprivation Syndrome" in *African-American Perspectives on Crime Causation, Criminal Justice Administration and Crime Prevention*, ed. Anne T. Sulton (Englewood, CO; Sulton Books, 1994).

2. See, "The Poverty," 183.

3. See Frank Schmalleger, *Trial of the Century: People of the State of California v. Orenthal James Simpson* (Upper Saddle River, NJ: Prentice Hall, 1996).

4. James R. Acker, Robert M. Bohm, and Charles S. Lanier, *America's Experiment with Capital Punishment: Reflections on the Past, Present, and Future of the Ultimate Penal Sanction*, (Durham, NC: Carolina Academic Press, 1998), 441.

5. Acker et al., *America's Experiment*, 442.

6. Acker, et al., *America's Experiment*, 445.

7. Acker, et al., *America's Experiment*, 444.

8. Acker, et al., *America's Experiment*, 445.

9. *Gideon v. Wainwright*, 372 U.S. 335 (1963).

10. Michael Mello and Paul J. Perkins, "Closing the Circle: The Illusion of Lawyers for People Litigating for Their Lives at the *Fin de Siecle*," in *America's Experiment with Capital Punishment*, ed. James Acker, Robert Bohm, and Charles Lanier (Durham, NC: Carolina Academic Press, 1998), 262.

11. *Burdine v. Texas* 719 S.W.2d 309 (Tex. Crim. App. 1986).

12. Nancy Cantor and Walter Mischel, "Prototypes in Person Perception," *Advances in Experimental Social Psychology* 12(1979): 3–4; Richard E. Nisbett, "The Dilution Effect: Nondiagnostic Information Weakens the Implications of Diagnostic Information," *Cognitive Psychology* 13(1981): 248–272; J. Frank Yates, *Judgment and Decision Making* (Englewood Cliffs, NJ: Prentice Hall, 1990).

13. Jody Armour, "Stereotypes and Prejudice: Helping Legal Decision-Makers Break the Prejudice Habit," *California Law Review* 83(1995): 733–772.

14. Information available on the Innocence Project website: www.innocenceproject.org

15. Armour, "Stereotypes," 733–772.

16. Allan G. Johnson, *The Blackwell Dictionary of Sociology: A User's Guide to Sociological Language* (Cambridge: Blackwell, 1995)

17. John H. Blume, Stephen Garvey, and Sheri Johnson, "Future Dangerousness in Capital Cases: Always at Issue." *Cornell Law Review* 86(2001): 404–410; William J. Bowers, "The Capital Jury Project: Rationale, Design, and Preview of Early Findings," *Indiana Law Journal* 70(1995): 1043–1102; Marla Sandys "Cross Overs—Capital Jurors Who Change Their Minds about Punishment: A Litmus Test for Sentencing Guidelines," *Indiana Law Journal* 70(1995): 1183–1221.

18. William J. Bowers, Marla Sandys, and Benjamin D. Steiner, "Foreclosed Impartiality in Capital Sentencing: Jurors' Predispositions, Guilt-Trial Experience, and Premature Decision-Making," *Cornell Law Review* 83(1998): 1476–1556; Craig Haney, "Taking Capital Jurors Seriously," *Indiana Law Journal* 70(1995): 1223–1232; Marla Sandys "Cross Overs—Capital Jurors Who Change their Minds About Punishment: A Litmus Test for Sentencing Guidelines" *Indiana Law Journal* 70(1995): 1183–1221.

~

CHAPTER EIGHT

The Impact on Jurors

In the end, we decided that he did . . . not with intent, but he did . . . he knew what he was doing. It was difficult and it wasn't right to kill in the instructions and we argued around quite a bit.

The Impact on Jurors

Interviews

Interviews with jurors in the *Colorado v. Page* case were conducted by the researcher in April of 2002. Two of the jurors agreed to be interviewed and the conversations were tape-recorded and transcribed. Supplemental information on what the jurors discussed and their opinions about the case is provided with interviews with six jurors that were conducted by the other investigators for the defense in November 2000, shortly after the guilty verdict in the case was announced. The interviews by the defense team were short. Some of them were done in person while others were conducted over the phone. The details of each conversation were provided to the defense attorneys in preparation for the penalty phase of the trial. Overall, interviews with eight jurors of varying detail were available for inclusion in this study (two conducted by this researcher and six by the defense team).

Several issues were raised with the juror interviews that were able to be investigated with the combined data set. It became clear, from the review of the interview reports, that (1) the jurors did not agree on the verdict or the sentence, at first, and that some degree of pressure was applied to jurors who tried to hold out against the guilty of first-degree murder verdict, (2) the jurors misunderstood some of the instructions and some of the evidence that were presented at trial, (3) the jurors used their own personal experiences and understanding of how human beings behave to draw conclusions about the defendant, (4) the jurors were glad that they did not have to sentence the defendant although some of them voiced opinions about the sentence that the judges ultimately rendered, (5) all of the participants in the trial (prosecutors, defense attorneys, judge, and victim) were viewed positively except the defendant, and (6) most of the jurors believed that justice was served by the life sentence in the *Page* case. Two of the interviews were conducted after the life sentence was announced.

Pressure

Jury deliberations are often influenced by factors that are not supposed to be part of the decisions the jury makes, that is, stereotypes,[1] pretrial publicity in the media,[2] confusion over instructions and expert witness testimony,[3] and lawyer performances,[4] among others. Little attention has been paid, however, to the influence of peer pressure on jury deliberations, that is, the influence that strong-willed jurors wield over weaker-willed jurors in the jury room. Interviews with jurors in the *Page* case revealed that some pressure was applied to "hold-out" jurors at various points during their deliberations. The pressure may have influenced the overall verdict, particularly the distinction they made between first- and second-degree murder.

Several jurors mentioned that the jury vote was split when the jury first went into the jury room to deliberate following the presentation of evidence. One juror suggested that the split was four to eight (with four against the first-degree murder conviction and in favor of second-degree), while another juror insisted that only two jurors were undecided as to the defendant's guilt on the first-degree murder charge. Both of the jurors admitted that the "holdout" jurors were pressured into changing their votes by the other jurors. When asked why pressure was applied to the "holdout" jurors, one juror said:

> They seemed to me . . . we found him guilty on the last three . . . in 15 minutes. And they kind of got off on why weren't there any fingerprints taken in her car? 'Cause they knew he did it! This was totally irrelevant, I thought. The jury foreman really had to keep people in line as to what was going on. Not that he didn't do it, they were trying to hash up some other little things.

And another juror said:

Then there was one lady who just my impression would be for religious reasons stood out very strongly right to the end and now I feel uncertain on guilt because I feel like she was sort of pushed into finally making it unanimous. There were clearly people who wanted to get it over and leave the courtroom and so forth.

With regard to pressure about the sentencing decision, one juror stated that the jury discussed the sentence during their deliberations about guilt. This was an issue that they were told not to discuss because that decision was supposed to be left up to the panel of judges. Nevertheless, when asked whether the jurors talked about whether or not the defendant would or should get the death penalty, one juror said:

I think some of the jurors wanted to really bad, but the point being, sane or insane, guilty or not guilty . . . and the judges would make this decision . . . there were three that were kind of holding out because they were afraid to say guilty really bad but see it wasn't up to us and that was good that we didn't have to dwell on that.

It appears, then, that pressure was applied to several jury members at several crucial points during their deliberations, particularly with regard to whether the defendant should be convicted of first-degree or second-degree murder (which would then determine whether the death penalty could be applied). Pressure placed on jurors to decide one way instead of another is unavoidable because it is difficult to get twelve people to agree on anything. In fact, judges routinely send jurors who have reached an impasse back into the jury room to try harder to reach a verdict. It is not surprising then that, to some extent, jurors' personalities played a role in determining the verdict in the current case because at least two jurors seemed pressured into voting with the majority of the jury members.

A strong-willed person such as the one holdout juror in the movie *Twelve Angry Men* may be able to persuade the majority of jurors to go along with her or him, in other words, but only after many hours of deliberation where people's lives and beliefs and values are unmercifully challenged.

Comprehension Issues

The Relationship between Child Abuse and Later Violence
It was clear from the review of the trial transcript that several jurors were confused as to what the expert witnesses had stated in their opinion of the defendant. For example, one juror said that Dr. Johnson, from the Colorado

State Hospital, "said that he didn't think Donta's childhood had any affect on how Donta behaved as an adult" even though Dr. Johnson was never asked about his opinion on the relationship between child abuse and later violence. Instead, Dr. Johnson's testimony was limited to the defendant's behavior at the hospital during evaluation, and the defendant's current mental state, specifically whether the defendant is insane. As such, it is clear that the juror who thought Dr. Johnson stated an opinion on the defendant's childhood and his behavior had either misunderstood Dr. Johnson's testimony, confused the doctors who testified at trial, or simply didn't remember which doctor she thought expressed that opinion.

To be fair, the juror recalled Dr. Johnson's testimony twenty-nine months after the testimony was offered in court. But review of the trial transcript indicates that *none* of the doctors who testified either for the defense or the prosecution stated that the defendant's abuse did not relate to his adult behavior. At best, one of the doctors who testified for the prosecution, Dr. Mayberg, said that she disagreed with the defense's experts who said that the defendant had frontal lobe damage to his brain. The defense's experts had run PET scans on the defendant's brain and enlarged, colorful props of the results of those scans were entered into evidence and shown to the jury. Dr. Mayberg, who testified for the prosecution said:

Prosecutor:	Dr. Mayberg, Dr. Raine testified that that video shows some abnormalities, or at least some reduced glucose metabolism in the orbital frontal area of Mr. Page's brain. Do you agree with Dr. Raine's conclusion on that score?
Dr. Mayberg:	I don't agree with his conclusion, no.
Prosecutor:	Could you explain to the jury why not?
Dr. Mayberg:	Well, I looked at the video this morning and saw the brain, not nine slices, but actually the original thirty slices stacked on top of each other in the computer. And then what the computer does it renders it into a three-dimensional object. So slices turned into a 3-D picture, which I saw, and I guess you saw. What one sees is that the most inferior part of the frontal lobe in the front, and not just the most extreme, but the relatively lower part is green on the video. Whereas on the normal controls it's more in the orange to amber color. And so when one looks at the spinning brain, you would say, I see a lot of green in the inferior part of the frontal lobe, and I see brighter color on the normals. And you can see it from all orientations. And it tips up and I appreciated that. The other thing I saw on the video was that actually Mr. Page's brain in the rest of the brain

was considerably brighter, so more red than was the normal controls. Now, I looked at that and said, well, you know, I've been looking at nine slices and the statistics, how can I reconcile the fact that the spinning brain actually looks like these areas of green . . . so I was trying to figure out why does it look one way when the statistics are telling me that the brain is not different because that's disconnected. When I looked at the scale that is on the video, the color scale, the color scale on the video is actually different than the color scale that's being presented on these sheets. So that what your eye is drawn to and what color it will be will change as a function of how you do the display. So there is a certain—it makes it look more abnormal than it is . . . so my conclusion is that, yes, I see a difference between Mr. Page and the normal control group in the three dimensional brain, but that it's—I'm being fooled as to how significant it is.

Later, the defense cross-examined Dr. Mayberg and established that she was not, in fact, offering an opinion as to whether the defendant had brain damage, but rather commenting on the opinion that the defense's experts had given:

Defense: Now, Doctor, you are not giving an opinion in this case as to whether Mr. Page has frontal lobe damage, are you?

Dr. Mayberg: No, I'm not.

Defense: And the reason you are not is because you didn't do anything to be able to make that opinion. You didn't do a physical exam. You didn't do a neurologic exam. You didn't do anything of that nature?

Dr. Mayberg: That is true. But I would put it a different way. I don't have an opinion as to a diagnosis. I've reviewed the medical records and I've reviewed the examinations done by your experts and other exams. And I have an opinion about whether or not there is evidence in the record that reflects that. But I don't have a diagnosis for Mr. Page; that is absolutely correct.

Defense: So your opinion is about their opinion?

Dr. Mayberg: My opinion is as a neurologist that studies behavior as to what is in the medical record from approximately age five through now, combined with what are the claims by the other experts as to how a storyline is put together as to whether or not a PET scan supports the fact that there is evidence of remote head injury that explains the circumstances of this case.

Two other doctors who testified for the prosecution, Dr. Jack Simon and Dr. Kenneth Kassover, said that they did not find evidence of frontal lobe brain damage in the defendant's PET scans and other neurological exams, but the prosecution never offered evidence during the guilt phase of the trial that the relationship between child abuse and later violence did not exist.

Interestingly, one investigator report of a juror interview stated that

> They all waited for one of our [the defense] experts to concretely state that Donta had a defect. The jurors didn't think any of the experts did. They thought Dr. Pincus was really credible but he didn't come out and say that Donta had something specific wrong with his brain.

But close inspection of the testimony of Dr. Dorothy Otnow-Lewis and Dr. Johnathan Pincus (see chapter 4) reveals that they both stated that "his function deteriorated rapidly" and that his "capacity to conform his behavior was impaired due to frontal lobe disease that the PET scan showed," respectively. Also, Dr. Opsahl said, "He certainly suffers from brain damage" (see chapter 7). It is unreasonable to assume that the jurors would remember each and every statement uttered by the defense's experts, but this juror suggested that *none* of the jurors recalled these statements. These experts were quite adamant in their pronouncements about the defendant's brain damage, not only because they stated that the brain damage existed, but also because they reiterated how the brain damage influenced his behavior.

Jury Instructions
Some of the *Page* jurors said that they fully understood the judge's instructions to the jury. Others did not. Two jurors stated that the instructions were confusing, specifically with regard to the definition of "deliberation." One investigator reported that

> She had a very difficult time with this decision. She struggled with "deliberate" and "intent." She didn't think Donta's actions were deliberate or intentional. She said she had a difficult time fitting the brain injury information into the instructions on sanity and mental state. The day before the verdict came in everybody had made his or her decision. They were waiting for her. She said she spent the day reading through the definitions and they didn't fit. She had a hard time understanding "reckless"—an act that is done deliberately and is not impulsive. She said she knew he didn't intend to kill Ms. Tuthill. She said she was holding out for "reckless." She finally changed her mind because the other jurors kept asking her why he would try to wash his clothes and clean up and she couldn't explain that.

Another juror said:

> We did get confused . . . because some of this stuff is confusing [referring to and
> reading from the judge's instructions packet that she was allowed to take home]
> . . . [such as] "He contends that because of mental illness and brain damage he
> could not form the culpable mental state developed in deliberation and in-
> tent." In the end, we decided that he did . . . not with intent, but he did . . .
> he knew what he was doing. It was difficult and it wasn't right to kill in the in-
> structions and we argued around quite a bit.

The same juror later commented that

> I really liked everybody, but the girl who was the chairman didn't have very
> much education. I don't think she understood totally what she was reading in
> the thing [gesturing to the instructions from which she had just read] and I'm
> not sure any of us fully understood.

The judge's instructions to the jury were supposed to explain the jury's
tasks and to clarify specific issues of law that they were expected to address
in their deliberations, including legal definitions. For that reason, comprehension of the instructions was required. These two jurors did not understand
some of the basic definitions that were being applied to the defendant's actions, an important aspect of the guilt decision. Not only did one of the jurors express that she felt pressured by the lack of clarity in the instructions,
but the other juror actually stated that she didn't think the other jurors or
the foreman fully understood the instructions either. These misunderstand-
ings alone could have influenced the jurors' decision on whether to convict
the defendant of capital murder, even if the physical evidence against the defendant had not been so clear and convincing.

In a capital case, "deliberation" and "intent" define the difference between first-degree and second-degree murder. Most capital juries do not have
DNA evidence and a taped confession to rely on when making decisions. Instead, jurors rely on expert and lay witness testimony and the judge's instructions to reach a verdict, particularly on the motive for the crime. Under
these circumstances, with the same types of comprehension errors, controversial capital convictions are likely to occur, that is, convictions where the
defendant's motive for the crime could be interpreted in two ways: in favor
of or against the defendant. Since motive is not usually established with
physical evidence, but rather with the opinions of experts and witnesses on
what they believe the defendant's motive to have been, jurors are likely to
form opinions about the defendant's motive based on personal beliefs about

the defendant and the experts that are called to testify about the same. Judges instructions that direct jurors to make their own decisions about the credibility and/or believability of witnesses all but ensure that stereotypes, familiarity, status, appearance, demeanor, and class will factor into the equation they use to assess credibility and/or believability.

Life without Parole
Some of the jurors expressed confusion over whether life imprisonment without the possibility of parole actually meant that the defendant would be incarcerated until the end of his life. A first-degree murder conviction allowed the defendant to be sentenced to death while a second-degree murder conviction allowed the defendant to receive life without the possibility of parole. The jury was not supposed to consider the sentence of the defendant in the *Page* case, though. Their only task was to decide whether to convict the defendant of first- or second-degree murder. Nonetheless, in Colorado, there is truth in sentencing, which means that the defendant would never be released from prison. That fact was never made clear to the jury. In fact, one investigator reported:

> She did say they talked about the sentence even though the judge said they weren't supposed to. Some of the jurors were concerned that Donta would get out at some point if they didn't find him guilty of first-degree murder. She said she knew he would be in jail for life.

And another juror interview revealed that

> Ms. _____ did understand that Donta would either be in the state hospital or prison for the rest of his life. She said she thought most of the jurors understood that. She said that Ms. _____ didn't understand that. Ms. _____ kept asking what would happen if he got out and did it again.

Another investigator reported that one of the jurors, after mentioning that she understood that life imprisonment without the possibility of parole meant that he would never get out of prison, expressed fear at the thought of him being free: "She does understand that a life sentence means that Donta wouldn't get out yet she made the comment that it would scare her if Donta were out." Moreover, a fourth juror made a distinction between life without parole in prison and in a mental institution: "I think we felt that if he had gone to a mental institution, he might have gotten out and that he would be a danger." The same juror also said "somehow we understood that it would be life plus *x* amount of years for some of the other offenses. So we felt it would be life."

A fifth juror, when asked whether jurors talked about how long the defendant would actually serve in prison if he did not get the death penalty, said: "I'm not sure we did. But I don't like that phrase . . . life without parole . . . I don't like it because I seem to keep reading in the paper that they got out before the time was up."

It appears, then, that there was some confusion over the sentence that may have affected conviction. Even though some of the jurors said that they understood what the sentence would be if he did not get the death penalty, their responses in interviews seemed to reveal otherwise, that is, that at least two of the jurors doubted that the defendant would actually die in prison. Perhaps this weighed into their decision about guilt because even with a second-degree guilty verdict, the defendant, in fact, was never going to be set free. The defense attorneys attempted to plea bargain with the prosecutors for a sentence of no less than life without the possibility of parole, and, it seems, that all of the participants, except the jury, were clear that life without parole means life without parole in the state of Colorado.

How the *Page* Jury Decided

The juror interviews also revealed that some of the *Page* jurors developed their own formula for deciding whether a first- or second-degree murder conviction was appropriate in the case, which seems appropriate given the fact that "deliberation" and "intent" (the deciding factors) are not usually established with physical evidence. The jury instructions allowed the jurors to determine the credibility of witnesses, but the instructions did not go so far as to say that the jury could simply dismiss entire portions of the defense's case because their experiences in life were different from what was being portrayed. Not only did some of the jurors openly and honestly assert that they paid no attention to the brain injury evidence and some of the doctors that were called to testify, but they also boldly stated that they knew people who suffered from the same types of problems that the defendant had (child abuse and neglect), but that since the people they knew had never committed crimes, the defendant was not excused.

> She then went into a long talk about being raised in a family of 12 children and not one of them steals or commits crimes. She said she was taught to work for what you want and, if you don't have the money for what you want, you do without. Ms. _____ said she is still going to school as is [sic] some of her brothers in order to better themselves and that Donta was given a second chance by being sent to Colorado. She said Donta was given the opportunity to start over

in Colorado, but he chose to take the wrong path and committed a horrible crime. He has to pay for the crime he committed.

Clearly, this juror applied her own upbringing to the case. She assumed that every person is raised with the same values that she was raised with and that when someone does something bad or wrong, that it is due to the fact that they made a rational choice to do it. This is the same argument that the prosecution used to portray the defendant as a willful murderer and incorrigible deviant—someone who simply chooses to break the law and deserves to be punished. It is perfectly reasonable for jurors to draw such conclusions about human behavior, too, because the law does not say that they cannot make character evaluations throughout the course of the trial and during jury deliberations. In fact, the entire purpose of trials seems to be for the jury to ultimately decide what to do with the defendant after listening to and evaluating the physical and sometimes anecdotal evidence provided.

Another juror claimed to have announced to the court during voir dire that she would not listen to any doctors during the trial: "She said she also told everyone she does not believe psychiatrists or psychologists and would not consider their testimony." Consequently, she may have dismissed the defense's entire case—most of it was presented by psychologists and psychiatrists who were called to testify about the defendant's brain damage and how it affected his judgment and behavior. Certainly, the lack of attention paid to 75 percent of one side's case resulted in a winning verdict for the other side in that juror's mind. The question becomes, then, why does the court allow evidence of a certain kind to be presented, but then also allow jurors to ignore it if they wish? To be sure, the judge cannot *make* the juror listen to and consider the testimony. Perhaps steps could be taken during jury selection to ensure that qualified jurors are willing to listen to and consider *all* of the evidence presented at trial, particularly experts who have been accepted by the court as an expert in some relevant field. It seems that the defense would not have had a chance from the beginning if jurors were not going to listen to the evidence they presented. It may not seem fair, but it is legal.

Still another juror, when asked about the prosecution's case, said that they did an excellent job but that she was "leery about the PET scans because I've been in the hospital for epilepsy and I know what they actually use them for. I didn't see the relevance of the different colors . . . especially since that guy said he had the same kind of scan as that murderer did" (referring to one of the prosecution's experts who testified that a PET scan is merely a composite of normal brains compared with the brain image of the defendant). The doctor showed a PET scan of his own brain in comparison to a composite of forty-one murderers' brains and his own scan looked similar to the murderers' brains. That same juror commented that there was so much brain evidence offered during the trial that it became boring: "It was almost like . . . in the jury room we'd call 'em *BRAIN* days . . . we knew it was going to be all of these PET scans and psychological . . . oh another long brain day."

As such, it is clear that this juror also, from personal experience, did not believe the testimony of some of the experts. Instead, she formed her own opinion on the issue of brain damage based on how she herself had been treated and what she had been told about her own brain. Again, it may not seem fair because her experience and her brain are not sufficient information on which to base conclusions about the defendant, but it is legal. The doctors stated that everyone's brain is different and most of them talked about specific differences in brains in general (including the contour, functioning, and position of the brain) that can make people act differently. Jurors who did not, for whatever reason, take into account the nuances of what the doctors said about most brains during the trial clearly missed the point of their testimony—to show that some brain differences influence behavior more than others.

To be fair, there was overwhelming physical evidence of the defendant's guilt, including a taped confession, DNA evidence drawn from his saliva and semen, fingerprints, shoe prints, and clothing found at the scene of the crime that pointed to his guilt. In fact, one juror stated that "the prosecution didn't have to come up with much . . . kind of interviewed the neuropsychologists later. They really didn't have to show much. They had the taped confession." Thus, the *Page* case was never about establishing guilt, but rather about establishing the *degree* of guilt, that is, first or second degree.

Most capital cases, however, do not have overwhelming physical evidence that ties the capital defendant to the crime. In the absence of a taped confession, with jurors using their own personal experience with people and doctors, and with jurors refusing to consider the testimony of experts during evidence portions of the trial, what chance does a capital defendant have? When asked about the defense's case, one juror said: "I think they tried to prove that he was mentally incapable of understanding what he was doing and brain damaged . . . which didn't have any effect on me because I know that you can get psychiatrists to argue anything because it's not an exact science." And another juror concluded: "The defense had to show much and they did a good job. We just didn't buy it." Unfortunately, then, it appears as though the defense was fighting a losing battle (on guilt/innocence) from the beginning, according to jurors.

The Sentence

Six jurors were interviewed before the sentence in the *Page* case was rendered. Two jurors were interviewed twenty-nine months after the sentence was imposed. The jurors' opinions on the sentence were mixed. It appears as though most of the jurors thought that most of the jurors wanted the defendant to get the death penalty, while a small minority of jurors thought that life imprisonment without the possibility of parole was appropriate. Three jurors refused to offer an opinion on the sentence, stating instead, for example, that "that is not my responsibility and I don't want to comment on it," "it was not for me to decide," or "leave that up to the judge." All of the jurors who were interviewed expressed relief that the sentencing decision was left up to the judges. In fact, one juror said, "I think we all sheltered behind the fact that the judges were going to make that decision because he made it very clear that we were not going to sentence him." Jurors who chose to comment on the sentence were brief even though they tried to explain their response. For example, one investigator reported that

> She thinks Donta should get the death penalty. She said it's upsetting to think about whether someone's life should be taken. She thought that the crime was brutal so she thought he should get the death penalty. She said she would rather get the death penalty than spend her life in prison. She said she didn't think Donta could do any good in prison.

This juror, at least in part, then, used her own feelings/opinion about the death penalty to render a decision about the defendant. The fact that the death penalty would be preferable to her if she were in the defendant's position allowed her to believe that it was the best punishment for him. Also, the "brutality" of the murder seemed to persuade her that death was the best punishment. But how brutal does a murder have to be to send someone to death row? The panel of judges debated this issue during the penalty phase of the trial.

One of the issues that the panel of judges struggled with in making their sentencing decision was whether to characterize the murder as "heinous." Heinousness requires that the murder be *shockingly atrocious or odious*.[5] As such, during the penalty phase of the trial, the judges questioned the prosecution as to why they thought the crime was heinous. The prosecution argued that since a lot of time (in their opinion) elapsed between the first time that the defendant and the victim encountered one another and the time that she supposedly died, the victim must have suffered for a long period of time. Long suffering, according to the prosecution, should render the murder heinous.

The defense argued, however, that some of the current Colorado death row inmates made their victims suffer longer than Ms. Tuthill would have suffered (some suffered for several days) and that the ways in which their victims were killed were much more brutal because they involved sodomy with foreign objects, torture, and kidnapping. The defense further argued that the amount of time that elapses between the point of contact and death does not, in and of itself, produce heinousness. The three-judge panel agreed and ruled that the murder in this case was not heinous.

One of the other jurors mentioned that she had trouble understanding the judges' ruling on heinousness, too. When asked whether she agreed with the sentencing decision, she said:

> At first I was appalled because to me it was very heinous. I mean I related to the mom. I have daughters. And this was just awful, but they're a lot smarter than I am and they're educated and they know what they're doing so if that's their decision . . . that's it.

Perhaps this juror would have been persuaded by other jurors during deliberations about the sentence if the decision had been left up to them. That is, jurors who feel that other jurors are "smarter" or "more educated" may defer to those jurors' opinions during deliberations. If so, jury decisions may actually be made based on the credentials or demeanor of the jurors rather than a fair assessment by all of the jurors of the facts in the case as presented by attorneys at trial.

Jurors who stated that they did not want the defendant to get the death penalty offered explanations of a moral or systematic kind; that is, they viewed the process and/or the penalty as unfair or erroneous. For example, one juror changed her mind about the death penalty after viewing a movie about the death penalty following the *Page* trial:

> I didn't refuse to serve because I thought I believed in the death penalty mostly because I was under the illusion which I gather is an illusion that it is more expensive to keep someone in jail for the rest of their life than to put them to death and I thought it made more sense to finish their life. Also I thought, I'm sure, I'd rather be put to death, I'm not sure by what means, than to have to spend the rest of my life at the age of twenty-four or whatever he was in prison. Afterwards, first of all, did you ever see that . . . I didn't see the movie, but I read the book of *Dead Man Walking* and I had particularly . . . had not read that, but I thought about it. I even bought the film and I said to my husband, "I'm on this trial and I'm not going to watch this because I think it could have an affect on me." But I looked at it about six months after the trial and I think now I would say that I don't believe in the death penalty.

This juror said that she *might have* voted for death in the *Page* case if the sentencing decision had been left up to the jury.

Two other jurors who were interviewed said that they would not have wanted the defendant to get the death penalty. Both of the jurors had been willing to sign affidavits to that effect for the defense attorneys to use during the penalty phase of the trial. Also, one of the "no comment" jurors said "to tell you the truth, I don't want to see anybody killed," which may be interpreted as a no vote on the death penalty if the decision had been left up to the jury. Perhaps the inability to decide between life and death weighs in favor of life without the possibility of parole in the jury room when jurors are forced to make a decision, but where there is no pressure to decide, people flirt with the idea as a form of justice. Literature on public opinion and the death penalty confirms that people, including law enforcement officials, support the death penalty in theory, but that fewer of them are willing to actually facilitate the imposition of it.[6] Hypothetically, then, they may believe that the penalty is just, but if they were forced to render a decision after hearing all of the facts in a particular case, their decision would favor life without the possibility of parole instead.

There is some evidence to suggest that the hypothetical sentencing decisions made by jurors during interviews had something to do with the jurors' views of how the defendant would behave in prison, too. Two jurors who said that they would have voted for death also said that it was, in part, due to the fact that they did not believe that the defendant would be a good prisoner. In fact, when asked how she thought the defendant would behave as a prisoner, one juror said:

> Terribly. Well, I wrote a letter for *Westword* magazine to Steve Jackson and I said that I was juror #1. He asked if he could publish it. I said [in the article] a lot of people go to prison and say that they better watch out for "Bubba." Well, I said, Donta Page *is* "Bubba." [*Westword* did not print that paragraph of the letter.]

Earlier in the interview, this juror had said, "No, no, no," when asked whether any of the images constructed by attorneys were stereotypical. She had also said, "I had not seen a picture of him prior and then I saw what he actually looked like with an afro and . . . wild looking! I mean it was hard to believe it was the same person."

Conversely, one of the jurors, when asked how the defendant would behave as a prisoner (and who also indicated that she would have voted for life without the possibility of parole instead of the death penalty), said:

I think to a certain extent it would depend on how the other prisoners treat him and how of course the wardens treat him. . . . I don't honestly know how he'll react. I think he might go to pieces, but I think he might be alright, but I think it depends on how he is treated.

This opinion may represent a more humanitarian view of the defendant in that his reaction to prison would depend on how he is treated. The previous opinion is more stereotypical in that it views the defendant statically or without variation; that is, the defendant acts violently because he is a certain kind of person, not because of the way he is treated. Stereotypes of this kind are dangerous because they assume that the defendant *cannot* behave properly or *cannot* be rehabilitated because he is innately violent. They dismiss the notion that he can be *provoked* into violence. That is not to say that the victim in this case provoked the defendant. She did not. But rather, the current study forwards that the defendant was provoked into responding violently to a threatening situation.

Overall, when stereotypes are a part of the ideology that supports sentencing decisions, it may be easier to conclude that people who cannot control themselves because they possess some innate inability to do so are unsalvageable and should be put to death, while those who act violently because they have been provoked in some way are salvageable and worthy of mercy. Stereotypes in this case may not have played a large role in the sentencing decision, but it is clear that they played a role in at least one juror's view of the defendant. When the sentencing decision in a capital case is given to a jury, perhaps steps should be taken to alleviate that bias.

Two jurors were asked whether they thought justice was ultimately served in the *Page* case since the defendant received LWOP. Both answered affirmatively, but they gave different reasons. One suggested that the attorneys might have made a difference: "Maybe if he'd had millions of money to spend on a defense attorney, he could have done something cleverer, but I think justice was served in the end." The other juror indicated that even though she thought the decision was just, she also thought that it was easy. When asked why she thought the judges might have given the defendant life instead of death she said:

I think it's awfully easy . . . and there were some of us in the jury room who said, "Well, he's dead" . . . [and] when it comes right down to it, I don't see how three judges can make that determination; ya know maybe they're religious or maybe this but just morally it would be hard to get three people together to say we need to kill this person.

Both respondents made it clear that they viewed judges as better qualified than jurors to make the life or death decision.

The Cases Presented by Attorneys

Witnesses

While most of the jurors viewed the prosecution's case as clear and convincing because of the physical evidence that they were able to collect at the scene of the crime and the taped confession, some jurors expressed disappointment with the way that the prosecution presented its case. For example, one of the prosecution's witnesses, Dr. Dan Martell, was not qualified to testify as the forensic specialist that the prosecution had presented him to be. He had failed the forensic specialist certification exam. Dr. Martell had lied about his board certification for the purpose of procuring employment as an expert witness in other criminal cases and the defense uncovered this deceit during questioning in the *Page* case. The defense did not object to his qualification as an expert, though, and the court decided to receive him as a forensic neuropsychologist following a lengthy discussion about his credentials:

Defense: Now, Doctor, are you board certified in forensic neuropsychology?
Martell: Yes, I am.
Defense: And who is that by?
Martell: American Board of Psychological Specialties.
Defense: Now, the American Psychological Association, is it called, the one you said was the one that you are a member of?
Martell: Yes.
Defense: That's like the granddaddy of psychological associations?
Martell: Yes, it is.
Defense: Now, they approve of only board certification from one board; is that right?
Martell: I'm not sure that that is right.
Defense: Well, are you familiar with a board that's the American Board of Professional Psychology?
Martell: Yes, I am.
Defense: Now, you are board certified by the American Board of Psychological Specialties, is what you said, right?
Martell: Yes, sir.
Defense: And that's a subdivision of a forensic group that has everything under it from fingerprint examiners to forensic teeth experts to nurses and forensic nurses, et cetera?
Martell: That's right.
Defense: You didn't have to pass any type of test to become board certified?

Martell: In my situation, I was what they call grandfathered, based on my training, my experience, and my contributions to the field.

Defense: When did you become grandfathered?

Martell: I believe it was October of last year.

Defense: Of '99?

Martell: Yes, sir.

Defense: Actually anybody who was a member of that organization could be grandfathered in prior to December 31st, '99, without ever having to do any kind of written test?

Martell: That's correct.

Defense: So it wasn't a special rule they applied to you?

Martell: No.

Defense: Now, you have been asked over the years about your board certifications by different lawyers through all these fifty or sixty cases; is that right?

Martell: Yes.

Defense: Now, I want to talk to you about what you've indicated about your board certification status. Prior to March of '99, you had—prior to March of '99, you also told attorneys that with respect to this one board, the one that's approved by American Psychological Association, that you were preparing and were attempting to get board certified; is that right?

Martell: That's correct.

Defense: And you have been attempting that since 1993?

Martell: I think '93 is a little early. I think maybe since 1995.

Defense: Do you recall testifying in 1993 in a case of *Idaho v. Langford* that you were preparing to become board certified?

Martell: I may have had an interest at that time. I don't think I had made my application to a board at that time.

Defense: But in any event, through the years up until March of '99, attorneys would ask you whether you were board certified and you would say you were preparing to become board certified, correct, or something of that nature?

Martell: I'm not sure I can answer the question. I don't think that was my testimony.

Defense: Okay. Well, what do you think your testimony was prior to March of '99 of last year?

Martell: In what situation?

Defense: When you were testifying about asking about being board certified?

Martell: Generally to say I'm not board certified.

Defense: Well, in March of last year, a local attorney by the name Lauren Cleaver had an interview with you. Do you remember that?

Martell: I do.

Defense: And she asked you about board certification and your response was that you weren't board certified because you hadn't scheduled your oral exams yet. Do you remember that?

Martell: Yes.

Defense: And then she confronted you with the fact that actually the reason you hadn't become board certified is because you had failed the written portion of the board certification; isn't that right?

Martell: That's not exactly right. But that's close. I have had—

Defense: Would you like to look at the interview?

Martell: Sure.

Defense: Doctor, if I could have you take a look at this and look at the highlighted blue portion.

Martell: Yes.

Defense: Ms. Cleaver asked you: "How many times have you applied for board certification?" You said, "Never." "Have you been rejected," she asked. "What is holding it up?" You said, "Holding it up? I need—I need to take my oral exams." Is that right?

Martell: Yes.

Defense: And then later on she confronted you with the fact that you had actually been denied because you failed the written portion of the certification program.

Martell: Yes.

Defense: And the reason you had been rejected is because you made a fundamental mistake in scoring—well, actually strike that. What happened was that during this certification program, in order to be certified, you gave them work samples for people from the board to look over to see if you scored things correctly.

Martell: That's one of things they look at, yes.

Defense: That's one. Just the portion that we are talking about with respect to that, you submitted a work sample and they looked at it?

Martell: Yes.

Defense: Now, you got to pick the work samples you submitted?

Martell: Yes, I did.

Defense: And you got rejected on that portion of the written part of the certification because you had made a fundamental mistake in scoring?

Martell: That's correct.

Defense: Now, prior to Ms. Cleaver talking to you about this in March of '99, you had never admitted in any courtroom when asked about the board certification process about this problem that you had with being certified, had you, Doctor?

Martell: I had never been asked and I never told anything but the truth.

Defense: When you were asked by Ms. Cleaver on February 22nd of '99, you said, "At least I need to take my oral exams."

Martell: That's correct.

Defense: So, in essence, Doctor, the reason that you were board certified by the one that didn't require a written exam prior to January 1st, 2000, but you are not board certified by the one that requires the written portion?

Martell: That's right.

Defense: And it's the one that requires the written portion that you have been trying to get in since 1995?

Martell: Well, I've only made one approach at it. I'm hoping to finish it soon.

Defense: Judge, I have no objection to Dr. Martell being qualified or accepted as an expert in the field of neuropsychology.

Court: All right. Dr. Martell will be accepted as an expert in that field and allowed to express his opinions.

Many of the jurors in the *Page* case remembered and commented on the embarrassment they felt about Dr. Martell's testimony because he was also exposed during his testimony for lying in an affidavit that he submitted to the court in another case and for having deceived his colleagues in that case. The affidavit alleged that Dr. Martell had secretly recorded a telephone conversation between colleagues and secretly gave the tape to the prosecution when the colleagues had been retained by the defense. In fact, the people that the affidavit referred to testified in the *Spivey* case that the information in the affidavit was deceitfully obtained and that parts of it were manufactured by Dr. Martell. Dr. Martell admitted that he had had difficulty procuring employment after the *Spivey* case:

Defense: Now, Doctor, I'm going to ask some specific questions. In the *Spivey* case, you were working for the United States Attorney's Office as a confidential expert; is that correct?

Martell: I'm not sure what you mean by confidential expert.

Defense: As an expert?

Martell: Yes.

Defense: Based upon disclosures that you made to attorneys from the United States Attorney's Office, the U.S. Attorney's Office put out a position paper that stated that the affidavit you filed in that case had been misleading to the Court; is that correct?

Martell: I don't believe so.

Defense: Do you remember testifying in the Lucas Samon trial?

Prosecution: Objection, Judge.

Court: Overruled.

Martell: Yes.

Defense: Do you remember testifying the U.S. Attorney's Office felt that the affidavit you filed in the *Spivey* case had been misleading?

Martell: I don't recall that testimony.

Defense:	Okay. Do you recall testifying in the case down in Colorado Springs, the U.S. Attorney's Office felt the affidavit you filed in the *Spivey* case had been misleading?
Martell:	Yes.
Defense:	That case ended up being settled in the middle of the trial after your affidavit problem became known?
Martell:	I don't believe the case was in trial at all.
Defense:	You don't believe the case was settled after that?
Martell:	The case was settled, but it was not a trial.
Defense:	It wasn't in the middle of trial?
Martell:	No, sir.
Court:	We are not going to go into that. That's beyond the scope of permissible impeachment.
Defense:	Doctor, there was an investigation into what had been done with this affidavit in the *Spivey* case by the United States Attorney's Regulatory Organization; is that correct?
Martell:	The Office of Professional Responsibility undertook an investigation at my request.
Defense:	At your request?
Martell:	Yes, sir.
Defense:	It was actually at the request of the judge?
Martell:	Not that I'm aware of.
Defense:	It's still pending, isn't it?
Martell:	As far as I know.
Defense:	Now, you have tried to get rid of this *Spivey* problem, in fact, and you have written a letter to the United States Attorney's Office to try to get them to hire you back on some cases; is that right?
Martell:	No.
Defense:	You didn't write a letter to the United States Attorney's Office?
Martell:	Your characterization as to try to get them to hire me back. I did write this to them. I explained the situation in this case, that I didn't feel it was handled appropriately and they have been conducting an investigation since that time.
Defense:	Well, let's go back and go over that just a little bit.
Martell:	Sure.
Defense:	When you wrote your letter to the United States Attorney's Office, you were aware that the U.S. Attorney from New Mexico, John Kelly, had notified the Attorney General's Office that he had information concerning you that would be used to substantially impeach your credibility as a key government witness in nuclear cases and, therefore, that their information must be disclosed to the defense in any other case.

Martell:	I don't believe that's my language.
Defense:	That was what you understood John Kelly, the U.S. Attorney, had written; is that right?
Martell:	I'm not sure that that is exactly right either.
Defense:	Are you aware of that letter from John Kelly?
Martell:	Am I aware Mr. Kelly wrote a letter? I'm not aware of him identifying me as some sort of key witness and that sort of language. I'm not aware of that.
Defense:	Do you remember him writing that he thought that there was information that would substantially impeach your credibility as a witness and that this information must be disclosed to the defense in any other cases?
Martell:	I'm not aware of that.
Defense:	You are not aware of that? Doctor, you wrote a letter dated June 10th, 1997, to the assistant attorney general; is that correct?
Martell:	I don't recall the date, but I think you have it in front of you. I trust that it's correct.
Defense:	By the way, Doctor, did you tell the prosecution about this *Spivey* situation here?
Martell:	Yes, I did.
Defense:	Would it surprise you that they didn't disclose it to the defense?
Prosecution:	Judge, this is—
Court:	Objection sustained. The jury is instructed to disregard that last remark which wasn't a question.

     *   *   *   *   *   *

Defense:	And one of the reasons you were concerned about clearing your name is because you had some pending work that you didn't want to lose?
Martell:	Yes, in part.
Defense:	And one of those cases was the—you had been retained by the United States government in the case of *U.S. v. Ted Kaczynski*; is that right?
Martell:	Yes, that's right.
Defense:	And you were worried about losing that work and other work?
Martell:	Yes.
Defense:	Because working for the United States government and prosecutors for the United States government was a substantial portion of your income?
Martell:	Well, now, I never said that.
Defense:	Well, you said you lost substantial income; is that correct?
Martell:	Substantial income, yes, but not that it's a substantial portion.
Defense:	Substantial income?

Martell:	Sure.
Defense:	By the time you had written that letter, you had already been taken off of several cases where you had been employed as an expert for the prosecution because of the *Spivey* problem?
Martell:	That's right.
Defense:	You have been taken off of a Connecticut case in the case of *United States v. Garfield Patterson*; is that right?
Martell:	Yes.
Defense:	That was a July '97 case, does that sound about right?
Martell:	I don't recall.
Defense:	And then March of '98 there is a case of *New Jersey United States Attorney's Office, United States v. Moses Clary* that you lost—
Martell:	Yes.
Defense:	—because of the *Spivey* problem?
Martell:	That's correct.
Defense:	You also believe that you were taken off a case in Virginia because of this *Spivey* problem?
Martell:	I'm not sure about that.
Defense:	*United States v. Gonzales*, which is three different cases in New Mexico, you were taken off of that also?
Martell:	I was.
Defense:	And the case in New Mexico, *United States v. DeLa Torre*; is that right?
Martell:	I think those were codefendants in the same case in New Mexico, but I'm not sure.
Defense:	But in any event, United States Attorney Tom English in New Mexico wrote a letter and told you that your services were no longer welcome in the *DeLa Torre* case?
Martell:	That's right.
Defense:	Now an additional case that you were removed from based on the *Spivey* incident was in Chicago in the case of Angelo Rugie?
Martell:	I'm not sure that that is true.
Defense:	How about *U.S. v. Barnetter*?
Martell:	I don't recognize the name.
Defense:	You were concerned when you wrote that letter of losing work with the United States Attorney's Office?
Martell:	Sure. They had been a good client, I was happy to work with them. I felt I had been treated poorly.
Defense:	And you wrote in that letter that you had been removed from major cases and lost significant income because of the *Spivey* matter?
Martell:	I think I've already answered that.

Defense:	As a result your income went down 5 to 10 percent?
Martell:	Maybe.
Defense:	You wrote in that letter that—Ted Kaczynski is the Unabomber case, right?
Martell:	Yes, it is.
Defense:	You indicated that that was a big one for you professionally; is that right?
Martell:	I think I indicated it was a big case for me and a big case for the government.
Defense:	Professionally?
Martell:	If you want to show me the language, I will endorse it. I don't recall what I said.
Defense:	If you can look at page 7.
Martell:	"This is obviously an extremely important case both for the government and for me professionally."
Defense:	Would it be safe to say you were determined to get your standing back with the prosecutors after the *Spivey* matter?
Martell:	I thought I was treated poorly in that case, and I didn't think it was fair. And so I followed the proper channels to file a complaint and say this isn't right.
Defense:	Doctor, that's why the Ted Kaczynski matter. You wanted to show the prosecutors that you were a good expert so badly that you secretly tape-recorded a conversation you had with a professional colleague by the name of Dr. Geard without Dr. Geard's permission, and then turned it over to the prosecution team in order to try to impeach Dr. Geard. Do you remember that?
Martell:	I don't know who Dr. Geard is. I did nothing secret to win the affection of the U.S. Attorney.
Defense:	Do you recall talking to Ms. Cleaver, again a local attorney, in February of '99?
Martell:	Yes.
Defense:	Do you recall talking to her about this tape-recording of an expert in the Kaczynski matter?
Martell:	I do.
Defense:	And you did that secretly, right?
Martell:	I did it because I was told it was all right by the FBI agent on the case.
Defense:	Did the other guy know about it?
Martell:	It was a conference call with several people on the line in different states. Nobody knew about it except me.
Defense:	Doctor, you said earlier that you hold yourself as a forensic psychologist in the highest of ethical standards?

Martell:	Absolutely.
Defense:	You consider it ethical to tape-record an opposing expert without their knowledge?
Martell:	There was no problem with it.
Defense:	No problem with it?
Martell:	No. If I had it to do over, I would have let him know. I think it was a mistake for me to have done that. But it was not immaterial, and it wasn't done for any nefarious or evil purpose other than to help me not have to take notes so fast.

Dr. Martell was discredited by the defense team during the *Page* trial and the jurors remembered and commented on the embarrassment that Dr. Martell's portion of the trial caused. When asked what she thought about the prosecution's case, for example, one juror said:

> Well, I thought it was fairly straightforward although obviously they expected it to be straightforward. I actually thought that towards the end they'd gotten rather sloppy about it because they were so sure they were gonna win . . . one of the last witnesses they had was such a scumbag in my opinion, ya know, if the clear police evidence and everything else hadn't been so clear I might have had doubts about what they were fighting for.

Later, this juror expressed amazement at how well the defense attorneys presented their case. This juror thought that the defense was much better prepared, communicated better with the jury, and fought harder to win the case, but in the end, she felt as though the prosecuting attorneys controlled the trial:

> I think it was fairly obvious that they had so much evidence going for them that they didn't really have to try as hard as the others and I think there was never much doubt in anyone's mind that he had done these things . . . he *was* guilty.

Another juror mentioned that "she was really embarrassed about Dr. Martell's testimony," and added that "if the D.A. was right, why couldn't he find a better expert to testify?" And a third juror, when asked which set of attorneys controlled the trial, said: "Prosecution . . . they're demeanor . . . it's just we all knew he did it . . . he never said he didn't do it so it was pretty easy for the prosecution to look like they were done and in a timely manner on their side."

Images
It was also clear from the juror interviews that the victim was angelically portrayed. The prosecution emphasized that her hopes and dreams had been cut

short, that her accomplishments were numerous, and that her personality was positive. In fact, it may have seemed as though the prosecution thought she was perfect because they attempted to arouse sympathy for her tragic death with pictures and letters and tearful characterizations of how much she will be missed. One juror commented on the props:

> The prosecuting attorneys did try to play on the sympathy for this young girl. They kept showing pictures of her, her roommate came forward and gave evidence all about what she was looking forward to. And it was a tragedy . . . it was pretty much a tragedy for him, too. Only I think possibly if you look back at his life we could see the tragedy getting worse and worse and an obvious ending.

And later, the same juror when asked to describe the victim said:

> Well, I thought she was an attractive girl. Full of hope and she'd just gotten a job that she thought would be great. And she was a pretty girl and one couldn't help feeling certain sympathy for someone who had all this going for them and had in no way provoked this assault. So you don't feel very sorry for him. I don't think she in any way provoked him.

It seems clear then that the victim's attractiveness and potential had something to do with whether this juror viewed the murder as tragic. Also, it seems that this juror's sympathy was to some extent aroused by the victim's passivity; that is, if she had done something to provoke the attack, the juror may have had less sympathy for her and may have, subsequently, not viewed the murder as heinous, requiring a second-degree murder conviction instead of a first-degree conviction that carries the death penalty. Consequently, it can be said that the prosecutors *had* to portray the victim in a perfect light to maximize the amount of sympathy that was aroused for her because decreasing the amount of social distance between the jury and the victim supported conviction. The extent to which sympathy could be aroused for the victim, then, may also be the extent to which the heinousness or brutality of a murder is assigned. Further research may even go so far as to uncover a direct correlation in that regard.

Another juror attributed the murder to the residential location of the victim by stating that the victim was a nice girl who unknowingly chose to live in a bad part of town. When asked what she remembered about the victim, for example, she said: "I remember her family . . . [and that she was] young, seemed very nice, nice roommates. Very terrible what he did to her. Bad part of town. Didn't know about that part of Denver. It was a bad area."

Interestingly, such characterizations of the victim were accurate in terms of what the victim had going for her, but it seems that negative things about the victim, that is, bad habits, mistakes she made, problems she encountered, and so forth, were never discussed. The portrayal of the victim was probably incomplete, in other words, and the imaginary boundary that was raised to protect her innocent and perfect portrayal was respected by all of the trial participants.

The portrayal of the defendant was also incomplete. To be sure, there were negative portrayals of the defendant such that one juror when asked how the defendant was portrayed by the prosecution said: "Well, I think basically an unscrupulous murderer. And rapist. And they brought a lot of pictures of the girl and obviously they wouldn't show any sympathy so they didn't." When asked how the defense portrayed him, the same juror said: "I think they tried to prove that he was mentally incapable of understanding what he was doing and brain damaged." Along the lines of mental competence, another juror said she thought the defendant was dumb:

Well, when he was sitting there, he never said anything. He was absolutely silent. I think he once looked up and smiled when his grandmother was there but otherwise he never showed any sort of reaction. The first time he came into court he had a lot of curly hair and then when it came nearer to the important part of the trial, I think he'd been spruced up presumably by the defense and he'd had his hair cut supposed to be looking a little smarter. My general impression, I think, would be of a not very intelligent person, but I don't know quite on what I'm basing that because all sorts of appearances can be particularly misleading. He didn't look sharp.

At least two jurors, then, characterized the prosecution's portrayal of the defendant as not very intelligent and unscrupulous. To be sure, the evidence presented at trial reinforced or at least lent credibility to these evaluations in that he did some very stupid and unscrupulous things, but the defense also brought up good things that the defendant had said and done in his life such as chores that he did for his mother and flowers that he bought for his girlfriend. There were times when the defendant bought clothes and furniture for his grandmother, too, and he oftentimes bought ice cream for his younger brothers. One of the residents of the Stout Street Foundation even testified that the defendant encouraged other residents to correct their behavioral problems so that they could improve their lives. However, such testimony was scarce, one-line comments mixed in with testimony about his bad side.

It is interesting to note the contrast, then, between the portrayal of the victim against the portrayal of the defendant. Only good things about the victim were mentioned while both good and bad things about the defendant surfaced during the trial. The defendant in the end, however, was clearly viewed as a completely bad person and some of the jurors seemed to minimize the nice things that he had done for other people. When the "thank you" letter to Dr. Johnson (from the Colorado State Hospital in Pueblo) was read aloud to the jury, for example, the fact that the defendant apologized to the doctor for some of his behavior and thanked the doctor for his help might not have had the effect on the jury that the defense had hoped, not because the jury did not hear it, but because the murder of Peyton Tuthill far outweighed any apology that he could have offered.

Besides, the letter that the defendant wrote to Dr. Johnson was a surprise. Dr. Johnson had found it in a stack of papers that he had in a file about the defendant. Neither set of attorneys knew about the letter until Dr. Johnson pulled it out of his coat pocket on the witness stand. A brief recess had been taken at that point in the trial so that both sets of attorneys could read the letter. The court decided to admit the letter into evidence and one of the defense attorneys read it aloud during closing statements (see chapter 7). The defendant's letter clearly stated that "there are no words." Some jurors may have viewed his apology as resulting from fear of punishment. Indeed, the prosecutor said that he was sorry that he had been caught, but not for committing the crime.

Two jurors expressed sympathy for the defendant's life situation, but they also commented that it did not matter much because other people have suffered the same plight and not committed crimes:

> Why would he do these things when other people who have similar drawbacks, difficulties in their lives don't do that? Therefore if you do them, you're wrong and anyway about four or five of us who said, "Well, wait a minute . . . look what he's gone through . . . [and] can you honestly say that you, if you'd gone through all of these things, that you're reaction would be the same as you around the table who are quite sure?" And we waffled a bit . . .

Clearly, there was room in the jury's deliberations made for the consideration of his life situation, but it did not outweigh the wrongfulness of the victim's death. One juror opined: "Donta was given the opportunity to start over in Colorado, but he chose to take the wrong path and committed a horrible crime. He has to pay for the crime he committed." And another interview mentioned that "she's known a lot of people who had a bad childhood and they didn't grow up to be murderers." The same juror went on to say that "she had her mind made up when she went into the jury room."

In sum, there is no doubt that the physical evidence presented at trial supported the jury's decision to convict the defendant of first-degree murder and that the expert witness testimony about the relationship between child abuse and later violence supported a conviction of second-degree murder. The question is whether the images presented by the prosecution and the defense at trial weighed into the jury's decision and whether those images are a fair assessment of or instrument by which to judge the defendant's attribution, particularly in capital cases where physical evidence is lacking.

Notes

1. Jody Armour, "Stereotypes and Prejudice: Helping Legal Decision-Makers Break the Prejudice Habit," *California Law Review* 83(1995): 733–772.

2. Nancy M. Steblay, Jasmina Besirevic, and Solomon Fulero, "The Effects of Pretrial Publicity on Juror Verdicts: A Meta-analytic Review," *Law and Human Behavior* 23(1999): 219–235.

3. Shari Seidman Diamond, Jonathan D. Casper, Cami L. Heiert, and Anna-Maria Marshall, "Juror Reactions to Attorneys at Trial," *Journal of Criminal Law and Criminology* 87(1996): 17–47; Bethany K. Dumas, "Jury Trials: Lay Jurors, Pattern Jury Instructions, and Comprehension Issues," *Tennessee Law Review* 67(2000): 701–742; Vicki L. Fishfader, Gary N. Howells, Roger C. Katz, and Pamela S. Teresi, "Evidential and Extralegal Factors in Juror Decisions: Presentation, Mode, Retention, and Level of Emotionality," *Law and Human Behavior* 20(1996): 565–572; Scott E. Sundby, "The Jury as Critic: An Empirical Look at How Capital Juries Perceive Expert and Lay Testimony," *Virginia Law Review* 83(1997): 1109–1188.

4. Michael J. Ahlen, "Opening Statements in Jury Trials: What Are the Legal Limits?" *North Dakota Law Review* 71(1995): 701–720; James W. McElhaney, "Finding the Right Script: Trial Lawyers Must Fit Their Cases to the Belief Patterns of Juries," *American Bar Association Journal* 81(1995): 90–92; Bryan Morgan, "The Jury's View," *University of Colorado Law Review* 67(1996): 983–988; Brian Reeves, "Jurors Judge Lawyers," *Kentucky Bench and Bar* 61(1997): 24–25.

5. Bryan A. Garner, *Black's Law Dictionary*, 7th ed. (St. Paul, MN: West Group, 1999).

6. Richard C. Dieter, "On the Front Line: Law Enforcement Views on the Death Penalty" (A report of the Death Penalty Information Center, Washington, D.C., 1995); Phoebe C. Ellsworth and Samuel R. Gross, "Hardening of the Attitudes: Americans' Views on the Death Penalty," in *The Death Penalty in America: Current Controversies*, ed. Hugo Adam Bedau (New York: Oxford University Press, 1997), 90–115; Robert Jay Lifton and Greg Mitchell, *Who Owns Death? Capital Punishment, The American Conscience, and the End of Executions* (New York: Harper Collins, 2002); Michael L. Radelet and Ronald L. Akers, "Deterrence and the Death Penalty: The Views of the Experts," *The Journal of Criminal Law and Criminology* 87(1996): 1–16.

CHAPTER NINE

~

Conclusion

The fundamental attribution error refers to the tendency to underestimate the impact of situational factors and to overestimate the importance of internal dispositional factors in judging the actions of another person.

Contributions

Some conclusions can be drawn from the data presented herein: (1) the attorneys in the *Page* case constructed an image of the defendant that was conducive to winning the trial, (2) the image of the defendant that the attorneys constructed left an impression on the jury, (3) the *Page* jurors discussed inappropriate topics and applied inappropriate standards to the decision in the case, and (4) the decision that the *Page* jurors made was based at least in part on a character evaluation of the defendant which, in turn, resulted in the internal attribution of guilt.

The attorneys in the *Page* case had different goals for the outcome of the trial. The prosecution wanted the jury to convict the defendant of first-degree murder and they wanted the panel of judges to sentence the defendant to death. The defense, on the other hand, wanted the jury to convict the defendant of second-degree murder and they wanted the panel of judges to sentence the defendant to a maximum of life imprisonment without the possibility of parole. In the end, each side could claim a partial victory.

We know from the two verdicts that the jury convicted the defendant of first-degree murder and that the panel of judges sentenced the defendant to life imprisonment without the possibility of parole, but whether the jury accepted the "savage beast" or the "troubled youth" portrayal necessarily requires some speculation. There may have been a mixed result in that regard as well, as twelve jurors can look at the same case from twelve different angles. Even though some of the jurors stated that the defendant was "wild looking" or that he "didn't look very bright," the jury may not have viewed the defendant as the defense and prosecution had hoped they would—perhaps some of them combined the features of the characterizations and decided that the defendant was a "savage youth" or a "troubled beast."

Some of the tactics and props that the attorneys used to reinforce the image that they presented of the defendant clearly influenced the jury's deliberations because several of the jurors mentioned the PET scan videos, the photographs of the victim, the scarring on the defendant, the words of the taped confession, and the demeanor of witnesses, but it is still unclear as to whether the jurors chose one image over the other when they voted to convict the defendant of first-degree murder. For that reason, a review of attribution theory has been added to interpret the results of this research.

The Attribution of Responsibility

As will be recalled from chapter 2, attribution theory suggests that people determine whether another person's actions are reasonable by evaluating the normality of the situation and person; that is, we look at what the person did in the context of who he or she is and where he or she was at the time of the act.[1] For example, a person who suddenly stands up and runs screaming from a room may be judged to be insane unless the fact that a twenty-foot-long snake slithered under his or her desk was made known to the people judging the situation. Without knowledge of the snake under the desk, a person who evaluates the actor's behavior is likely to internally attribute the behavior (and label the person crazy). But, when knowledge of the snake is had, the person evaluating the behavior is likely to externally attribute the behavior and excuse it (referring to Scott and Lyman's (1968) work on "accounts"). To be sure, "when people have the same information, they agree about causality. When new information is introduced, people agree about its bearing on causality."[2] The task for the prosecutors in the current case was to define the defendant so as to internally attribute the crime, whereas the task of the defense attorneys was to define the situation so as to externally attribute the crime.

Tasks of the Attorneys

In the current case, the prosecuting attorneys attempted to internally attribute responsibility for the crime by focusing on the defendant's behavior, including what he did on the day of the crime, his criminal history, his lack of observable remorse, his attempt to avoid detection, and his overall negative lifestyle. By suggesting to the jury that the defendant was simply an evil wrongdoer who chose to act irresponsibly and criminally (having thwarted attempts by his family and social agencies to help himself and improve his life) the prosecutors attempted to internally attribute responsibility for the crime—the murder of Peyton Tuthill was solely the result of the defendant's will to do wrong. Therefore, according to prosecutors, the defendant was rightfully convicted of first-degree murder.

The defense, on the other hand, attempted to externally attribute responsibility for the crime. They tried to focus the jury's attention on social forces in the defendant's life that influenced his behavior such as the child abuse, brain damage that resulted from the abuse, violent and impoverished living conditions, overwhelmed social services, and the lack of familial support—a "justification," according to Scott and Lyman.[3] By shifting the blame for his circumstances away from him and onto his family and neighborhood, the defense attempted to externally attribute responsibility for the crime to win a second-degree murder conviction.

Tasks of the Jury—How Causality May Have Been Determined
Attribution theory requires interpretation of the actor's situation. The defendant, Donta Page, had broken into Peyton Tuthill's home. There was no reason for him to go into the house. He was waiting for a bus that would take him back to the East Coast. All he had to do was wait to go home. Instead, he decided to rob a house to get money and the chips fell from there. Any reasonable person could conclude that breaking into a stranger's home to obtain money is not only illegal, but also risky because crimes rarely happen as they are planned. The fact that the murder occurred during the commission of a felony was not discussed by jurors in the current case, but it certainly influenced the way that the defendant was viewed by them, that is, as a thief.

The defendant had a previous criminal record. The prosecutor made mention of his previous criminal record in the opening statement and brought evidence (in the form of witness testimony and a video of him robbing a convenience store during the penalty phase) of his having committed violent crimes in the past. The defense attorneys did not try to remove the images of the defendant robbing a convenience store from the judges' minds after they viewed the videotape of the robbery. Instead, the defense asserted that the defendant did those things because he was desperate for money and food and clothing. Nonetheless, the jury was forced to conclude that the defendant had been involved in violent crimes before. Combined with incarceration records that showed that the defendant had attempted to break out of jail before, the jury was also able to conclude that the defendant posed a future danger to society.

In contrast, the jury was asked to view the defendant as a victim of his own life history. They were expected to believe the expert witnesses that testified that the horrible beatings he endured as a child damaged his brain, which then affected his ability to control his emotions, think, plan, make judgments, and be successful. The jury was given the opportunity to lessen the degree of culpability they attributed to the defendant by showing mercy on him and his family because they were so dysfunctional. The jury decided not to believe the defense experts on child abuse, though, which tipped the scales of judgment in favor of internal attribution and a first-degree murder conviction.

The jury's final task was to weigh their view of the situation that the defendant was in against the person they thought him to be. Certainly, "the judges have gradually, by means of a process that goes back very far indeed, taken to judging something other than crimes, namely, the 'soul' of the criminal."[4] As such, a character evaluation was made. Who is this defendant? Is he an evil killer or a negligent thief? The prosecution argued that the defendant was an evil killer: they showed the bloodiness of the crime, the long suffering of the victim, the haphazard clean up, and his attempt to avoid detection. The defense argued that the defendant is a negligent thief. He was not smart enough to premeditate and plan and to successfully avoid detection for the crime. In fact, the defendant did not avoid detection very well because his steps were traced all the way back to Maryland where he had already been arrested for another crime. A negligent or incompetent thief, according to the defense, should be found guilty of second-degree murder because the murder was not premeditated.

After having evaluated the evidence and listened to the judge's instructions on what is relevant to consider in their deliberations, the jury reached a verdict: guilty of first-degree murder. Their decision could have been based solely on the physical evidence presented at trial. To be sure, the defense conceded early in the trial that the defendant had committed the murder. Why didn't their affirmative defense of neurological impairment as a result of child abuse work? The fundamental attribution error may shed light on this topic.

The Fundamental Attribution Error

As previously mentioned, the "fundamental attribution error" refers to the tendency to "underestimate the impact of situational factors and to overestimate the importance of internal dispositional factors."[5] In the current case, an argument can be made that the jury overestimated the evilness of the defendant and underestimated the desperateness of his situation—the impact on the defendant of being verbally abused at the Stout Street Foundation and being kicked out on the street for the night: he had no money, no friends, and no place to sleep. He had experienced homelessness, poverty, and isolation before and he had taken care of himself by committing crimes. For that reason, he chose to rob a house to get money for the trip back home.

Feelings of fear drove the defendant to commit the crime of burglary, in other words, while his lack of intelligence, lack of self-control, brain damage, and abusive childhood probably escalated the burglary to rape and murder because he was unable to control his emotions when the victim came home surprising him. The jury was shown evidence of how these factors can influence and increase the likelihood of violent behavior in some people, but they "just didn't buy it." Why not?

The fundamental attribution error represents an easy way to judge people that people don't want to take the time to understand. Stereotypes are also an easy way to judge people without having to think about who they really are. When jurors are forced to make difficult decisions, they may become lazy, relying on stereotypes and dispositional factors to make decisions instead of situational factors and individual character evaluations, which, though legal, may not be the result of unbiased assessments; that is, if it looks like a duck, quacks like a duck, and acts like a duck, it must be a duck. But that is not necessarily true. The defendant in the current case was shown to have emotional problems. Perhaps the jury "didn't buy it" because they would have had to view several other social facts differently, too. For example, if it is true that some murderers act irrationally and violently because they are brain damaged and cannot control themselves, random violence is not only likely to continue to occur, but the randomness of it somehow becomes more clear. To jurors, that may be an uncomfortable thought.

Also, if the defendant really grew up in such horrible circumstances (constant beatings, impoverished conditions, and no one to care for him) and if there are others being raised in the same conditions, our society is not as good and safe and humane as we might have previously thought. That, too, is an uncomfortable thought for jurors. Further, if the defendant is really a good person deep down inside, but never really had a chance to live and simply adapted his lifestyle to the social forces that most influenced him, executing him or incarcerating him is a temporary solution to an ongoing and increasing problem because there may be many more like him until we fix the social problems that caused him to act (and react) violently. Again, that is an uncomfortable thought for jurors.

In short, it is much easier to believe that individuals are rotten or evil or bad (because they choose to be) than to believe that their environment or society plays a role in their behavior, in part, because we can incarcerate or execute the troublemakers and still feel like we have addressed the problem. Contrarily, if *society* is to blame, how do we fix it? Psychological explanations and internal attributions, therefore, are easier to make than sociological explanations and external attributions. The problem, however, is that the same kinds of people are being incarcerated and executed when little attention is paid to their individual problems.

When people make shortcut character evaluations, oftentimes the result is reached by use of stereotypes. "Stereotypes not only shape public attitudes and behavior toward deviants, but guide the very choice of individuals who are to be so defined and processed.[6] In this society, blacks have historically been stereotyped to represent the inferior, criminal, violent, unintelligent, incompetent, and sexually deviant element. In fact, the lives of blacks have been shown to be less valuable than the lives of whites in numerous studies about the death penalty and race.[7] For that reason, it can be said that our society views the incarceration and execution of blacks who kill whites as less of a problem than fixing the social problems that have historically plagued the population such as discrimination, oppression, poverty, unemployment, illiteracy, and hopelessness as a result of them. No one is going to organize a protest against the lifetime incarceration of the defendant in the current study for two reasons: (1) he did it, and (2) nothing is lost by his absence in society (that is, he doesn't matter). As long as society continues to view certain populations (poor minorities) this way—as disposable and not worth the hassle to redeem [or] to allow contributions to society—some of the problems of crime and criminality in our society, particularly violent crime, will never be addressed.

Normalcy

People tend to favor psychological explanations for behavior over sociological ones because they are easier to fix. That is, when a person misbehaves, it is easier to deal with that one person than to analyze and evaluate the external causes of the behavior. For that reason, it can be concluded that the prosecuting attorneys in the current study had an easier time convincing the jurors of the defendant's guilt, not only because the physical evidence was overwhelming, but also because the internal attribution was normal. Put another way, the defendant was what many people would call a "normal" murderer in terms of race, gender, income, life history, education level, family background, and age. In fact, Swigert and Farrell would classify him as a "normal primitive" who "represents a conception of criminality that combines both class and race characteristics. The imagery suggests a group of people whose style of life and innate attributes predispose them to violence."[8] Following is a "clinical description" of the "normal primitive":

The "normal primitive" comes largely from the foreign-born and black populations. Their lives are characterized by impoverished economic conditions which, as with their behavior, may be described as "primitive." Occupational achievements center around unskilled, menial labor, and these careers are often sporadic. Educational levels are minimal and testing indicates borderline to low-average intelligence . . . the offspring of the black population seem unaffected by improved educational and social opportunities. The personality characteristics of the "normal primitive" are childlike or juvenile, the behavior and attitude being similar to that of an eight- to twelve-year-old boy. At the same time, acceptance as a *man* by his group is very important. In this regard, the "normal primitive" is sensitive and takes offense to any question of his masculinity . . . the primitive man is comfortable and without mental illness. He has little, if any, education and is of dull intelligence. His goals are sensual and immediate—satisfying his physical and sexual needs without inhibition, postponement or planning. There is little regard for the future—extending hardly beyond the filling of his stomach and the next payday or relief check. His loyalties and identifications are with a group that has little purpose in life, except surviving with a minimum of sweat and maximum of pleasure. He has the ten-year-old boy's preoccupation with muscular prowess and "being a man." Unfortunately, he lacks the boy's external restraint and supervision so that he is more or less an intermittent community problem and responsibility.[9]

Thus, the prosecution's portrayal of the defendant did not require a stretch of the jurors' imaginations. There were no surprises in the trial with regard to physical evidence or witness testimony. All the jury had to do was show up, be alert, and then vote the way that most citizens probably would have voted even if they had not attended every day of the trial. From the moment that the defendant's and the victim's photos were splashed across local newspapers and the defendant was arrested and followed by news media down the corridors of the courthouse wearing handcuffs and escorted by sheriffs, the stereotype of criminality in our society was affirmed. At that point, Donta Page became less of an individual and more of a category.

"Normal crimes" are defined by David Sudnow as "those occurrences whose typical features, e.g., the ways they usually occur and the characteristics of persons who commit them (as well as the typical victims and typical scenes), are known and attended to by the [public defender]."[10] In discussing the effect that such convenient categorizations have on the legal representation of offenders, he observes:

For in their actual use, categories of crime, as we have reiterated continuously above, are, at least for this legal establishment, the shorthand reference terms for that knowledge of the social structure and its criminal events upon which the task of practically organizing the work of "representation" is premised. That knowledge includes, embodied within what burglary, petty theft, narcotics violations, child molestation and the rest actually stand for, knowledge of modes of criminal activity, ecological characteristics of the community, patterns of daily slum life, psychological and social biographies of offenders, criminal histories and futures; in sum, practically tested criminological wisdom.[11]

Such "wisdom" affects how juries view and consider evidence that is presented by attorneys, particularly the images of the defendant. In the current case, the image of a savage beast fit nicely with the normality of the crime. The jury did not have to deliberate long to figure out that the defendant looked and acted like the proverbial duck. Besides, the physical evidence supported that conclusion.

Alternatively, the jury could have viewed the defendant as a negligent thief and that may have paved the way for a second-degree murder verdict (because premeditation was lacking). But the image that the defense tried to portray competed against the image that the prosecution portrayed and the latter image was much more comfortable to employ because it was normal. If the jury had lent credibility to the "abuse excuse," not only would they have to convict the defendant of second-degree murder, but millions of other murderers' cases might have to be reconsidered because many death row inmates claim to have been emotionally, physically, and sexually abused. The jurors may have been reluctant to open the floodgates to such appeals or to revamp social policy to rectify those cases.

Implications

There are two main implications for the current study: (1) further research is warranted around the relationship between the designation of a crime as heinous and the perfect image of the victim, and (2) further research could uncover a correlation between race and socioeconomic status (SES) of the defendant and the rate at which juries internally attribute responsibility for violent crimes.

Heinousness and the Victim's Halo

During the trial, numerous references to the "heinousness" of the crime were made by the prosecution. To be sure, the prosecutor tried to drive home the point that the victim suffered for a long period of time, that she did not provoke the attack, that she had a lot to live for, and that the defendant showed no mercy in killing and raping her. In the end, the court was not convinced that the facts set forth by the prosecutors were relevant to the discussion of heinousness.

Heinous is defined as *a crime that is shockingly atrocious or odious*.[12] As such, the jurors and the panel of judges were asked, by the prosecution, to view the murder as one of the "worst that had ever occurred in Denver" for the aforementioned reasons. The defense, however, argued that the murder was "run of the mill" because the six inmates who then sat on Colorado's death row had multiple victims and the murders for which they had been sentenced to death involved kidnapping and torture as well as brutality. That is, they argued that this murder was categorically different from "the worst of the worst." The panel of judges agreed that the murder, though horrible, was not shockingly atrocious or odious and denied that it was heinous.

Observation of the trial, however, indicated that the supposed "shock" value of the crime actually came as much from the perfection of the victim as from the brutality of the crime. To be sure, people have been stabbed to death in their homes in Denver before, but the point that the prosecutors seemed to be trying to make was not only that the stabbing death of Peyton Tuthill was horrible, but also that she did not deserve to be stabbed to death because she had lived and had the potential to continue to live the "American dream." The image of Peyton Tuthill as a pretty, educated, caring, loved, loving, and charitable person was propped up against the image of the defendant as an unattractive, uneducated, selfish, unloved, and evil person; the prosecution used photographs, witness testimony, and victim impact statements to accomplish this task. In the end, it was the victim's goodness that the prosecution used to try to convince the judges that the crime was atrocious, rather than the actual stabbing death. Clearly, this was a murder of a person of high status (broadly defined) by a person of low (or no) status.

Perhaps further research into the relationship between the designation of a crime as heinous and the portrayal of the victim's perfection would uncover a direct correlation in that regard; that is, the more perfect and pretty the victim is deemed to be, the more heinous the jury or panel of judges may deem the crime to be. But, in the current case, the argument for heinousness, based in part on the victim's perfection, failed.

Race/SES of Defendant and Internal Attribution

Internal attributions suggest that the actor is solely responsible for the behavior under discussion. In order to internally attribute behavior to an actor rather than to a situation (external attribution), the situation must have low distinctiveness; that is, it is a normal situation in which people find themselves (such as a party, a ball game, or a funeral) or high distinctiveness (an abnormal situation) with high consensus (people who are like the defendant are capable of murder) and high consistency (people who are like the defendant are capable of murdering other people *often*). In the current case, the situation was highly distinctive in that the defendant was robbing a house. But whether people like the defendant are capable of murder and whether people like the defendant are thought to murder people *often* are character evaluations.

If the defendant in the current case had been a white, middle-aged rabbi, for example, the jury would be able to conclude that white, middle-aged rabbis are not often arrested and charged with the crime of murder—and if they are, it is because the situation (money problems, an unhappy marriage, a drinking problem, or drugs, for example) caused or provoked them into doing it. But since the defendant was a poor, black male, the jury was able to conclude that the defendant was probably highly responsible for the murder precisely because poor, black males are oftentimes arrested and charged with the crime of murder (notwithstanding physical evidence of the person's guilt). Again, this speaks to the "normality" of the crime. Recall that "normal crimes" are oftentimes judged much quicker by decision-makers like public defenders and with little emphasis placed on the actual differences between them.

Race and SES, particularly the stereotypes surrounding poor, black men, may predispose jurors to internal attributions of guilt for certain crimes. Put another way, poor minorities are viewed as people who simply choose to be violent instead of being viewed as people who can be *provoked* to violence by their situations. Further research into this relationship is warranted.

Policy Suggestion
The current study has provided data that suggests that capital decision-makers need more help in making life and death decisions because some human factors, like stereotyping and discussions about irrelevant factors (future dangerousness, prior criminal record, life without parole during the guilt phase, etc.) still infect the decisions that are being made. For that reason, one recommendation is submitted for consideration: improved guided discretion.

Improved Guided Discretion
It is clear from the comments of jurors in chapter 5 that the *Page* jurors did not always follow the rules of jury deliberation that were spelled out to them by the judge before they were allowed to discuss the case. Several jurors mentioned that they discussed the defendant's prior criminal record; that they did not understand the judge's instructions to the jury, but failed to notify the

judge so that he could explain them; that they discussed the sentence when the judge told them not to; and that they dismissed entire portions of the defense's case. For this reason, it is clear that the guided discretion statutes that were approved in the *Gregg, Jurek,* and *Proffit* decisions are not enough to avoid the capriciousness and arbitrariness that they were designed to prevent.

That is not to say that the *Page* decision was capricious or arbitrary (because there was plenty of physical evidence pointing to the guilt of the defendant) but rather that the types of irrelevant considerations that juries made prior to those decisions seem to be the same types of irrelevant discussions that juries are having in the jury room today. Any attempt to rectify this situation may be futile but guided discretion could include the following rules: (1) stereotypes should be acknowledged and discussed openly so as to prevent or at least discourage jurors from falling victim to them while they are considering a case; (2) there should be no rush to judgment by imposing a minimum time limit on deliberations for a capital case (that is, the jury should deliberate for no less than one week and no more than one month, for example), (3) bullying should be discouraged, but acknowledged as an unavoidable consequence of the dynamics between members of groups who make decisions (holdout jurors, in other words, should feel comfortable discussing contentious matters with other jurors while simultaneously being encouraged to reach a consensus with them); and (4) a jury referee who is also sworn to confidence and who has the power to stop or refocus the jury's discussion should be allowed to participate in the trial.

Problems with this recommendation include the inability to determine whether stereotypes are being used to make decisions even if they are acknowledged and discouraged (as well as identifying the stereotypes when they are deeply embedded in the psyche of jurors), the inconvenience and possible uselessness of forcing jurors to deliberate for specified periods of time, the difficulty in distinguishing between "bullying" and the use of persuasive discussion techniques to reach consensus, and the difficulty in maintaining the integrity of jury referees who may have vested interests in the outcome of the trial.

Nevertheless, this recommendation would serve to streamline the jury selection process, focus and maintain clarity on the issues that juries are suppose to consider, improve the fairness of the trial process, and even the playing field for poor and minority capital defendants, among other important functions. Reflecting upon the purpose of the criminal justice system in America, it seems appropriate to take steps to insure that the rights and privileges of all citizens, including those accused of capital crimes, are protected by the process even if not from the public opinion of the masses.

Notes

1. Roger Brown, *Social Psychology* (New York: The Free Press, 1986).

2. Brown, *Social Psychology*, 167.

3. Marvin B. Scott and Stanford M. Lyman, "Accounts," *American Sociological Review* 33(1968): 46–62.

4. Michel Foucault, *Discipline and Punish* (New York: Vintage Books, 1977), 19.

5. Brown, *Social Psychology*, 169.

6. Victoria Lynn Swigert and Ronald A. Farrell, "Normal Homicides and the Law," *American Sociological Review* 42(1977): 17.

7. Samuel R. Gross and Robert Mauro, *Death and Discrimination: Racial Disparities in Capital Sentencing* (Boston, MA: Northeastern University Press, 1989); *McCleskey v. Kemp* 106 S.Ct. 3331 (1986); James McCloskey, "The Death Penalty: A Personal View," *Criminal Justice Ethics* 15(1996):70–75; Michael L. Radelet, "Executions of Whites for Crimes Against Blacks: Exceptions to the Rule?" *The Sociological Quarterly* 30(1989): 529–543.

8. Victoria Lynn Swigert and Ronald A. Farrell, "Normal Homicides and the Law." *American Sociological Review* 42(1977), 19.

9. Swigert and Farrell, "Normal Homicides," 19.

10. David Sudnow, "Normal Crimes: Sociological Features of the Penal Code in a Public Defender Office," *Social Problems* 12(1964):255–276.

11. Sudnow, "Normal Crimes," 257.

12. Bryan A. Garner, *Black's Law Dictionary*, 7th ed. (St. Paul, MN: West Group, 1999).

Bibliography

Acker, James R., Robert M. Bohm, and Charles S. Lanier. *America's Experiment with Capital Punishment: Reflections on the Past, Present, and Future of the Ultimate Penal Sanction.* Durham, NC: Carolina Academic Press, 1998.

Adler, Patricia A. and Peter Adler. *Membership Roles in Field Research.* Newbury Park, CA: Sage Publications, 1987.

Ahlen, Michael J. "Opening Statements in Jury Trials: What Are the Legal Limits?" *North Dakota Law Review* 71 (1995): 701–720.

Armour, Jody. "Stereotypes and Prejudice: Helping Legal Decision-makers Break the Prejudice Habit." *California Law Review* 83 (1995): 733–772.

Babbie, Earl. *The Practice of Social Research.* 8th ed. Belmont, CA: Wadsworth, 1998.

Bailey, William C., and Ruth D. Peterson. "Murder, Capital Punishment, and Deterrence: A Review of the Literature." Pp. 135–161 in *The Death Penalty in America: Current Controversies,* edited by Hugo Adam Bedau. New York: Oxford University Press, 1997.

Bartels, Lynn. "Paige couldn't change life in Denver rehab." /*Denver Rocky Mountain News*/ . March 21, 1999, page 5A.

Batson v. Kentucky, 476 U.S. 79 (1986).

Beccaria, Cesare. *On Crimes and Punishments.* Indianapolis: Bobbs-Merrill, 1963.

Becker, Howard S. *Outsiders: Studies in the Sociology of Deviance.* New York: Free Press, 1963.

———. "Whose Side Are We On?" *Social Problems* 14(1967): 239–247.

Bedau, Hugo Adam. *The Death Penalty in America: Current Controversies.* New York: Oxford University Press, 1997.

Bedau, Hugo Adam, and Michael L. Radelet. "Miscarriages of Justice in Potentially Capital Cases." *Stanford Law Review* 40 (1987): 27–31.

———. "The Myth of Infallibility: A Reply to Markman and Cassell." *Stanford Law Review* 41 (1988): 161–170.

Bell, Scott. "Hearts and Minds: For Success at Trial, Appeal to a Jury's Rationality as well as its Sympathy." *The Los Angeles Daily Journal* 110 (1997): S1.

Berger, Peter L., and Thomas Luchmann. *The Social Construction of Reality: A Treatise in the Sociology of Knowledge.* New York: Doubleday, 1966.

Blume, John H., Stephen Garvey, and Sheri Johnson. "Future Dangerousness in Capital Cases: Always At Issue." *Cornell Law Review* 86 (2001): 404–410.

Bohm, Robert M. "American Death Penalty Opinion: Past, Present, and Future." Pp. 25-46 in *America's Experiment with Capital Punishment,* edited by J. Acker, R. Bohm, and C. Lanier. Durham, NC: Carolina Academic Press, 1998.

Borgida, E., and R. Park. "The Entrapment Defense: Juror Comprehension and Decision-making." *Law and Human Behavior* 12 (1988): 19–40.

Bowers, William J. *Legal Homicide: Death as Punishment in America, 1864–1982.* Boston: Northeastern University Press, 1984.

———. "The Capital Jury Project: Rationale, Design, and Preview of Early Findings." *Indiana Law Journal* 70 (1995): 1043–1102.

Bowers, William J., and Glenn L. Pierce. "Arbitrariness and Discrimination Under Post-Furman Capital Statutes." *Crime and Delinquency* 26 (1980): 626–629.

Bowers, William J., Marla Sandys, and Benjamin D. Steiner. "Foreclosed Impartiality in Capital Sentencing: Jurors' Predispositions, Guilt-Trial Experience, and Premature Decision-Making." *Cornell Law Review* 83(1998): 1476–1556.

Bowers, William J., Benjamin D. Steiner, and Marla Sandys. "Death Sentencing in Black and White: An Empirical Analysis of the Role of Jurors' Race and Jury Racial Composition." *University of Pennsylvania Journal of Constitutional Law* 3 (2001): 171–274.

Bridges, George S., and Sara Steen. "Racial Disparities in Official Assessments of Juvenile Offenders: Attributional Stereotypes as Mediating Mechanisms." *American Sociological Review* 63 (1998): 554-570.

Bright, Stephen B. "Counsel for the Poor: The Death Sentence Not for the Worst Crime but for the Worst Lawyer." Pp. 275–318 in *The Death Penalty in America: Current Controversies,* edited by Hugo Adam Bedau. New York: Oxford University Press, 1997a.

———. "Neither equal nor just: the rationing and denial of legal services to the poor when life and liberty are at stake." *Annu. Survey Am. Law,* 1997b: 783–836.

Brown, Roger. *Social Psychology.* 2nd ed. New York: The Free Press, 1986.

Burdine v. Texas, 513 U.S. 1185 (1995).

Burns, Robert P. *A Theory of the Trial.* Princeton, NJ: Princeton University Press, 1999.

Cantor, Nancy, and Walter Mischel. "Prototypes in Person Perception." *Advances in Experimental Social Psychology* 12 (1979): 3–4.

Colorado Revised Statutes. Vol. 6. Titles 16–21. *Criminal Code.* Denver: Bradford Publishing Company, 2001.

Conklin, John E. *New Perspectives in Criminology.* Boston, MA: Allyn and Bacon, 1996.

Cromwell, Paul. *In Their Own Words: Criminals on Crime.* 2nd ed. Los Angeles, CA: Roxbury Publishers, 1996.

Curtis, Olga. "Denver's First Murderer." *Empire Magazine* 5 (1978): 33.

Diamond, Shari Seidman, Jonathan D. Casper, Cami L. Heiert, and Anna-Maria Marshall. "Juror Reactions to Attorneys at Trial." *Journal of Criminal Law and Criminology* 87 (1996): 17–47.

Dieter, Richard C. "On the Front Line: Law Enforcement Views on the Death Penalty." A report of the Death Penalty Information Center. Washington, D.C., 1995.

———. "Sentencing for Life: Americans Embrace Alternatives to the Death Penalty." Pp. 116-134 in *The Death Penalty in America: Current Controversies,* edited by Hugo Adam Bedau. New York: Oxford University Press, 1997.

Doob, A., and H. Kirshenbaum. "Some Empirical Evidence on the Effect of Section 12 of the Canada Evidence Act Upon the Accused." *Criminal Law Quarterly* 15 (1972): 88–96.

Dooley, David. *Social Research Methods.* 4th ed. Upper Saddle River, NJ: Prentice Hall, 2001.

Dumas, Bethany K. "Jury Trials: Lay Jurors, Pattern Jury Instructions, and Comprehension Issues." *Tennessee Law Review* 67 (2000): 701–742.

Ekland-Olson, Sheldon. "Structured Discretion, Racial Bias and the Death Penalty: The First Decade after Furman in Texas." *Social Science Quarterly.* 69 (1988): 853–873.

Ellsworth, Phoebe C. and Samuel R. Gross. "Hardening of the Attitudes: Americans' Views on the Death Penalty." Pp. 90–115 in *The Death Penalty in America: Current Controversies*, edited by Hugo Adam Bedau. New York: Oxford University Press, 1997.

Emerson, Robert, Rachel Fretz, and Linda Shaw. *Writing Ethnographic Fieldnotes.* Chicago, IL: University of Chicago Press, 1995.

Farrell, Ronald, and Malcolm D. Holmes. "The Social and Cognitive Structure of Legal Decision-Making." *The Sociological Quarterly* 32 (1991): 529–542.

Fast, Joseph M., and Ray Doyle. "A View from the Jury Box." *For the Defense* 37 (1995): 20–21.

Feagin, Joe R., Anthony M. Orum, and Gideon Sjoberg. *A Case for the Case Study.* Chapel Hill, NC: University of North Carolina Press, 1991.

Fins, Deborah. *Death Row USA*, NAACP Legal Defense Fund. Washington, D.C. Winter 2007.

Fishfader, Vicki L., Gary N. Howells, Roger C. Katz, and Pamela S. Teresi. "Evidential and Extralegal Factors in Juror Decisions: Presentation, Mode, Retention, and Level of Emotionality." *Law and Human Behavior* 20 (1996): 565–572.

Fiske, Susan T., and Shelley E. Taylor. *Social Cognition.* New York: McGraw-Hill, 1991.

Foucault, Michel. *Discipline and Punish.* New York: Vintage Books, 1977.

Fox, James Alan, Michael Radelet, and Julie L. Bonsteel. "The Death Penalty Opinion in the Post-Furman Years." *New York University Review of Law and Social Change* XVIII (1990): 499–528.

Furman v. Georgia 408 U.S. 238 (1972).

Gallop, George, Jr. *Gallup Poll 2000.* Wilmington, DE: SR Books, June 28, 2001.

Garfinkel, Harold. "Research Note on Inter and Intra-Racial Homicides." *Social Forces* 27 (1949): 120–123.

Garner, Bryan A. Editor in Chief. *Black's Law Dictionary.* 7th ed. St. Paul, MN: West Group, 1999.

Gary, Lawrence E. "Drinking, Homicide and the Black Male." *Journal of Black Studies* 17 (1986): 15–31.

Geimer, William S., and Jonathan Amsterdam. "Why Jurors Vote Life or Death: Operative Factors in Ten Florida Death Penalty Cases." *American Journal of Criminal Law* 15 (1988):1–54.

Giddens, Anthony. *Emile Durkheim: Selected Writings.* New York: Cambridge University Press, 1972.

Gideon v. Wainwright, 372 U.S. 335 (1963).

Givelber, Daniel. "The New Law of Murder." Indiana Law Journal. 69 (1994): 375–391.

Goffman, Erving. *The Presentation of Self in Everyday Life.* New York: Doubleday, 1959.

———. *Asylums: Essays on the Social Situation of Mental Patients and Other Inmates.* Chicago, IL: Aldine Publishing, 1961.

———. *Stigma: Notes on the Management of Spoiled Identity.* Englewood Cliffs, NJ: Prentice Hall, 1963.

Gomm, Roger, Martyn Hammersley, and Peter Foster. *Case Study Method: Key Issues, Key Texts.* London: Sage Publications, 2000.

Gouldner, Alvin W. "The Sociologist as Partisan: Sociology and the Welfare State." *The American Sociologist* 3 (1968): 103–116.

Green, Edith, and Mary Dodge. "The Influence of Prior Record Evidence on Juror Decision-Making." *Law and Human Behavior* 19 (1995): 67–78.

Gregg v. Georgia 428 U.S. 153 (1976).

Gross, Samuel R. "Update: American Public Opinion on the Death Penalty—It's Getting Personal." *Cornell Law Review* 83 (1998): 1448–1475.

Gross, Samuel R. and Robert Mauro. "Patterns of Death: An Analysis of Racial Disparities in Capital Sentencing and Homicide Victimization." *Stanford Law Review* 37 (1984): 895–911.

———. *Death and Discrimination: Racial Disparities in Capital Sentencing.* Boston, MA: Northeastern University Press, 1989.

Gusfield, Joseph R. *Symbolic Crusade: Status Politics and the American Temperance Movement.* Ubana, IL: University of Illinois Press, 1963.

Haney, Craig. "Taking Capital Jurors Seriously." *Indiana Law Journal* 70 (1955): 1223–1232.

Hans, Valerie P. "How Juries Decide Death." *Indiana Law Journal* 70 (1995): 1233–1240.

Hans, V., and A. Doob. "Section 12 of the Canada Evidence Act and the Deliberations of Simulated Juries." *Criminal Law Quarterly* 18 (1976): 235–253.

Heider, Fritz. *The Psychology of Interpersonal Relations.* New York: Wiley, 1958.

Hill, Gary D., Anthony R. Harris, and JoAnn Miller. "The Etiology of Bias: Social Heuristics and Rational Decision Making in Deviance Processing." *Journal of Research in Crime and Delinquency* 22 (1985): 135–162.

Hoffman, Joseph L. "Where's the Buck? Juror Misperception of Sentencing Responsibility in Death Penalty Cases." *Indiana Law Journal* 70 (1995): 1137–1160.

Humphreys, Laud. *Tearoom Trade: Impersonal Sex in Public Places.* New York: Aldine Publishing Company, 1975.

Hunt, Darnell. "Reaffirming Race: Reality, Negotiation, and the Trial of the Century." *The Sociological Quarterly* 38 (1997): 399-422.

Johnson, Allan G. *The Blackwell Dictionary of Sociology: A User's Guide to Sociological Language.* Cambridge, MA: Blackwell Publishers, 1995.

Johnson, Robert. *Death Work: A Study of the Modern Execution Process.* Belmont, CA: Wadsworth Publishing, 1998.

Jones, E. E., and K. E. Davis. "From Acts to Dispositions: The Attribution Process in Person Perception." In L. Berkowitz (ed.), *Advances in Experimental Social Psychology.* Orlando, FL: Academic Press, 1965: 219–266.

Jurek v. Texas 428 U.S. 262 (1976).

Kaplan, Abraham. *The Conduct of Inquiry.* San Francisco, CA: Chandler Publishing, 1964.

Kappeler, Victor, Merle Blumberg, and Gary Potter. *The Mythology of Crime and Criminal Justice.* 2nd ed. Prospect Heights, IL: Waveland, 1996.

Karson, Jill, ed. *Criminal Justice Opposing Viewpoints.* San Diego, CA: Greenhaven Press, 1998.

Kelley, Harold H. "Attribution Theory in Social Psychology." In D. Levine (ed.), *Nebraska Symposium on Motivation.* Lincoln, NE: University of Nebraska Press, 1967.

———. "Attribution in Social Interaction". In E. E. Jones, D.E. Kanouse, H. H. Kelley, R.E. Nisbett, S. Valins, and B. Weiner (eds.), *Attribution: Perceiving the Causes of Behavior.* Morristown, NJ: General Learning Press, 1972: 79–94.

King, William M. *Going to Meet A Man: Denver's Last Legal Public Execution, 27 July 1886.* Niwot, CO: University of Colorado Press, 1990.

Kvale, Steinar. *Interviews: An Introduction to Qualitative Research Interviewing.* Thousand Oaks, CA: Sage, 1996.

Lewis, Dorothy Otnow. *Guilty By Reason of Insanity: Inside the Minds of Killers.* New York: Ivy Books, 1998.

Lewis, F. M., and L.H. Daltroy. "How Causal Explanations Influence Health Behavior: Attribution Theory" in Glanz, K., Lewis, F.M. and Rimer, B.K. (eds.) *Health Education and Health Behavior: Theory, Research and Practice*. San Francisco, CA: Jossey-Bass Publishers, 1990: 92–114.

Liebow, Elliot. *Tally's Corner: A Study of Negro Street Corner Men*. Boston, MA: Little Brown, 1967.

Lifton, Robert Jay, and Greg Mitchell. *Who Owns Death? Capital Punishment, The American Conscience, and the End of Executions*. New York: Harper Collins Publishers, 2002.

Lincoln, Yvonna S., and Egon G. Guba. "The Only Generalization Is: There Is No Generalization" Pp. 27–44 in Roger Gomm, Martyn Hammersley, and Peter Foster (eds.) *Case Study Method: Key Issues, Key Texts*, London: Sage, 2000.

Lockett v. Ohio, 434 U.S. 889 (1977).

Lofland, John, and Lyn H. Lofland. *Analyzing Social Settings: A Guide to Qualitative Observation and Analysis*. 3rd ed. Belmont, CA: Wadsworth, 1995.

Luginbuhl, James, and Julie Howe. "Discretion in Capital Sentencing Instructions: Guided or Misguided?" *Indiana Law Journal*. 70 (1995): 1161–1181.

Lutz, Robin. "Experimenting with Death: An Examination of Colorado's Use of the Three-Judge Panel in Capital Sentencing." *University of Colorado Law Review* 73 (2002): 227-287.

Mandell, Mark. "Overcoming Juror Bias: Is There an Answer?" *Trial* 36 (2000): 28.

Martinez v. Colorado, 234 St. Ct. 336 (2002).

Masur, Louis P. *Rites of Execution: Capital Punishment and the Transformation of American Culture 1776-1865*. New York: Oxford University Press, 1989.

May, Hazel. "Murderers' Relatives: Managing Stigma, Negotiating Identity." *Journal of Contemporary Ethnography* 29 (2000): 198–221.

———. "Who Killed Whom: Victimization and Culpability in the Social Construction of Murder." *British Journal of Sociology* 50 (1999): 489–506.

McCleskey v. Kemp 106 S.Ct. 3331 (1986).

McCloskey, James. "The Death Penalty: A Personal View." *Criminal Justice Ethics* 15 (1996):70–75.

McElhaney, James. W. "Finding the Right Script: Trial Lawyers Must Fit Their Cases to the Belief Patterns of Juries." *American Bar Association Journal* 81 (1995): 90–92.

Mello, Michael. *Against the Death Penalty: The Relentless Dissents of Justices Brennan and Marshall*. Boston, MA: Northeastern University Press, 1996.

Mello, Michael, and Paul J. Perkins. "Closing the Circle: The Illusion of Lawyers for People Litigating for Their Lives at the *Fin de Siecle*." Pp. 245–284 in *America's Experiment with Capital Punishment*, edited by J. Acker, R. Bohm, and C. Lanier. Durham, NC: Carolina Academic Press, 1998.

Monk, Richard C. *Taking Sides: Clashing Views on Controversial Issues in Crime and Criminology*. 6th ed. Norwalk, CT: Dushkin/McGraw-Hill, 2001.

Morgan, Bryan. "The Jury's View." *University of Colorado Law Review* 67 (1996): 983–988.

Myers, Robert D., Ronald S. Reinstein, and Gordon M. Griller. "Complex Scientific Evidence and the Jury." *Judicature* 83 (1999): 150-157.

Nisbett, Richard E. "The Dilution Effect: Nondiagnostic Information Weakens the Implications of Dignostic Information." *Cognitive Psychology* 13 (1981): 248–272.

Packard, Robyn. "Judging Jurors." *Canadian Lawyer* 20 (1996): 12–15.

Perruso, Roxane J. "And Then There Were Three: Colorado's New Death Penalty Sentencing Statute." *University of Colorado Law Review* 68 (1997): 189–227.

Peterson, Ruth D., and William C. Bailey. "Is Capital Punishment an Effective Deterrent for Murder? An Examination of Social Science Research." Pp. 157–182 in *America's Experiment* with *Capital Punishment*, edited by J. Acker, R. Bohm, and C. Lanier. Durham, NC: Carolina Academic Press, 1998.

Pojman, Louis P., and Jeffrey Reiman. *The Death Penalty: For and Against*. Lanham, MD: Rowman and Littlefield, 1998.

Pokorak, Jeffrey J. "Probing the Capital Prosecutor's Perspective: Race of the Discretionary Actors." *Cornell Law Review* 83 (1998): 1811–1820.

Prejean, Sister Helen. *Dead Man Walking*. New York: Random House, 1993.

Pritchard, David. "Homicide and Bargained Justice: The Agenda Setting Effect of Crime News on Prosecutors." *Public Opinion Quarterly* 50 (1986): 143–159.

Proffitt v. Florida 428 U.S. 242 (1976).

Radelet, Michael L. "Executions of Whites for Crimes Against Blacks: Exceptions to the Rule?" *The Sociological Quarterly* 30 (1989): 529–543.

Radelet, Michael L., and Glenn L. Pierce. "Choosing Those Who Will Die: Race and the Death Penalty in Florida". *Florida Law Review* 43 (1991): 1-34.

Radelet, Michael L., and Ronald L. Akers. "Deterrence and the Death Penalty: The Views of the Experts." *The Journal of Criminal Law and Criminology* 87 (1996): 1–16.

Rector, Neil A., Michael Bagby, and R. Nicholson. "The Effect of Prejudice and Judicial Ambiguity on Defendant Guilt Ratings." *The Journal of Social Psychology* 133 (1993): 651.

Reeves, Brian. "Jurors Judge Lawyers." *Kentucky Bench and Bar* 61 (1997): 24–25.

Reichert, Jennifer L. "Lawyers Face the Hurdle of Overcoming Juror Biases, Survey Shows." *Trial* 35 (1999): 96–101.

Riedel, Marc. "Discrimination in the Imposition of the Death Penalty: A Comparison of the Characteristics of Offenders Sentenced Pre-Furman and Post-Furman." *Temporal Law Quarterly* 49 (1976): 230–258.

Rimer, Sara. "In Dallas, Dismissal of Black Jurors Leads to Appeal by Death Row Inmate," New York Time, February 13, 2002, query.nytimes.com/gst/fullpage.html?res= 9D01E0DF163FF 930A25751C0A9649C8B63

Ring v. Arizona, 536 U.S. 584 (2002).

Ritzer, George. *Modern Sociological Theory*. 4th ed. New York: McGraw-Hill, 1996.

Rose, Jeremy. 1999. "How Jurors See Expert Witnesses." *Trial Lawyer* 22 (1999): 420–426.

Ross, Lee. "Blacks, Self-Esteem, and Delinquency" in *African-American Perspectives on Crime Causation, Criminal Justice Administration and Crime Prevention*. Anne T. Sulton, ed. Englewood, CO: Sulton Books, 1994: 53–68.

Ryan, William. *Blaming the Victim*. New York: Pantheon Books, 1971.

Sandys, Marla. "Cross Overs—Capital Jurors Who Change Their Minds About Punishment: A Litmus Test for Sentencing Guidelines." *Indiana Law Journal* 70 (1995): 1183-1221.

Sarat, Austin. "Violence, Representation, and Responsibility in Capital Trials: The View from the Jury." *Indiana Law Journal* 70 (1995): 1103–1135.

Salekin, Randall T., James R. P. Ogloff, Cathy McFarland, and Richard Rogers. "Influencing Jurors' Perceptions of Guilt: Expression of Emotionality During Testimony." *Behavioral Sciences and the Law* 13 (1995): 293–305.

Schek, Barry, Peter Neufield, and Jim Dwyer. *Actual Innocence: Five Days to Execution and Other Dispatches from the Wrongly Convicted*. New York: Doubleday, 2000.

Schmalleger, Frank. *Trial of the Century: People of the State of California v. Orenthal James Simpson*. Upper Saddle River, NJ: Prentice Hall, 1996.

Scott, Marvin B., and Stanford M. Lyman. "Accounts." *American Sociological Review* 33 (1968): 46–62.

Sellin, Thorsten. *The Penalty of Death*. Beverly Hills, CA: Sage, 1980.

Sherman, Steven J. "The Capital Jury Project: The Role of Responsibility and How Psychology Can Inform the Law." *Indiana Law Journal* 70 (1995): 1241–1248.

Slobogin, Christopher. "Should Juries and the Death Penalty Mix?: A Prediction About the Supreme Court's Answer." *Indiana Law Journal* 70 (1995): 1249–1270.

Snell, Tracy L. Capital Punishment 2000. Bureau of Justice Statistics, Office of Justice Programs, U.S. Department of Justice, Washington, D.C. 2001.

Stake, Robert E. "The Case Study Method in Social Inquiry" Pp. 19–26 in Roger Gomm, Martyn Hammersley, and Peter Foster (eds.) *Case Study Method: Key Issues, Key Texts*. London: Sage, 2000.

Steblay, Nancy M., Jasmina Besirevic, and Solomon Fulero. "The Effects of Pretrial Publicity on Juror Verdicts: A Meta-Analytic Review." *Law and Human Behavior* 23 (1999): 219–235.

Steiker, Carol S., and Jordan M. Steiker. "Judicial Developments in Capital Punishment Law." Pp. 47–76 in *America's Experiment with Capital Punishment*, edited by J. Acker, R. Bohm, and C. Lanier. Durham, NC: Carolina Academic Press, 1998.

Strickland v. Washington, 466 U.S. 668 (1984).

Sudnow, David. "Normal Crimes: Sociological Features of the Penal Code in a Public Defender Office." *Social Problems* 12 (1964): 255-276.

Sulton, Anne T. *African-American Perspectives on Crime Causation, Criminal Justice Administration and Crime Prevention*. Englewood, CO: Sulton Books, 1994.

Sundby, Scott E. "The Jury as Critic: An Empirical Look at How Capital Juries Perceive Expert and Lay Testimony." *Virginia Law Review* 83 (1997): 1109–1188.

Swigert, Victoria Lynn, and Ronald A. Farrell. "Normal Homicides and the Law." *American Sociological Review* 42 (1977): 16–32.

Thomas, William I., and Dorothy S. Thomas. *The Child in America: Behavior Problems and Programs*. New York: Knopf, 1928.

U.S. Bureau of Justice Statistics. *Capital Punishment 2000*. Washington, D.C.: U.S. Government Printing Office, 2000.

Van Wormer, Katherine. "Those Who Seek Execution: Capital Punishment as a Form of Suicide." *USA Today* 123 (1995): 92–3.

Vidmar, Neil J., and Regina A. Schuller. "Juries and Expert Evidence: Social Framework Testimony." *Law and Contemporary Problems*. 52 (1989): 133–176.

Von Drehle, David. "Miscarriage of Justice: Why the Death Penalty Doesn't Work." *The Washington Post Magazine* 33 (1995): 33–36.

Whyte, William Foote. *Street Corner Society: The Social Structure of an Italian Slum*. Chicago: University of Chicago Press, 1955.

Wissler, R. L. and M. J. Saks. "On the Inefficacy of Limiting Instructions: When Jurors Use Prior Conviction Evidence to Decide on Guilt." *Law and Human Behavior* 9 (1985): 37-48.

Yates, J. Frank. *Judgment and Decision Making*. Englewood Cliffs, NJ: Prentice Hall, 1990.

Zeisel, Hans. "Race Bias in the Administration of the Death Penalty: The Florida Experience." *Harvard Law Review* 95 (1981): 459–460.

Index

abuse excuse, 117, 120, 123, 192
acquittal, 5, 7, 41, 73
active member, membership, 56
adversarial balance, imbalance, 20, 21, 150–52
African-Americans, 21–23, 25, 27, 118, 123, 190
aggravated robbery, 3, 147
aggravating circumstances (aggravators), 16, 72, 83, 116, 120, 130, 154, 155
alternatives to the death penalty, 16, 22, 24, 34, 198
anomie, 48
appellate review, 10, 16
arbitrariness, 10, 195; and capriciousness, 17, 154–55
arguments for death, 30
arguments for life, 28
attorney/lawyer performances, 4, 23, 26, 28, 158
attorney tactics, 68
attribution theory, 7, 42–44, 60, 186–87
automatic appeal, 29

autopsy report, 1; photographs and, 69, 117, 121

Batson v. Kentucky, 28
Beccarria, Cesare, 16
Becker, Howard S., 11
bias, 4, 41, 44, 63, 171, 189; juror, 4, 42; racial 21, 24
bifurcated trial, 10
Blackmun, Justice Harry, 30
blacks. See African-Americans
Brennan, Justice William, 21
Brimmer, Phillip, 2, 152
Brown, Sergeant Darryl, 129–30
Burdine v. Texas, 152

Canney, Randy, xvi, 2, 62, 140, 144, 148, 152
capital jury, xvii, 6, 9, 24, 28, 41, 163; capital jury project, 10, 20, 27, 39, 56; decision making and, 4, 10, 17, 24
capital murder, 3, 116, 150–52, 163
capital punishment, xii, 8–10, 16, 19, 23, 28–29, 31, 115

capital trial, 4, 6, 10, 19, 39, 40, 49, 71, 116, 152, 154
capriciousness, 17, 154, 155, 195
case study, 11, 12, 50, 56, 62; methodology, 3, 10, 50–51, 56
Castle, Jim, xvii, 2, 62, 90–91, 139, 149, 152
causal judgments, 7, 43
Colorado v. Page, 2, 125, 157
competition, xvii, 12
confession, 47, 69, 80, 99, 135, 152, 153; taped, 80, 83, 86, 117, 163, 167, 172, 186
conscience collective, 8, 48, 49
conviction, 2, 5, 7, 10, 12, 16, 17, 41, 71–73, 80, 115, 151, 153, 163, 181, 184, 188; erroneous, 16; felony, 119; murder, 2, 67, 72, 88, 95, 124, 158, 164–65, 181, 187; prior, 42
Cooper, Henry, 2, 152
credentials, 5, 70, 169, 172
credibility, 68, 119, 164, 182, 192; of witnesses, 3, 73, 165, 176–77
crime scene, 2, 5, 69, 79, 85, 117–18, 127, 150
criminal history, 5, 186
criminal justice system, xiii, 23, 195
cruel and unusual punishment, 10, 15, 16
cycle of violence, xiii, 112–13, 148

death penalty, 23–24, 26–27, 29–31, 40, 43–44, 49, 51–52, 55, 63, 67, 101, 115–18, 125, 130, 138, 151, 159, 165, 168–70, 181, 190; abolition of, 15–16, 63; attitudes about, 9, 23; cost of, 18; deterrent value of, xii, 22, 29; process, 11, 56; sentencing, 11, 117–18. *See also* capital punishment
death row, 8, 10, 16, 18–19, 22, 28, 116, 130, 139, 168, 192; and African-Americans, 8, 18, 21; and Colorado, 18, 125–26, 130, 169, 193; inmates, 116, 125–26, 169, 192
defense attorneys, xii, 2, 3, 5, 11, 42–45, 58–60, 62, 67, 87–88, 107, 113, 124–25, 149–52, 155, 157–58, 165, 170, 180, 183, 186–87
Denver county jail, xv, 52, 61, 129, 130
discreditable stigma, 7, 46
discrimination, 40, 43, 50, 87, 190
District of Columbia, xvi, 110. *See also* Washington, D.C.
DNA, 79–80, 150, 153; evidence, 16, 152, 163, 167; testing, 16, 79
dramaturgy, 45, 46
drugs, 2, 29, 50, 52–53, 134, 136–37, 194
Durkheim, Emile, 8, 48

education, xvii, 8, 19, 23, 52, 113, 163, 190–91
Eighth Amendment, 10, 15, 16. *See also* cruel and unusual punishment
execute, xii, xiii, 6, 9–10, 12, 16–19, 21, 22, 28–29, 31, 42–43, 55, 63, 190
exhibits, xvii, 55, 61, 68–69, 98, 100, 112, 118, 150
expert witnesses, 3, 6, 25, 58, 70, 95–96, 101, 106–07, 150–52, 158–59, 172, 184, 188
external loci, 7, 43

felony murder, 3, 84, 116, 120, 147
first-degree burglary, 3, 147
first-degree murder, 3, 9, 17, 44, 67–68, 72, 84, 95–96, 107, 124, 147, 158, 164, 184–88
Foucault, Michel, 46–47
Fourteenth Amendment, 20–21, 125. *See also* Eighth Amendment
frontal lobe damage/disease, 95, 103, 105–07, 126, 160–62

fundamental attribution error/flaw, 44, 185, 188–89
Furman v. Georgia, 10
future dangerousness, 8–9, 25, 31, 39, 46, 108, 117, 120–21, 154, 194

gender, 7, 23, 45, 49, 138, 190
General Equivalency Diploma (GED), xv, 52, 62, 112, 155
Gideon v. Wainwright, 152
Gill, Josephine, 120
Goffman, Erving, 46, 50, 68–69
Gregg v. Georgia, 10, 16–17
guided discretion, 10, 16–17, 56, 154–55, 194–95. See also *Gregg v. Georgia, Jurek v. Texas*, and *Proffit v. Florida*

heinousness, 117, 120, 168–69, 181, 192–93
homelessness, 2, 95, 138, 189

incarceration, xi, 18, 29, 42, 47, 49–50, 55, 121, 129, 136, 153–54, 187, 190
inmates, xv, 28–29, 52, 54, 128, 129–30, 153, 155, 193
insanity, 3, 50, 96, 146
intent, xiv, 2, 4, 20, 43, 67, 71, 80, 84, 87, 88, 96, 125, 139, 157, 162–63, 165
internal loci, 7, 43–44
interviews, 3, 10, 98; qualitative, 51; with defendant, 52–53, 57; with jurors, 9–10, 56–57, 157–58, 165, 170, 180
investigator, xv, xvi, 53–55, 57–58, 62, 113, 120, 129, 150, 152, 157, 162, 164, 168

Jenny, Carol, 125, 128
Johnson, David, 126
Jurek v. Texas, 16
jury: comprehension, 25; decision-

making, 4, 10, 17, 23–24, 26–27, 49, 71, 153; instructions, 162, 165; selection, 4, 56, 58, 142, 166, 195

Kempe Children's Center, 125, 128

law enforcement, ii, 23, 151, 170
legal process, xi, xii
legal representation, 19, 22, 191
lethal injection, 15, 18, 47
lex talionis, 30–31
life without the possibility of parole (LWOP), 3, 9, 24, 29–31, 116, 164, 168, 171, 185
Lisak, David, 125
Lockett v. Ohio, 20, 125

Marshall hypothesis, 22
Marshall, Justice Thurgood, 21–22
Martell, Dan, 172
McCleskey v. Kemp, 21
media, xi–xii, 3, 9, 25, 48, 76, 158, 191
mercy, 4, 6, 55, 101, 137, 154, 171, 188, 193
methodology, 3, 10, 50–51, 56
mission, 52, 75, 87, 115, 125
mitigating circumstances (mitigators), 16, 20, 72, 88, 116, 120, 125, 154–55
motive, 71, 80, 83–84, 86, 95, 101, 107, 163
murder rates, xvi, 129

neurological impairment, 88, 96, 188
news broadcast, xv
newspaper, xiii, xvii, 61, 191
normal crimes, 191, 194
normal primitive, 60, 190–91

Opsahl, Charles, 101, 106, 143, 162
Otnow-Lewis, Dorothy, xvii, 58, 96, 124, 162
Owens, Lawrence, 119

Page, Linda, xvii, 58, 88–91, 110, 112–13, 129, 140, 142
Page, Patricia, 93–94, 110, 113, 128
panel of judges, 3, 11–12, 18, 43, 120–23, 126, 129, 150, 159, 168, 185, 193
Parker-Lewis, Beverly A., 110–12
participant observation, 11–12, 51
pecuniary gain, 72, 83–84, 116, 118, 120, 154
penalty phase, 120, 125–126, 152, 154, 157, 168, 170, 187
Penny, Erica, xvii, 58, 91, 93, 113
personal front, 7, 45
Pincus, Johnathan, 101, 124, 162
plea bargain, 9, 67, 165
poverty deprivation syndrome, 138–39
poverty rates, xvi
prejudice, xii, xiv, 25–26, 40, 44, 76, 150,
premeditation, 4, 67–68, 80, 88, 96, 107, 119–20, 126, 192
presentation of self in everyday life, 7, 44
prevention, ii, xii, 128
Priest, Jon, 78
prior record, 20, 42, 49, 60, 125, 150, 153–54, 199
prison, 31, 47, 52, 55, 61, 72, 117, 119–21, 125, 127–28, 130, 153–55, 164–65, 168–71
Proffitt v. Florida, 16
proportionality review, 10, 117–18, 130
props, 4, 68–70, 73, 150–51, 155, 160, 181, 186
prosecutors, 2–4, 9, 11, 28, 44, 55, 59, 72, 80, 134, 135, 149, 150–51, 154, 158, 165, 179, 181, 186–87, 193
psychiatrists, 2, 79, 107, 151, 166–67
psychological evaluation, 108, 110
public executions, 15, 17, 47
public opinion, 22, 24, 26, 170, 195
public wrath, 8, 48

racial bias, 21, 24
racial stereotypes, 9
rebuttal, 2, 3, 6, 68, 149
records, xvii, 22, 58, 98–99, 105, 124–25, 128, 130, 136, 161, 187
rehabilitation program, 1, 119
Rehnquist, Justice William, 20
revenge, just deserts, 30
Ring v. Arizona, 18
role model, 61, 126, 129
Rosequist, Patti, 123–24

sanctions, 48
savage beast image, 5–6, 11, 112, 186, 192
scars/scarring, 96, 104, 106, 123–24, 127, 144, 186
Scottsboro decision, 152
second-degree murder, 2, 3, 67–68, 72, 88, 95–96, 107, 124, 158–59, 163–65, 181, 184–85, 187–88, 192
sexual assault, 1, 118; second-degree sexual assault, 3, 147
social construction of reality, 40–41, 49
social control, 15, 48
social distance, 11–12, 52, 60, 71–73, 85, 95, 181
social facts, 6, 40, 49, 189
social forces, xi, 8, 87, 114, 189
social services, 5, 110, 113, 128, 187; social service system, xvi
social solidarity, 48
social worker, xv, 134, 143
socioeconomic status (SES), 192–94
sociological explanations/analysis, xi, xii, 8, 190
statutory guidelines, 11–12
stereotypes, 5, 9, 12, 25, 39–40, 42, 44, 49, 60, 76, 85–86, 137, 152–54, 158, 164, 171, 189–90, 194–95
stigma (stigmatization), 7, 12, 45–46
Strickland v. Washington, 19

theory of the crime, 2, 3, 46, 75
therapy, xiii, 108, 109, 112, 126, 137
threshold statute, 16
torture, 5, 16, 48, 77, 127, 130, 169, 193
trial transcripts, xvii, 51, 58, 60, 71, 73, 89, 159–60
troubled youth image, 5, 6, 11, 107, 112, 149, 186
trust, xiii, 46, 54, 91, 109, 177
truth in sentencing, 31, 164
Tuthill, Peyton, 1, 62, 76–80, 85–87, 112, 135–36, 139, 183–87, 193

U.S. Supreme Court, 10, 16, 18–19, 28, 152

values, xiii, 8, 29, 45, 48, 73, 150, 159, 166
verdict, xiv, xvii, 3, 5, 8, 11–12, 25–27, 43, 49–50, 57, 68, 73, 137, 147, 149–50, 153–55, 157–59, 162–63, 165–66, 185, 188, 192
victim impact statements, 120–23, 193
victimization, xii, 6
violent behavior (violence), xiii, 2, 5, 7, 9, 11, 41, 44, 52, 79, 88, 92, 95, 96, 107, 112–13, 120, 125–26, 128, 141, 143, 147–49, 159–60, 162, 171, 184, 189, 191, 194

Washington, D.C., xvii, 101, 110, 113, 128–29
White, Justice Byron, 20
whites, 21–23, 27–28, 50, 190
Witherspoon, Frederick, xvii, 58, 93–95, 113, 128

xenophobia, 25, 60

About the Author

Dr. Allison M. Cotton is assistant professor of criminology at the Metropolitan State College of Denver. A Colorado native, Dr. Cotton received a Bachelor's Degree in Sociology from the University of Colorado at Boulder in 1991, a Master's Degree in Sociology from Howard University in Washington, D.C. in 1995, and a Ph.D. in Sociology from the University of Colorado at Boulder in 2002. Dr. Cotton has published several papers on criminal justice topics, including but not limited to the death penalty, eye-witness identifications, lethal behavior, and expert witnesses. Her research interests include the death penalty; juvenile justice; wrongful convictions; and gender, race, and crime. *Effigy: Images of Capital Defendants* is her first book, which will be followed by a second (coauthored) book called *Racialized Perceptions of Crime* in the summer of 2010 by New York University Press. Dr. Cotton's teaching interests include race, class, gender, the media, and crime.

Since beginning her academic career, Dr. Cotton has received two Fulbright-Hays Scholars Abroad awards: the first award was to study the relationship between physical and social structures in China in the summer of 2005. The second award has been granted to study female genital mutilation in Egypt during the summer of 2008. She has been nominated several times in her career for Faculty of the Year Awards, including the "People's Choice" Award for Female Faculty at Prairie View A&M University in 2005 and, most recently, she won an "Outstanding Faculty Leadership Award" for campus involvement at the Metropolitan State College of Denver in 2008. She is also currently nominated for the "School of Professional Studies Out-

211

standing Professional Development Award" of 2008 for the work that she has done on her books and other publications. Dr. Cotton is a member of the Academy of Criminal Justice Sciences, the American Society of Criminology, and Coloradans Against the Death Penalty. She continuously supports community service projects focusing on educational development and criminal justice reform through active membership in the Denver Alumnae Chapter of Delta Sigma Theta Sorority, Inc.